Towards Semi-Supervised and Reinforced Task-Oriented Dialog Systems (SereTOD 2022)

Beijing, China and Online
7 December 2022

ISBN: 978-1-7138-9147-5

Printed from e-media with permission by:

Curran Associates, Inc.
57 Morehouse Lane
Red Hook, NY 12571

Some format issues inherent in the e-media version may also appear in this print version.

Printed with permission by Curran Associates, Inc. (2024)

Association for Computational Linguistics
209 N. Eighth Street
Stroudsburg, Pennsylvania 18360

Phone: 1-570-476-8006
Fax: 1-570-476-0860

acl@aclweb.org

Additional copies of this publication are available from:

Curran Associates, Inc.
57 Morehouse Lane
Red Hook, NY 12571 USA
Phone: 845-758-0400
Fax: 845-758-2633
Email: curran@proceedings.com
Web: www.proceedings.com

SereTOD 2022

Towards Semi-Supervised and Reinforced Task-Oriented Dialog Systems

Proceedings of the Workshop

December 7, 2022

The SereTOD organizers gratefully acknowledge the support from the following sponsors.

Gold

Introduction

Welcome to the Workshop - Towards Semi-Supervised and Reinforced Task-Oriented Dialog Systems (SereTOD), co-located with EMNLP 2022!

Task-oriented dialog (TOD) systems are designed to assist users to accomplish their goals. Recently, neural generative approaches have received increasing attention. Unfortunately, building TOD systems remains as a label-intensive and time-consuming task. The process still heavily relies on manually labeled dialog data and annotated task-related knowledge base. However, unlabeled data are often easily available in many forms such as human-to-human dialogs, open-domain text corpus, and unstructured knowledge documents. The purpose of this Workshop is to invite researchers from both academia and industry to share their perspectives on building semi-supervised and reinforced TOD systems, discuss challenges and advance the field in joint effort.

In parallel, we open up a challenge, in which we collect and share a newly released, large-scale, human-human dialog dataset, called the MobileCS (Mobile Customer Service) dataset to foster this line of research. The Challenge consists of two tracks: Information extraction from dialog transcripts (Track 1), and Task-oriented dialog systems (Track 2). Congratulations to the 15 teams, who submitted effective results, out of the total of 62 teams registered for the SereTOD Challenge!

We received submissions from all levels of methodologies, algorithms, models, system developments, applications and datasets towards semi-supervised and reinforced TOD systems. Given the high-quality submissions received and the capacity of the Workshop, the selection process was very competitive. We accepted 11 papers accounting for 47% of the submissions. Further, authors of a total of 13 Findings papers on Dialog have confirmed to present at the Workshop (as nonarchival presentations). In total, we have 24 papers included in the program, splitting into 4 oral sessions and 1 poster session.

SereTOD Workshop is co-located with EMNLP on December 7, 2022 (virtually with EMNLP main venue and on-site in Beijing). In additional to the paper presentations, the program also features 3 invited talks, a panel, as well as awards for the SereTOD Challenge.

We would like to take this opportunity to thank the Program Committee for their support and thorough reviews. We are deeply honored to have excellent talks from our invited speakers - Pascale Fung, Dilek Hakkani-Tur, and Jason Williams. We are especially thankful for the support from Joint Institute of Tsinghua University - China Mobile Communications Group Co. Ltd. Finally, we are grateful for the extensive help from EMNLP 2022 workshop co-chairs, Daniel Hershcovich and Asli Celikyilmaz.

We sincerely hope you will enjoy a memorable SereTOD Workshop!

The SereTOD Workshop General Chairs,
Zhijian Ou, Tsinghua University
Junlan Feng, China Mobile
Juanzi Li, Tsinghua University

Organizing Committee

Organizers

Zhijian Ou, Tsinghua University
Junlan Feng, China Mobile
Juanzi Li, Tsinghua University

Program Committee

Reviewers

Lu Chen, Shanghai Jiaotong University
He He, New York University
Yi Huang, China Mobile Research
Bing Liu, Facebook
Yang Liu, Amazon
Verena Rieser, Heriot-Watt University
Rui Yan, Renmin University of China
Koichiro Yoshino, RIKEN
Kai Yu, Shanghai Jiaotong University
Jiangjiang Zhao, China Mobile Online Services

Keynote Talk: Ingesting Knowledge from Diverse Sources to Open Domain Social Conversations

Dilek Hakkani-Tur
Amazon

Abstract: Following the recent advancements in language modeling and availability of large natural language datasets, the last decade has been flourishing for conversational AI research. The progress also helped emphasize the importance of reasoning over a diverse set of external knowledge and task completion resources for forming relevant, informative, and accurate responses, discussing with the users when the available solutions/information are not sufficient, and making proactive suggestions. For ingesting knowledge in conversations, recent work has mainly grounded conversational responses on knowledge snippets from wikipedia and web documents, with the goals of preventing hallucination and providing users diverse and accurate responses. However, much of the world's knowledge is dynamic and it is spread across diverse resources. Some of these are already structured, such as knowledge graphs. But a majority of them are not structured, for example, news articles and books. And some of them also include subjective information, such as customer reviews. In this talk, I will discuss our recent work on integrating knowledge to conversation responses from such a diverse set of resources, challenges associated with these, and progress we made so far.

Bio: Dilek Hakkani-Tür is a senior principal scientist at Amazon Alexa AI focusing on enabling natural dialogues with machines. Prior to joining Amazon, she was a researcher at Google Research, Microsoft Research, International Computer Science Institute at University of California, Berkeley, and AT&T Labs - Research. She received her BSc degree from Middle East Technical Univ., and MSc and PhD degrees from Bilkent Univ., Department of Computer Engineering. Her research interests include conversational AI, natural language and speech processing, spoken dialogue systems, and machine learning for language processing. She has over 80 patents that were granted and co-authored more than 300 papers in natural language and speech processing. She received several best paper awards for publications she co-authored on conversational systems, from IEEE Signal Processing Society, ISCA, EURASIP and others. She served as an associate editor for IEEE Transactions on Audio, Speech and Language Processing (2005-2008), a member of the IEEE Speech and Language Technical Committee (2009-2014), an area editor for speech and language processing for Elsevier's Digital Signal Processing Journal and IEEE Signal Processing Letters (2011-2013), the Editor-in-Chief of the IEEE/ACM Transactions on Audio, Speech and Language Processing (2018-2021), and an IEEE Distinguished Industry Speaker (2021). She also served on the ISCA Advisory Council (2015-2019) and the IEEE Signal Processing Society Fellows Committee (2019-2022). She was elected as a fellow of the IEEE (2014) and ISCA (2014).

Keynote Talk: Insights on the relationship between usage frequency, user proficiency, and interaction quality for a virtual assistant

Jason D. Williams
Apple

Abstract: For a virtual assistant, it seems clear that users who have a higher-quality experience would tend to use the assistant more. But causality is less obvious — for example, does higher usage frequency result from higher-quality interactions, or is higher usage frequency a reflection of higher user proficiency? How does user proficiency change over time? In this talk I'll cover a quantitative investigation into the relationships between usage frequency, user proficiency, and interaction quality for a real-world virtual assistant. The insights from this study may help inform reward or loss functions for virtual assistants optimized with reinforcement or semi-supervised learning. This is joint work with colleagues Zidi Xiu, Kai-Chen Cheng, David Q. Sun, Jiannan Lu, Hadas Kotek, Paul McCarthy, Yuhan Zhang, Christopher Klein, and Stephen Pulman.

Bio: Jason D. Williams leads a team that builds language understanding for Siri at Apple, where he has been since 2018. Prior to Apple, he was a Research Manager at Microsoft Research, leading research groups on conversational systems and reinforcement learning. Jason has published over 60 peer-reviewed papers on dialog systems and related areas, with over 8,000 citations and five best paper/presentation awards. Jason initiated the Dialog State Tracking Challenge series in 2012; shipped components of the first release of Microsoft Cortana in 2014; and launched Microsoft's Language Understanding Service (www.luis.ai (http://www.luis.ai/)) in 2015. Jason has previously served as an elected member of the IEEE Speech and Language Technical Committee (SLTC) in the area of spoken dialogue systems for 3 terms, President of SIGDIAL, senior area chair at ACL and EMNLP, and general chair and technical chair of IEEE ASRU.

Keynote Talk: Responsible & Empathetic Human Robot Interactions

Pascale Fung
Hong Kong University of Science & Technology

Abstract: Conversational AI (ConvAI) systems have applications ranging from personal assistance, health assistance to customer services. They have been in place since the first call centre agent went live in the late 1990s. More recently, smart speakers and smartphones are powered with conversational AI with similar architecture as those from the 90s. On the other hand, research on ConvAI systems has made leaps and bounds in recent years with sequence-to-sequence, generation-based models. Thanks to the advent of large scale pre-trained language models, state-of-the-art ConvAI systems can generate surprisingly human-like responses to user queries in open domain conversations, known as chit-chat. However, these generation based ConvAI systems are difficult to control and can lead to inappropriate, biased and sometimes even toxic responses. In addition, unlike previous modular conversational AI systems, it is also challenging to incorporate external knowledge into these models for task-oriented dialog scenarios such as personal assistance and customer services, and to maintain consistency. In this talk, I will introduce state-of-the-art generation based conversational AI approaches, and will point out remaining challenges of conversational AI and possible directions for future research, including how to mitigate inappropriate responses. I will also present some ethical guidelines that conversational AI systems can follow.

Bio: Pascale Fung is a Professor at the Department of Electronic & Computer Engineering and Department of Computer Science & Engineering at The Hong Kong University of Science & Technology (HKUST). Prof. Fung received her PhD in Computer Science from Columbia University in 1997. She worked and studied at AT&T Bell Labs (1993 1997), BBN Systems & Technologies (1992), LIMSI, CNRS, France (1991), Department of Information Science, Kyoto University, Japan (1989 1991), and at Ecole Centrale Paris, France(1988). She is an elected Fellow of the Association for Computational Linguistics (ACL) for her significant contributions towards statistical NLP, comparable corpora, and building intelligent systems that can understand and empathize with humans. She is an Fellow of the Institute of Electrical and Electronic Engineers (IEEE) for her contributions to human-machine interactions and an elected Fellow of the International Speech Communication Association for fundamental contributions to the interdisciplinary area of spoken language human-machine interactions. She served as Editor and Associate Editor for Computer Speech and Language, IEEE ACM Transactions on Audio, Speech and Language Processing, Transactions for ACL, IEEE Signal Processing Letters. She served as a Committee Member of the IEEE Signal Processing Society Speech and Language Technology Committee (SLTC) for six years. She is a past president t and a Board Member of the ACL Special Interest Group on Linguistics Data and Corpus Based Approaches in NLP (SIGDAT).

Table of Contents

Program

Wednesday, December 7, 2022

04:50 - 05:00	*Opening Remarks*
05:00 - 05:40	*Invited Talk 1 - Dilek Hakkani-Tur*
05:40 - 06:00	*Break*
06:00 - 07:00	*Oral Session 1 (Semi-Supervised Dialogue Systems)*
	Semi-Supervised Knowledge-Grounded Pre-training for Task-Oriented Dialog Systems Weihao Zeng, Keqing He, Zechen Wang, Dayuan Fu, Guanting Dong, Ruotong Geng, Pei Wang, Jingang Wang, Chaobo Sun, Wei Wu and Weiran Xu
	Prompt Learning for Domain Adaptation in Task-Oriented Dialogue Makesh Narsimhan Sreedhar and Christopher Parisien
	DIALOGIC: Controllable Dialogue Simulation with In-Context Learning Zekun Li, Wenhu Chen, Shiyang Li, Hong Wang, Jing Qian and Xifeng Yan
	Robust Task-Oriented Dialogue Generation with Contrastive Pre-training and Adversarial Filtering Shiquan Yang, Xinting Huang, Jey Han Lau and Sarah Erfani
07:00 - 08:00	*Oral Session 2 (Information Extraction and Knowledge-Grounded Dialogue Systems)*
	Information Extraction and Human-Robot Dialogue towards Real-life Tasks A Baseline Study with the MobileCS Dataset Hong Liu, Hao Peng, Zhijian Ou, Juanzi Li, Yi Huang and Junlan Feng
	Explainable Slot Type Attentions to Improve Joint Intent Detection and Slot Filling Kalpa Gunaratna, Vijay Srinivasan, Akhila Yerukola and Hongxia Jin
	Topic-Aware Response Generation in Task-Oriented Dialogue with Unstructured Knowledge Access Yue Feng, Gerasimos Lampouras and Ignacio Iacobacci
	Doc2Bot: Accessing Heterogeneous Documents via Conversational Bots Haomin Fu, Yeqin Zhang, Haiyang Yu, Jian Sun, Fei Huang, Luo Si, Yongbin Li and Cam-Tu Nguyen

Wednesday, December 7, 2022 (continued)

08:00 - 09:00 *Lunch*

09:00 - 09:40 *Invited Talk 2 - Jason Williams*

09:40 - 10:40 *Oral Session 3 (Reinforced Dialogue Systems)*

A Generative User Simulator with GPT-based Architecture and Goal State Tracking for Reinforced Multi-Domain Dialog Systems
Hong Liu, Yucheng Cai, Zhijian Ou, Yi Huang and Junlan Feng

Offline-to-Online Co-Evolutional User Simulator and Dialogue System
Dafeng Chi, Yuzheng Zhuang, Yao Mu, Bin Wang, Jianzhu Bao, Yasheng Wang, Yuhan Dong, Xin Jiang, Qun Liu and Jianye Hao

State-Aware Adversarial Training for Utterance-Level Dialogue Generation
Yi Huang, Xiaoting Wu, Wei Hu, Junlan Feng and Chao Deng

Is MultiWOZ a Solved Task? An Interactive TOD Evaluation Framework with User Simulator
Qinyuan Cheng, Linyang Li, Guofeng Quan, Feng Gao, Xiaofeng Mou and Xipeng Qiu

10:40 - 11:00 *Break*

11:00 - 11:40 *Invited Talk 3 - Pascale Fung*

11:40 - 12:40 *Oral Session 4 (Dialogue Datasets)*

CMCC: A Comprehensive and Large-Scale Human-Human Dataset for Dialogue Systems
Yi Huang, Xiaoting Wu, Si Chen, Wei Hu, Qing Zhu, Junlan Feng, Chao Deng, Zhijian Ou and Jiangjiang Zhao

DOROTHIE: Spoken Dialogue for Handling Unexpected Situations in Interactive Autonomous Driving Agents
Ziqiao Ma, Ben VanDerPloeg, Cristian-Paul Bara, Yidong Huang, Eui-In Kim, Felix Gervits, Matthew Marge and Joyce Chai

AssistSR: Task-oriented Video Segment Retrieval for Personal AI Assistant
Stan Weixian Lei, Difei Gao,, Yuxuan Wang, Dongxing Mao, Zihan Liang, Lingmin Ran and Mike Zheng Shou

	DialogUSR: Complex Dialogue Utterance Splitting and Reformulation for Multiple Intent Detection Haoran Meng, Xin Zheng, Tianyu Liu, Zizhen Wang, He Feng, Binghuai Lin, Xuemin Zhao, Yunbo Cao and Zhifang Sui
12:40 - 13:40	*Poster Session*
	A GlobalPointer based Robust Approach for Information Extraction from Dialog Transcripts Yanbo J. Wang, Sheng Chen, Hengxing Cai, Wei Wei, Kuo Yan, Zhe Sun, Hui Qin, Yuming Li and Xiaochen Cai
	A Token-pair Framework for Information Extraction from Dialog Transcripts in SereTOD Challenge Chenyue Wang, Xiangxing Kong, Mengzuo Huang, Feng Li, Jian Xing, Weidong Zhang and Wuhe Zou
	Disentangling Confidence Score Distribution for Out-of-Domain Intent Detection with Energy-Based Learning Yanan Wu, Zhiyuan Zeng, Keqing He, Yutao Mou, Pei Wang, Yuanmeng Yan and Weiran Xu
	Oh My Mistake!: Toward Realistic Dialogue State Tracking including Turnback Utterances Takyoung Kim, Yukyung Lee, Hoonsang Yoon, Pilsung Kang, Junseong Bang and Misuk Kim
	History-Aware Hierarchical Transformer for Multi-session Open-domain Dialogue System Tong Zhang, Yong Liu, Boyang Li, Zhiwei Zeng, Pengwei Wang, Yuan You, Chunyan Miao and Lizhen Cui
	Modeling Complex Dialogue Mappings via Sentence Semantic Segmentation Guided Conditional Variational Auto-Encoder Bin Sun, Shaoxiong Feng, Yiwei Li, Weichao Wang, Fei Mi, Yitong Li and Kan Li
	Diving Deep into Modes of Fact Hallucinations in Dialogue Systems Souvik Das, Sougata Saha, Yiwei Li and Rohini Srihari
	Keep Me Updated! Memory Management in Long-term Conversations Sanghwan Bae, Donghyun Kwak, Soyoung Kang, Min Young Lee, Sungdong Kim, Yuin Jeong, Hyeri Kim, Sang-Woo Lee, Woomyoung Park and Nako Sung
13:40 - 13:50	*SereTOD Challenge Awards*
13:50 - 14:30	*Panel, Closing*

Oh My Mistake!: Toward Realistic Dialogue State Tracking including Turnback Utterances

Takyoung Kim[†], **Yukyung Lee**[†], **Hoonsang Yoon**[†], **Pilsung Kang**[†], **Junseong Bang**[‡], **Misuk Kim**[§]
Korea University, Seoul 02841, Republic of Korea[†]
Electronics and Telecommunications Research Institute, Daejeon 34129, Republic of Korea[‡]
Sejong University, Seoul 05006, Republic of Korea[§]
{takyoung_kim, yukyung_lee, hoonsang_yoon, pilsung_kang}@korea.ac.kr
misuk.kim@sejong.ac.kr

Abstract

The primary purpose of dialogue state tracking (DST), a critical component of an end-to-end conversational system, is to build a model that responds well to real-world situations. Although we often change our minds from time to time during ordinary conversations, current benchmark datasets do not adequately reflect such occurrences and instead consist of over-simplified conversations, in which no one changes their mind during a conversation. As the main question inspiring the present study, "Are current benchmark datasets sufficiently diverse to handle casual conversations in which one changes their mind after a certain topic is over?" We found that the answer is "No" because DST models cannot refer to previous user preferences when template-based turnback utterances are injected into the dataset. Even in the the simplest mind-changing (turnback) scenario, the performance of DST models significantly degenerated. However, we found that this performance degeneration can be recovered when the turnback scenarios are explicitly designed in the training set, implying that the problem is not with the DST models but rather with the construction of the benchmark dataset.

1 Introduction

The dialogue state tracking (DST) module is a part of a task-oriented dialogue system, the main role of which is to extract essential information of user preferences from various conversational situations. Based on the given information from the previous module, the DST module finds appropriate slot-value pairs to understand the current conversational situations, and these pairs are then delivered to the next module to continue the conversation. Hence, building an accurate DST model is a key success factor of the overall task-oriented dialogue system not only because it can convince users that the system perfectly understands what they are talking about, but also because appropriate responses can be generated based on the result of the DST model. As in other natural language processing (NLP) tasks, two main components are mandatory to build a good DST model: (1) well-structured machine learning models and (2) sufficiently large datasets that contain various real-world conversational situations with fewer biases for training the model. Since the introduction of Transformer and BERT (Vaswani et al., 2017; Devlin et al., 2018), various breakthrough model structures have been designed for DST, such as SUMBT and SOM-DST (Lee et al., 2019; Kim et al., 2020), and have shown an excellent performance. With respect to DST-specific datasets, by contrast, some benchmark datasets, such as WOZ (Wen et al., 2017) and MultiWOZ (Budzianowski et al., 2018), have been introduced; however, their sizes and coverage are not yet satisfactory owing to the relatively high labeling cost. For example, the MultiWOZ only consists of approximately 10,000 dialogues from some different domains, which is significantly smaller than other NLP datasets such as SQuAD or IMDB (Rajpurkar et al., 2016; Maas et al., 2011).

Whereas the MultiWOZ has been used as a standard benchmark dataset for DST, there has been an increasing number of recent studies reporting the concerns regarding the inherent limitations of this dataset. First, newer versions of MultiWOZ have been proposed to address certain issues such as annotation errors, typos, standardization, annotation consistency, and other factors (Eric et al., 2019; Zang et al., 2020; Han et al., 2020; Ye et al., 2021). In addition, Qian et al. (2021) pointed out an entity bias issue, i.e., only a small number of values in the ontology account for the majority of labels. For example, a large number of *'train-destination'* slots take the value *'cambridge'* in the MultiWOZ (Qian et al., 2021). In addition, with CoCo (Li et al., 2020), an overestimation of the held-out accuracy was pointed out by showing that the training and evaluation sets of the MultiWOZ

Proceedings of the Towards Semi-Supervised and Reinforced Task-Oriented Dialog Systems (SereTOD), pages 1 - 12
December 7, 2022 ©2022 Association for Computational Linguistics

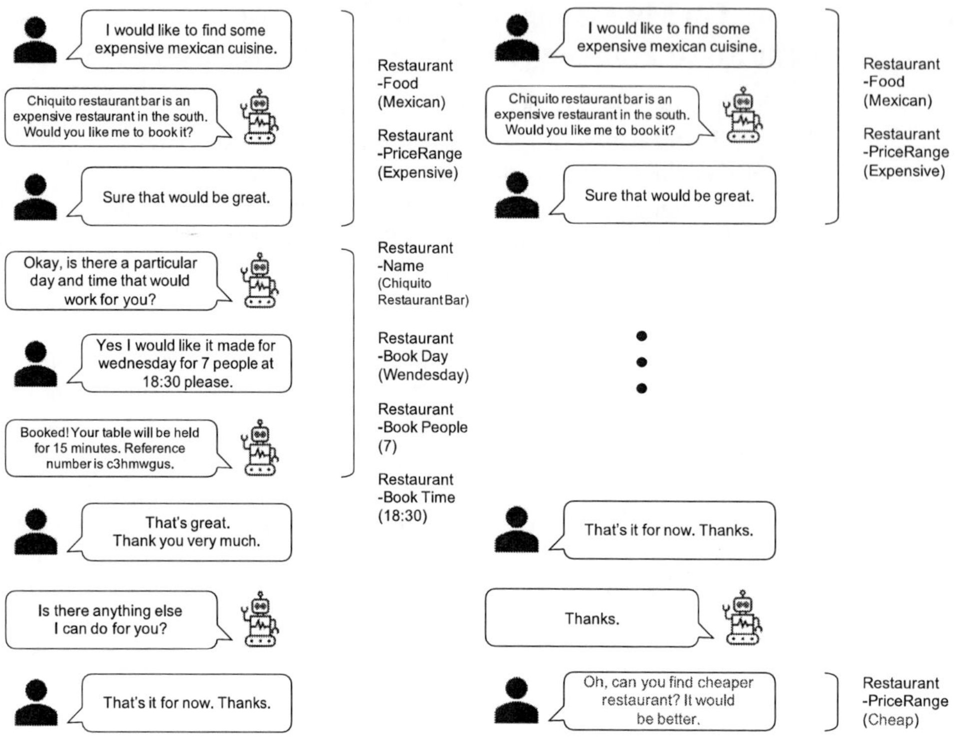

Figure 1: Dialogue flow example of MultiWOZ 2.1 (MUL1514.json).

have a similar distribution, and controllable counterfactual goals were proposed that do not change the original dialogue flow but generate a new dialogue with different responses.

Although previous studies have raised inherent problems in the MultiWOZ, most have tended to focus on correcting the annotation inconsistency or entity biases, which enforces the dialogue in the dataset to be more idealistic. However, in real-world conversations, the dialogue flow between two speakers is not always as fluent as those in the MultiWOZ, e.g., one can occasionally change one's mind during a conversation. For example, Figure 1a shows a sample dialogue in the MultiWOZ. No slot that appears once appears again in the subsequent dialogue turns. As the main hypothesis motivating this study, real conversations do not always continue as shown in Figure 1a, but often continue as shown in Figure 1b. Individuals change their mind during a conversation, and thus some slot-value pairs (same slot but different values) repeatedly appear in an entire dialogue. This hypothesis has led us to raise the main question of this paper: *"Can the current benchmark dataset handle a situation in which users change their mind after a certain amount of turn?"* Our assumption is that the turnback situation of a user will hamper the robust evaluation of DST models because such models do not have a chance to learn the situation in which the values of specific slots are changed during the conversation. To experimentally verify our assumption, we investigate how DST models handle additional turnback dialogues by injecting template-based utterances under different scenarios on the MultiWOZ.

It is common for users to change their decisions in various ways in the real world, and thus we define four turnback situations as follows:

- **SINGLE TURNBACK** : This is the simplest form in which the user changes the decision of a single slot only once.
- **RETURN TURNBACK** : This is the reverse of a decision twice but returning to the original value of a single slot.
- **DUAL-VALUE TURNBACK** : The decision for a single slot is changed twice and thus the corresponding values are also changed twice.
- **DUAL-SLOT TURNBACK** : The decision for

two slots are sequentially changed. The corresponding values are changed only once.

The remaining states are more complicated variants of the simplest versions by modifying the number of repetitions or slots. There are some ways to generate turnback utterances such as manually annotating dialogues or generating with the help of language models (Raffel et al., 2020). In this study, we injected turnback utterances at the end of the existing dialogue using pre-defined templates for two reasons. First, locating turnback utterances at the end of the dialogue is a better way to verify the ability handling long-range contexts for the model. Second, template-based-generated utterances explicitly mention the information of `domain`, `slot`, and `value` in a raw text, which can play a role as the minimal form of turnback scenarios. We found even these simple and explicit forms of turnback utterances are sufficient to disclose the problem.

In this paper, we evaluate the performance of turnback situations with TRADE, SUMBT, and Transformer-DST (Wu et al., 2019; Lee et al., 2019; Zeng and Nie, 2021). The results show that existing models cannot detect changing user preferences when injecting turnback utterances in the test set; the same trends are also shown in all variants of turnback scenarios. We further determined that including turnback utterances appropriately during the training phase can make a model robust because the model performance rebounds. To summarize, the main contributions of this paper can be summarized as follows:

- We define the problem that the current benchmark cannot handle, i.e., the change in decision of the user after a certain topic is over, which must be considered when constructing an realistic conversational system.

- We quantitatively and qualitatively evaluate three representative DST models to verify the effect of the turnback situation by injecting template-based utterances into the existing dataset.

- We explore the effect of various turnback proportions in both the training and testing datasets: When turnback utterances appear in the test set, models trained with the data including turnback utterances become more robust.

2 Related Work

2.1 Limitation of Benchmark Dataset

MultiWOZ (Budzianowski et al., 2018) is one of the most popular multi-domain task-oriented dialogue datasets. Although a new task-oriented dialogue dataset, such as SGD (Rastogi et al., 2020), has been recently proposed, most previous studies still evaluate the performance based on MultiWOZ (Kim et al., 2022). However, it has been revealed that the MultiWOZ has inherent errors and biases, and several studies have been proposed to resolve the reported issues.

Annotation error Even the recent versions of MultiWOZ still have incorrect labels and inconsistent annotations (Eric et al., 2019; Zang et al., 2020; Han et al., 2020; Ye et al., 2021). These noises are the primary reason why it is challenging to accurately evaluate the model performance. Fortunately, the benchmark is continuously updated by progressively correcting any annotation errors found.

Biased slots The slots in MultiWOZ are biased. The slots in the training and test sets overlap by more than 90%, and the co-occurrence between slots in the test set is also unequally distributed. DST models are vulnerable to unseen slots because biased slots do not consider rare but realistic slot combinations. To relieve this assumption, CoCo (Li et al., 2020) generates counterfactual dialogues to allow the existing dataset to cover realistic conversation scenarios.

Biased entities Entities in the MultiWOZ are also significantly biased. The test dataset has most of the entities that appear in the training dataset, and existing models are vulnerable to unseen entities (e.g., *"cambridge"* appearing in 50% of the destination cities in the *train* domain) (Qian et al., 2021). Thus, the new test dataset consisting of unseen entities is proposed, which also results in a decrease in performance (Qian et al., 2021).

Change my mind During a real conversation, people often change their minds. For example, when making a reservation for a restaurant, one might change the number of visitors, arrival time, or menu. When catching a taxi, the rider might ask the driver to go to their office first, and suddenly decide to go home to take a rest instead. Someone might want to sleep more, so they might delay their departure time. There are many other examples in which speakers change their mind or decision

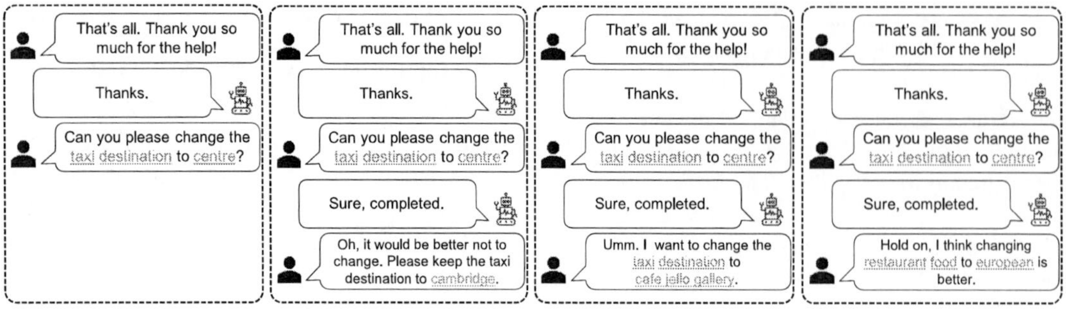

(a) SINGLE TURNBACK (b) RETURN TURNBACK (c) DUAL-VALUE TURNBACK (d) DUAL-SLOT TURNBACK

Figure 2: An example of proposed turnback situations. Text in orange denotes a domain, blue denotes a slot, and green denotes a value.

[Train]
1: Umm. I think it's better to change {domain} {slot} to {value}.
2: Can you change {domain} {slot} to {value}? I forgot it.
3: Oh, I need to change {domain} {slot} to {value}. Please fix it.

[Validation]
1: Oh, I took a mistake. Change {domain} {slot} to {value} please.
2: It would be better to change {domain} {slot} to {value}. Can you make it?
3: I forgot about it, I want to change {domain} {slot} to {value}.

[Test]
1: I think {value} is better. I want to change {domain} {slot} to {value}.
2: Wait, it might be better to change {domain} {slot} to {value}.
3: Hold on, I've been thinking about it and I think changing {domain} {slot} to {value} will be better.

Figure 3: Template utterances of each phase (train, validation, and test).

during a conversation. Unfortunately, the current well-known DST benchmark dataset does not seem to take these scenarios into serious consideration. All conversations continue naturally, and no one reverses what they have said. Some approaches reflect changing decisions of the user but only cover changes in the same dialog topic (Bordes et al., 2017; Mosig et al., 2020). Our contention regarding the conditions of a good DST benchmark dataset is that the conversations in the dataset should reflect more realistic situations, e.g., frequent turnback utterances, which are a main component of ordinary conversations in the real world.

This paper is partially related to Jakobovits et al. (2022), which points out the current task-oriented dialogue benchmark only considers short-term context rather than long history. Our turnback scenarios are the representative phenomena that show the lack of *conversationality* of the benchmark dataset, defined in Jakobovits et al. (2022).

3 Method

To test whether the model trained with the current DST dataset can track the change in value of the turnback situation, we assume four turnback scenarios and inject these turnback utterances at the end of every dialogue, as represented as Figure 2. In other words, each data containing dialogue of t turns can be formulated as $X_t = \{(U_1^{sys}, U_1^{usr}), \ldots, (U_t^{sys}, U_t^{usr})\}$, and we then append an extra template-generated turn with one of the aforementioned turnback situations at the end of the existing data, resulting in $X_k = \{(U_1^{sys}, U_1^{usr}), \ldots, (U_k^{sys}, U_k^{usr})\}$, where $k = t{+}1$ for a single turnback situation or $k = t{+}2$ for multiple situations. Figure 3 shows examples of a turnback used in each dataset. Note that we used different templates for different datasets to avoid an overlap across the datasets. Whenever applying a template-based utterance generation, the arbitrary template of each phase is selected at each turn of dialogue.

As the main purpose of this paper is to investigate whether the model can follow the user's mind-changing utterances, we designed the simplest form of turnback utterances: injecting them to the last turn and generating utterances using templates. The former is to assume the mind-changing within the longest history in a single dialogue, and the latter is to show that models cannot track changing values when even the most informative turnback utterances are explicitly provided. Accordingly, we defined four variants of turnback situations as follows:

SINGLE TURNBACK Users change the value of a particular slot only once, as shown in Figure 2a. Basically, a single turnback utterance is constructed using the last turn of the dialogue because it contains accumulated belief states that appeared throughout the dialogue. Figure A1 shows the process of generating a single turnback utterance and skipping the process when there is no belief stated

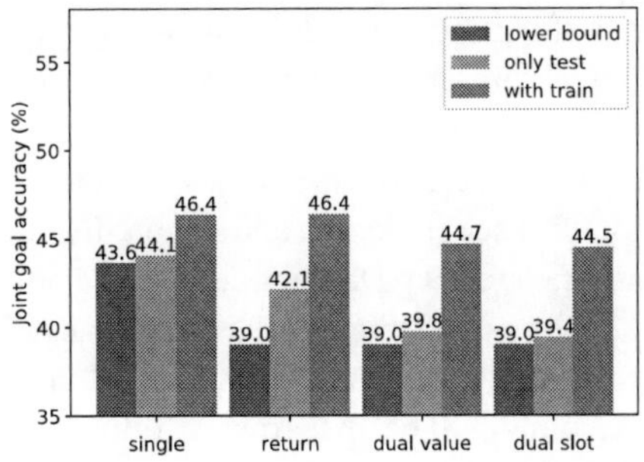

(a) TRADE

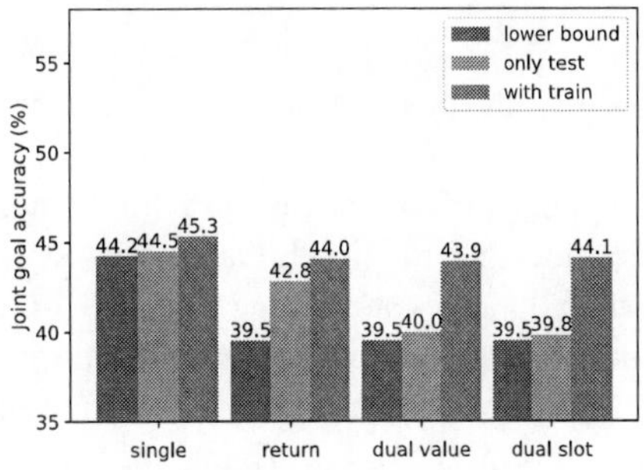

(b) TRADE + CoCo

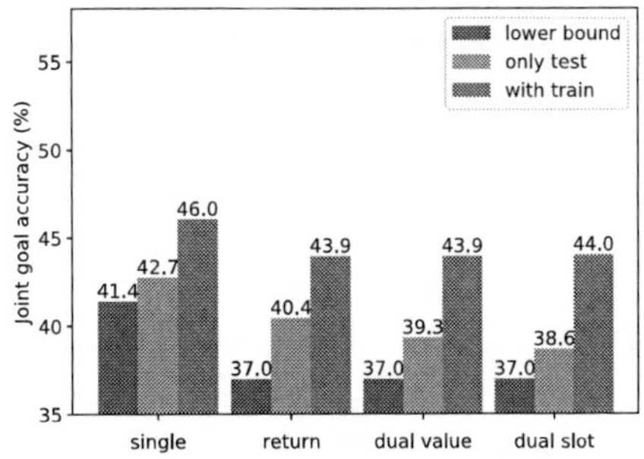

(c) SUMBT

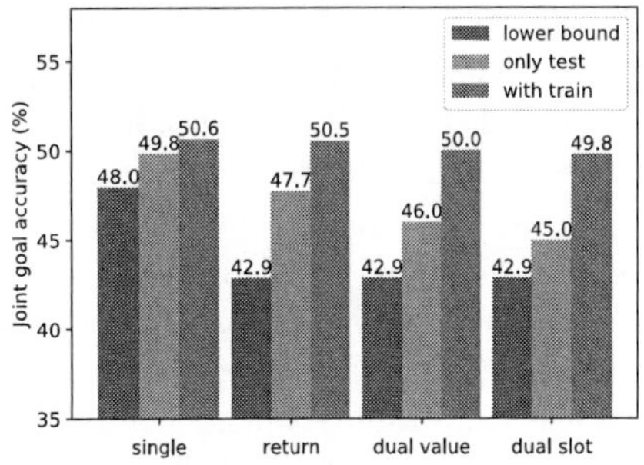

(d) Transformer-DST

Figure 4: Performance gap based on the existence of turnback in the training data. Lower bound indicates the performance of not correctly predicting additional turnback turns at all.

during the dialogue.

RETURN TURNBACK Users change the value of a particular slot but return to the original value again, as shown in Figure 2b. This means that the final belief state after injecting a return turnback utterance is the same as the belief state of the original dataset. In this case, the first turnback utterance can be generated like a single turnback process, and the second turnback utterance is then generated identically by simply replacing the changed value with the original value.

DUAL-VALUE TURNBACK Users sequentially change the value of a particular slot twice, as shown in Figure 2c. Dual value turnback utterances can be generated in the same way as return turnback utterances, but can be generalized to a triple or quadruple value turnback if there are more than two available values in the slot on the ontology.

DUAL-SLOT TURNBACK Users first change the value of a particular slot and then also change the value of a different slot, as represented in Figure 2d. This can be generated simply by applying a single turnback twice; however, there must be more than two total belief states to apply this scenario.

4 Experiments

4.1 Experimental setup

We verified our hypothesis using the MultiWOZ 2.1 (Eric et al., 2019), the most commonly used DST dataset in previous studies. As a performance metric, the joint goal accuracy was employed. The joint goal accuracy is a standard criterion used to check if the model tracks the triplet of `(domain, slot, value)` precisely. When tracked correctly, the joint goal accuracy is marked as 1, and is otherwise 0. The numbers of training, validation, and test sets are 8420, 1000, and 999, respectively. The open-source code for the TRADE model was from CoCo repository[1], while the code for SUMBT[2] and Transformer-DST[3] was from the original author, respectively. For the TRADE model, we also considered the model trained jointly with CoCo-augmented dataset (Li et al., 2020). All the experiments explained later were conducted using a machine with the NVIDIA GeForce RTX 3090 GPU.

[1]https://github.com/salesforce/coco-dst

[2]https://github.com/SKTBrain/SUMBT

[3]https://github.com/zengyan-97/Transformer-DST

4.2 Main results

Figure 4 shows the main results. As the extra turnback utterances are appended to the original dataset, we reported the performance lower bound where the model does not predict the additional states of turnback utterances at all (blue color). In other words, the joint goal accuracy of every turn of turnback scenarios is zero in the lower bound setting. The performance of the original model with turnback-included test set is reported with the orange color. Compared to the lower bound, the model trained with the original set correctly predicts only a few altered dialogue states. In the case of multiple turnbacks (i.e., RETURN TURNBACK , DUAL-VALUE TURNBACK , and DUAL-SLOT TURNBACK), the models with RETURN TURNBACK resulted in relatively better performance than the others. This is not because the model predict the state values in the turnback utterance correctly, but because RETURN TURNBACK has the same value with the original state value. Note that these turnback utterances generated using templates are the *easiest* form of the situation, explicitly providing the entire information of `domain`, `slot`, and `value`.

4.3 Including turnback dialogues in the training set

Because the main hypothesis was sufficiently supported by the first experiment, we further investigated whether including turnback situations in the training dataset can prevent the model from not being able to trace the changing values. We inserted turnback utterances at the end of all training train and validation data, and different template utterances were randomly used for the training and validation phases, as illustrated in Figure 3.

The green-colored bar in Figure 4 shows the joint goal accuracy for each turnback scenario before and after the turnback utterance are included in the training and validation datasets with a performance lower bound of newly added turnback turns. The performance always improves irrespective of the turnback scenarios and DST models. Also note that the performance recovery is more significant for more complicated turnback scenarios. Injecting turnback utterances increases the joint goal accuracy by 1.83%p on average for a single turnback, whereas the average improvement is 4.90%p for the dual slot turnback.

In addition to achieving a quantitative rebound in performance, we also conducted a qualitative comparison of the model predictions before and after the turnback injection in the training and validation datasets. Table 1 shows an example of dual slot turnback dialogue, and the predicted states of the Transformer-DST model are as shown in Table 2. The prediction results of the remaining three turnback situations are also provided in Tables A1, A2, and A3. The first row of Table 2 is the last turn of the original dialogue, and we can see that both the original and dual-trained model predict the belief states correctly. In the second and third rows of the same table, when the values of two slots are sequentially changed, the original model can catch only one changing value (*'finches bed and breakfast'*). Not being able to follow all changes is frequently detected with the original model in other test dialogues. By contrast, the model trained with the turnback utterances can correctly predict the entire belief state, as shown in the last row and the last column of Table 2.

Based on the results shown in Figure 4 and Table 2, we can conclude that the performance degeneration of the DST models is not because the DST model structures are incorrect but because they do not have a chance to train such turnback utterances with the current benchmark DST dataset, which means that the MultiWOZ dataset does not have a sufficient coverage yet for dialogues in the realworld.

4.4 Difference in performance according to turnback proportion

We also conducted an ablation study on how the turnback utterance proportions in the training and test dataset affect the DST performance. We evaluate five different proportions of turnback-injected training and test datasets (i.e., 0%, 30%, 50%, 70%, and 100%) with corresponding turnback-test situations, resulting in a total of 25 combinations of training-test turnback proportions. We named each turnback-mixed dataset *phase-N%*. For example, Train-30% denotes the dataset in which 30% of the turnback utterances are applied to the existing dialogues, and the remaining 70% of the original dialogues are unmodified. The performances of Transformer-DST are shown in Table 3. The performance of the other models are provided in Tables A4, A5, and A6. The last column of the table is the difference between the best-proportion model performance and the original performance.

Turn #	Dialogue History
1	System: " " User: "I need a taxi. I'll be departing from la raza."
2	System: "I can help you with that. When do you need to leave?" User: "I would like to leave after 11:45 please."
3	System: "Where will you be going?" User: "I'll be going to restaurant 17."
4	System: "I have booked for you a black volkswagen, the contact number is 07552762364. Is there anything else I can help you with?" User: "No, that's it. Thank you!"
5	System: "Completed." User: "Wait , it might be better to change **taxi leave at** to **15:00**."
6	System: "Sure. Anything else?" User: "Hold on , I've been thinking about it and I think changing **taxi destination** to **finches bed and breakfast** will be better."

Table 1: Sample dialogue of test set with additional DUAL-SLOT TURNBACK situation (SNG01367.json).

Gold state (label)	Predicted state (original model)	Predicted state (DUAL-SLOT-trained model)
"taxi-departure-la raza", "taxi-leaveat-11:45", "taxi-destination- restaurant 17"	"taxi-departure-la raza", "taxi-leaveat-11:45", "taxi-destination- restaurant 17"	"taxi-departure-la raza", "taxi-leaveat-11:45", "taxi-destination- restaurant 17"
"taxi-departure-la raza", "taxi-leaveat-**15:00**", "taxi-destination- restaurant 17"	"taxi-departure-la raza", "taxi-leaveat-11:45", "taxi-destination- restaurant 17"	"taxi-departure-la raza", "taxi-leaveat-**15:00**", "taxi-destination- restaurant 17"
"taxi-departure-la raza", "taxi-leaveat-**15:00**", "taxi-destination- **finches bed and breakfast**"	"taxi-departure-la raza", "taxi-leaveat-11:45", "taxi-destination- **finches bed and breakfast**"	"taxi-departure-la raza", "taxi-leaveat-**15:00**", "taxi-destination- **finches bed and breakfast**"

Table 2: The model prediction on DUAL-SLOT TURNBACK situation at turn 4, 5, and 6 (SNG01367.json).

	SINGLE TURNBACK					
	Train-0%	Train-30%	Train-50%	Train-70%	Train-100%	Difference
Test-0%	**54.47**	54.40	54.32	54.44	52.80	-0.03%p
Test-30%	53.04	53.81	53.84	**54.00**	52.22	0.96%p
Test-50%	52.06	53.44	53.36	**53.46**	51.88	1.40%p
Test-70%	50.90	**52.81**	52.78	52.73	51.12	1.91%p
Test-100%	49.84	51.98	52.23	**52.32**	50.65	2.48%p

* Bold denotes the best, and underline denotes the second-best performance.

Table 3: Joint goal accuracy (%) of Transformer-DST with different SINGLE TURNBACK proportions.

Based on Table 3, we can draw the following observations. First, adding moderate turnback utterances does not significantly affect the performance on Test-0%, which is the original test dataset. The joint goal accuracies of Train-30%, Train-50%, and Train-70% are very close to that of Train-0%. Second, high proportions of turnback utterances in the training set help recover the performance in most cases. With regard to turnback ratio in the training dataset, above 70% of the turnback utterance show the best performance in Table 3, A4, and A6. In the case of Table A5, we expect that conterfactual slot combinations provided in CoCo-augmented dataset can assist the model's robust prediction.

5 Conclusion

A DST model should focus on properly reacting to unpredictable scenarios from a human speaker. From this perspective, using realistic benchmark datasets for the model is crucial. To validate recent DST models trained on the commonly used DST benchmark dataset, we first designed a template-based (but enough to verify the hypothesis) data injection method to create a turnback situation and modified the test dataset by appending one of four trunback scenarios to the end of the dialogue. Our experiment showed that the current model trained using the existing benchmark cannot track the changing values well when users change their decisions. We also conducted additional experiment to investigate whether the model performance can be recovered if the turnback utterances are properly included in the training dataset. Experimental results showed that the joint goal accuracy was improved for all turnback scenarios when the models were trained on the dataset with turnback utterances. The ablation study shows that moderately including the turnback utterances can manage a broader range of turnback proportions. Our experimental results emphasize that constructing a right benchmark dataset is as important as developing an advanced model structure in NLP tasks.

Despite the meaningful results, we argue that the turnback utterance is just one of many situations that can happen in a real-world conversation. If more diverse realistic dialogue scenarios are reflected in the DST benchmark dataset, the bias of models trained on it can be significantly reduced.

Acknowledgment

This research was supported and funded by the Korean National Police Agency. [Pol-Bot Development for Conversational Police Knowledge Services / PR09-01-000-20]

References

Antoine Bordes, Y-Lan Boureau, and Jason Weston. 2017. Learning end-to-end goal-oriented dialog. In *Proceedings of the 5th International Conference on Learning Representations*.

Paweł Budzianowski, Tsung-Hsien Wen, Bo-Hsiang Tseng, Iñigo Casanueva, Stefan Ultes, Osman Ramadan, and Milica Gašić. 2018. MultiWOZ - a large-scale multi-domain Wizard-of-Oz dataset for task-oriented dialogue modelling. In *Proceedings of the 2018 Conference on Empirical Methods in Natural Language Processing*, pages 5016–5026, Brussels, Belgium. Association for Computational Linguistics.

Jacob Devlin, Ming-Wei Chang, Kenton Lee, and Kristina Toutanova. 2018. Bert: Pre-training of deep bidirectional transformers for language understanding. In *Proceedings of the 57th Annual Meeting of the Association for Computational Linguistics: Tutorial Abstracts*, page 4171–4186.

Mihail Eric, Rahul Goel, Shachi Paul, Abhishek Sethi, Sanchit Agarwal, Shuyang Gao, and Dilek Hakkani-Tür. 2019. Multiwoz 2.1: Multi-domain dialogue state corrections and state tracking baselines. *CoRR*, abs/1907.01669.

Ting Han, Ximing Liu, Ryuichi Takanobu, Yixin Lian, Chongxuan Huang, Wei Peng, and Minlie Huang. 2020. Multiwoz 2.3: A multi-domain task-oriented dataset enhanced with annotation corrections and co-reference annotation. *arXiv preprint arXiv:2010.05594*.

Alice Shoshana Jakobovits, Francesco Piccinno, and Yasemin Altun. 2022. What did you say? task-oriented dialog datasets are not conversational!?

Sungdong Kim, Sohee Yang, Gyuwan Kim, and Sang-Woo Lee. 2020. Efficient dialogue state tracking by selectively overwriting memory. In *Proceedings of the 58th Annual Meeting of the Association for Computational Linguistics*, pages 567–582, Online. Association for Computational Linguistics.

Takyoung Kim, Hoonsang Yoon, Yukyung Lee, Pilsung Kang, and Misuk Kim. 2022. Mismatch between multi-turn dialogue and its evaluation metric in dialogue state tracking. In *Proceedings of the 60th Annual Meeting of the Association for Computational Linguistics (Volume 2: Short Papers)*, pages 297–309, Dublin, Ireland. Association for Computational Linguistics.

Hwaran Lee, Jinsik Lee, and Tae-Yoon Kim. 2019. SUMBT: Slot-utterance matching for universal and scalable belief tracking. In *Proceedings of the 57th Annual Meeting of the Association for Computational Linguistics*, pages 5478–5483, Florence, Italy. Association for Computational Linguistics.

Shiyang Li, Semih Yavuz, Kazuma Hashimoto, Jia Li, Tong Niu, Nazneen Rajani, Xifeng Yan, Yingbo Zhou, and Caiming Xiong. 2020. Coco: Controllable counterfactuals for evaluating dialogue state trackers. In *Proceedings of the 8th International Conference on Learning Representations*.

Andrew L. Maas, Raymond E. Daly, Peter T. Pham, Dan Huang, Andrew Y. Ng, and Christopher Potts. 2011. Learning word vectors for sentiment analysis. In *Proceedings of* the 49th Annual Meeting of the Association for Computational Linguistics: Human Language Technologies, pages 142–150, Portland, Oregon, USA. Association for Computational Linguistics.

Johannes E. M. Mosig, Shikib Mehri, and Thomas Kober. 2020. STAR: A Schema-Guided Dialog Dataset for Transfer Learning. *arXiv e-prints*.

Kun Qian, Ahmad Beirami, Zhouhan Lin, Ankita De, Alborz Geramifard, Zhou Yu, and Chinnadhurai Sankar. 2021. Annotation inconsistency and entity bias in multiwoz. In *Proceedings of the 22nd Annual Meeting of the Special Interest Group on Discourse and Dialogue*. Association for Computational Linguistics.

Colin Raffel, Noam Shazeer, Adam Roberts, Katherine Lee, Sharan Narang, Michael Matena, Yanqi Zhou, Wei Li, and Peter J. Liu. 2020. Exploring the limits of transfer learning with a unified text-to-text transformer. *Journal of Machine Learning Research*, 21(140):1–67.

Pranav Rajpurkar, Jian Zhang, Konstantin Lopyrev, and Percy Liang. 2016. SQuAD: 100,000+ questions for machine comprehension of text. In *Proceedings of the 2016 Conference on Empirical Methods in Natural Language Processing*, pages 2383–2392, Austin, Texas. Association for Computational Linguistics.

Abhinav Rastogi, Xiaoxue Zang, Srinivas Sunkara, Raghav Gupta, and Pranav Khaitan. 2020. Towards scalable multi-domain conversational agents: The schema-guided dialogue dataset. In *Proceedings of the AAAI Conference on Artificial Intelligence*, volume 34, pages 8689–8696.

Ashish Vaswani, Noam Shazeer, Niki Parmar, Jakob Uszkoreit, Llion Jones, Aidan N Gomez, Łukasz Kaiser, and Illia Polosukhin. 2017. Attention is all you need. In *Advances in neural information processing systems*, pages 5998–6008.

Tsung-Hsien Wen, David Vandyke, Nikola Mrkšić, Milica Gašić, Lina M. Rojas-Barahona, Pei-Hao Su, Stefan Ultes, and Steve Young. 2017. A network-based end-to-end trainable task-oriented dialogue system. In *Proceedings of the 15th Conference of the European Chapter of the Association for Computational Linguistics: Volume 1, Long Papers*, pages 438–449, Valencia, Spain. Association for Computational Linguistics.

Chien-Sheng Wu, Andrea Madotto, Ehsan Hosseini-Asl, Caiming Xiong, Richard Socher, and Pascale Fung. 2019. Transferable multi-domain state generator for task-oriented dialogue systems. In *Proceedings of the 57th Annual Meeting of the Association for Computational Linguistics*, pages 808–819, Florence, Italy. Association for Computational Linguistics.

Fanghua Ye, Jarana Manotumruksa, and Emine Yilmaz. 2021. Multiwoz 2.4: A multi-domain task-oriented dialogue dataset with essential annotation corrections to improve state tracking evaluation. *arXiv preprint arXiv:2104.00773*.

Xiaoxue Zang, Abhinav Rastogi, Srinivas Sunkara, Raghav Gupta, Jianguo Zhang, and Jindong Chen. 2020. Multiwoz 2.2: A dialogue dataset with additional annotation corrections and state tracking baselines. In *Proceedings of the 2nd Workshop on Natural Language Processing for Conversational AI, ACL 2020*, pages 109–117.

Yan Zeng and Jian-Yun Nie. 2021. Jointly optimizing state operation prediction and value generation for dialogue state tracking.

A Appendix

System Utterance: "Is there anything to help?"
User Utterance: "No, that's all. Thanks."
Turn Index: 7
Belief State:

{
    'restaurant-food': 'european',
    'taxi-destination': 'cambridge',
    'hotel-name': 'lensfield hotel'
}

(a) Get the last turn's dialog.

System Utterance: "Is there anything to help?"
User Utterance: "No, that's all. Thanks."
Turn Index: 8
Belief State:

{
    'restaurant-food': 'european',
    'taxi-destination': 'cambridge',
    'hotel-name': 'lensfield hotel'
}

(b) Duplicate dialog and randomly select belief state.

System Utterance: "Is there anything to help?"
User Utterance: "No, that's all. Thanks."
Turn Index: 8
Belief State:

{
    'restaurant-food': 'european',
    'taxi-destination': **'stansted airport'**,
    'hotel-name': 'lensfield hotel'
}

(c) Replace the value of selected belief state with a different value on ontology.

System Utterance: "Thanks."
User Utterance: "Wait, it might be better to change taxi destination to stansted airport."
Turn Index: 8
Belief State:
{
    'restaurant-food': 'european',
    'taxi-destination': 'stansted airport',
    'hotel-name': 'lensfield hotel'
}

(d) Change system utterance and apply a template to user utterance.

Figure A1: Process of SINGLE TURNBACK dialogue generation.

Gold state (label)	Predicted state (original model)	Predicted state (SINGLE-trained model)
"taxi-departure-la raza", "taxi-leaveat-11:45", "taxi-destination- restaurant 17"	"taxi-departure-la raza", "taxi-leaveat-11:45", "taxi-destination restaurant 17"	"taxi-departure-la raza", "taxi-leaveat-11:45", "taxi-destination restaurant 17"
"taxi-departure-, **london liverpool street**", "taxi-leaveat-11:45", "taxi-destination- restaurant 17"	"taxi-departure- la raza", "taxi-leaveat-11:45", "taxi-destination- restaurant 17"	"taxi-departure- **london liverpool street**", "taxi-leaveat-11:45", "taxi-destination- restaurant 17"

Table A1: Model prediction on SINGLE TURNBACK situation at turns 4 and 5 (SNG01367.json).

Gold state (label)	Predicted state (original model)	Predicted state (RETURN-trained model)
"taxi-departure-la raza", "taxi-leaveat-11:45", "taxi-destination- restaurant 17"	"taxi-departure-la raza", "taxi-leaveat-11:45", "taxi-destination- restaurant 17"	"taxi-departure-la raza", "taxi-leaveat-11:45", "taxi-destination- restaurant 17"
"taxi-departure-, **the copper kettle**", "taxi-leaveat-11:45", "taxi-destination- restaurant 17"	"taxi-departure- la raza", "taxi-leaveat-11:45", "taxi-destination- restaurant 17"	"taxi-departure- **the copper kettle**", "taxi-leaveat-11:45", "taxi-destination- restaurant 17"
"taxi-departure-**la raza**", "taxi-leaveat-11:45", "taxi-destination- restaurant 17"	"taxi-departure-**la raza**", "taxi-leaveat-11:45", "taxi-destination- restaurant 17"	"taxi-departure-**la raza**", "taxi-leaveat-11:45", "taxi-destination- restaurant 17"

Table A2: Model prediction on RETURN TURNBACK situation at turns 4, 5, and 6 (SNG01367.json).

Gold state (label)	Predicted state (original model)	Predicted state (DUAL-VALUE-trained model)
"taxi-departure-la raza", "taxi-leaveat-11:45", "taxi-destination- restaurant 17"	"taxi-departure-la raza", "taxi-leaveat-11:45", "taxi-destination- restaurant 17"	"taxi-departure-la raza", "taxi-leaveat-11:45", "taxi-destination- restaurant 17"
"taxi-departure-la raza", "taxi-leaveat-**10:15**", "taxi-destination- restaurant 17"	"taxi-departure-la raza", "taxi-leaveat-**10:15**", "taxi-destination- restaurant 17"	"taxi-departure-la raza", "taxi-leaveat-**10:15**", "taxi-destination- restaurant 17"
"taxi-departure-la raza", "taxi-leaveat-**12:00**", "taxi-destination- restaurant 17"	"taxi-departure-la raza", "taxi-leaveat-10:15", "taxi-destination- restaurant 17"	"taxi-departure-la raza", "taxi-leaveat-**12:00**", "taxi-destination- restaurant 17"

Table A3: Model prediction on DUAL-VALUE TURNBACK situation at turn 4, 5, and 6 (SNG01367.json).

	SINGLE TURNBACK					
	Train-0%	Train-30%	Train-50%	Train-70%	Train-100%	Difference
Test-0%	**49.55**	48.47	48.25	48.11	48.81	-0.74%p
Test-30%	**47.82**	47.41	47.16	47.16	**47.82**	0.00 %p
Test-50%	46.52	46.62	46.41	46.67	**47.24**	0.72%p
Test-70%	45.31	45.92	45.63	45.85	**46.50**	1.19%p
Test-100%	44.05	45.12	45.13	45.29	**46.36**	2.31%p

* Bold denotes the best, and underline denotes the second-best performance.

Table A4: Joint goal accuracy (%) of TRADE with different SINGLE TURNBACK proportions.

	SINGLE TURNBACK					
	Train-0%	Train-30%	Train-50%	Train-70%	Train-100%	Difference
Test-0%	**50.21**	48.40	49.80	47.73	48.05	-0.41%p
Test-30%	48.36	47.30	**48.74**	46.81	47.22	0.38%p
Test-50%	47.13	46.57	**48.16**	46.07	46.62	1.03%p
Test-70%	46.02	45.57	**47.42**	45.38	45.89	1.40%p
Test-100%	44.49	44.75	**46.73**	44.75	45.30	2.24%p

* Bold denotes the best, and underline denotes the second-best performance.

Table A5: Joint goal accuracy (%) of TRADE + CoCo with different SINGLE TURNBACK proportions.

	SINGLE TURNBACK					
	Train-0%	Train-30%	Train-50%	Train-70%	Train-100%	Difference
Test-0%	46.99	46.24	46.32	**47.16**	47.10	0.17%p
Test-30%	45.59	46.57	46.17	47.18	**47.38**	1.79%p
Test-50%	44.80	46.29	45.70	46.70	**47.22**	2.42%p
Test-70%	43.73	45.54	45.13	46.11	**46.39**	2.66%p
Test-100%	42.72	45.01	44.70	45.62	**46.04**	3.32%p

* Bold denotes the best, and underline denotes the second-best performance.

Table A6: Joint goal accuracy (%) of SUMBT with different SINGLE TURNBACK proportions.

A GlobalPointer based Robust Approach for Information Extraction from Dialog Transcripts

Yanbo J. Wang[1], **Sheng Chen**[1], **Hengxing Cai**[2], **Wei Wei**[3], **Kuo Yan**[1], **Zhe Sun**[1], **Hui Qin**[1], **Yuming Li**[4] and **Xiaochen Cai**[5]

[1]LYZD-FinTech Co., LTD, Beijing, China
[2]4Paradigm Inc., Beijing, China
[3]School of Computer Science and Engineering, Xi'an University of Technology, Xi'an, China
[4]The University of Auckland, Auckland, New Zealand
[5]Nanjing University, Nanjing, China

Abstract

With the widespread popularisation of intelligent technology, task-based dialogue systems (TOD) are increasingly being applied to a wide variety of practical scenarios. As the key tasks in dialogue systems, named entity recognition and slot filling play a crucial role in the completeness and accuracy of information extraction. This paper is an evaluation paper for SereTOD 2022 Workshop challenge (Track 1: Information extraction from dialog transcripts). We proposed a multi-model fusion approach based on GlobalPointer, combined with some optimisation tricks, finally achieved an entity F1 of 60.73, an entity-slot-value triple F1 of 56, and an average F1 of 58.37, and got the highest score in SereTOD 2022 Workshop challenge[1].

1 Introduction

Task-oriented dialogue (TOD) systems are designed for specific application areas and have gained more and more attention in both academia and industry recently (Gao et al., 2019).

As a branch of the dialogue systems, TOD systems are different from question-and-answer (QA) systems and chat-oriented dialogue systems. TOD system needs to determine the user's intent through understanding, analysis, information extraction, and clarification. Then complete a round of dialogue through natural language generation or APIs.

According to the work of Zhao et al. (Zhao and Eskenazi, 2016) and Zhang et al. (Zhang et al., 2020), the structure of a traditional TOD system is shown in Figure 1, which can be divided into three modules, Spoken Language Understanding (SLU), Natural Language Generation (NLG), and Dialogue Manager.

The SLU Module converts language into semantic representations, the purpose is to obtain the semantic information of user input speech. The downstream module of SLU is the dialogue manager module. The task of this module is to decide how the system responds to the input speech (McTear, 2004) and then the system updates its internal state, and then the system determines the system behaviour through policies. In order to provide information to the user, the dialogue manager usually needs to query the knowledge base or the Internet, and it also needs to consider the historical data in the multi-round dialogue. Finally, the NLG module translates the decisions of the system into natural language-based dialogues. Among them, the state variables contain variables that track the dialogue process, as well as slots that represent user needs.

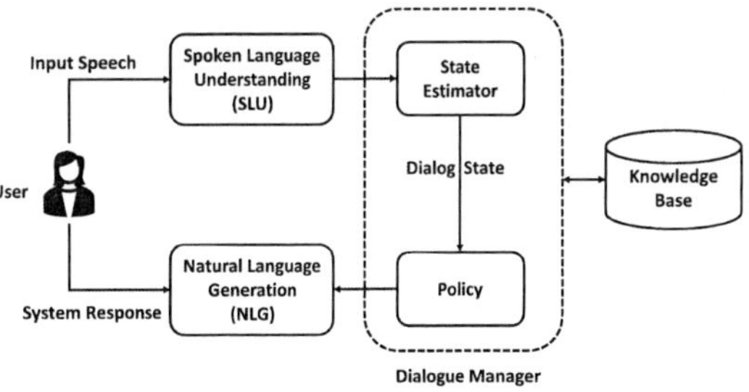

Figure 1: The data samples in the product catalogue in the Shopping Queries Data Set.

1.1 Task description

The task of SereTOD 2022 Workshop challenge consists of 2 tracks, and we focus on track 1 (Information extraction from dialogue transcripts) in this paper. There are four sub-tasks for track 1:

- **Entity Extraction.** Extract entity mentions in real-life dialogues according to the entity types defined in the schema (including related data package plan and services, a total of nine categories).
- **Entity Coreference Resolution.** Since an entity might be mentioned in different surface

[1]https://docs.google.com/spreadsheets/d/1w28AKkG6Wjmuo15QlRlRyrnv859MT1ry0CHV8tFxY9o/edit?usp=sharing

Proceedings of the Towards Semi-Supervised and Reinforced Task-Oriented Dialog Systems (SereTOD), pages 13 - 18
December 7, 2022 ©2022 Association for Computational Linguistics

```
{
  "id": "94bba9d63c097df1800482d827287e47",
  "content": [
    {
      "[SPEAKER 1]": "你好，很高兴为您服务",
      "[SPEAKER 2]": "唉你好，我想问一下，我想办那个半年_六个G那个包，我想问问那个包那个不是属于全国漫游嘛",
      "客服意图": "问候",
      "用户意图": "问候,求助-查询（ent-1-流量范围）",
      "info": {
        "ents": [
          {
            "name": "半年_六个G那个包",
            "id": "ent-1",
            "type": "流量包",
            "pos": [
              [
                2,
                15,
                24
              ]
            ]
          }
        ],
        "triples": [
          {
            "ent-id": "ent-1",
            "ent-name": "半年 六个G那个包",
            "prop": "业务时长",
            "value": "半年",
            "pos": [
              2,
              15,
              17
            ]
          },
          {
            "ent-id": "ent-1",
            "ent-name": "半年 六个G那个包",
            "prop": "流量总量",
            "value": "_六个G",
            "pos": [
              2,
              17,
              21
            ]
          }
        ]
      }
    },
```


Figure 2: A basic unit of the MobileCS (mobile customer-service) dialog dataset.

forms, for example, "100元的流量包", "那个流量包", "100元的那个业务", "刚才那业务" may refer to the same entity " 100元流量包 (100 Yuan data package plan)". Thus we need to represent the entities with coreference relationships in a unified id.

- **Slot Filling.** Extract the slot value corresponding to the entity slots (including the specific content of the package or business and the status of the user, etc.). For example, in the dialogue "10GB套餐的月费用是50元 (The price for the 10GB data package plan is 50 Chinese Yuan per month)", "50元 (50 Chinese Yuan)" will be the value for the monthly price slot.

- **Entity Slot Alignment.** Align entities and slot values with corresponding relationships.

1.2 Data description

The data for this challenge is ***MobileCS (mobile customer-service) dialog dataset*** (Ou et al., 2022) around 100K dialogues (in Chinese), which come from real-world dialogue transcripts between real users and customer-service staffs from China Mobile, with privacy information anonymised.

The official data includes three parts: training data, dev data and test data. A basic unit of the data sample is shown in Figure 2. In which Speaker ID such as "**[SPEAKER 1]**" and "**[SPEAKER 2]**" refer to the speaker of the dialogue, "用户意图" represents the user intent, "客服意图" represents the system intent, the entities and triples are the information mentioned in this turn.

2 Approach

In this paper, we focus on the baseline (Liu et al., 2022) and practical business difficulties of and dialogue system, and propose suitable solutions. The difficulties can be summarised as follows:

- In the slot value extraction stage, the length of the slot value to be extracted is relatively long, the categories are complex, and the general sample repetition is relatively small. Especially for the categories '业务规则' and '持有套餐'.

- The problem of label scope coverage nesting. Labels from class A may be overwritten by labels from class B.

- The distribution of training data, dev data, and test data has an obvious difference.

- Some single-turn dialogues with entities contain very little information, but there are many entities containing business rules need to be identified.

According to the above-mentioned difficulties, our solutions can be summarised as follows:

- We apply the GlobalPointer to the Entity Extraction and Slot Filling tasks , set different loss weights for positive and negative samples.

- Data pre-processing: The addition of global context information, split the paragraphs into single characters, merge the original training data and dev data to train.

- We add training data and dev data to the Pretrained Masked Language Model.

- We optimized the Entity Slot Alignment task to increase the cross-validation score by 9 percentage points.

- In the Entity Extraction task, we trained some models with different maximum token length (384, 256, 280). The differences between models bring benefits to fusion.

- We truncate the 256×256 token probability matrix according to the maximum entity length and fuse it to greatly reduce memory consumption.

- For the overlapping nested entities in the Entity Extraction task, we do post-processing to eliminate them.

2.1 Model and tricks

In the challenge, we found that nested entities and non-nested entities coexist in training data and dev data. The sequence-to-sequence method in baseline cannot handle the situation of nested entities, therefore, we use the end-to-end method to solve this tough issue. In entity extraction and slot filling, we are mainly based on GlobalPointer (Su et al., 2022), a novel efficient span-based approach for named entity recognition, which uses global normalisation for named entity recognition, and can identify nested and non-nested entities indiscriminately.

For any sentence, GlobalPointer constructs an upper triangular matrix to traverse all valid spans, as shown in Figure 3, each grid corresponds to an entity span. Assuming that after the input sentence

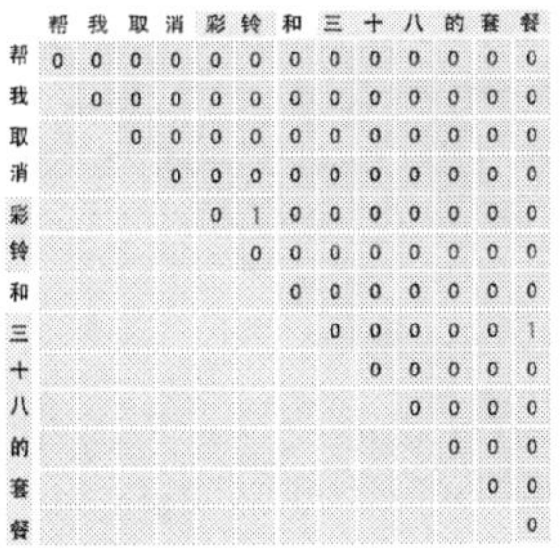

Figure 3: Schematic diagram of GlobalPoniter multi-head identification of nested entities.

passes through the encoder, the representations at positions i and j are h_i and h_j, and the query vector q_i and key vector k_j of the two are obtained through the fully connected layer:

$$q_i = W_q h_i + b_q$$

$$k_j = W_k h_j + b_k$$

Then the score of each span $s(i,j)$ predicted as an entity is:

$$s(i,j) = q_i^T k_j$$

On this basis, GlobalPointer incorporates the Rotational Position Encoding (RoPE) mechanism to explicitly introduce relative position information to the prediction of span pairs. For position m, RoPE calculates an orthogonal matrix R_m, then multiply R_m by q to rotate q. According to the matrix multiplication rule, if k is also multiplied by the RoPE. At this time, the score $s(i,j)$ of the span will have relative position information R_{n-m}:

$$(R_m q_i)^T (R_n k_j) = q_i^T R_m^T R_n k_j = q_i^T R_{n-m} k_j$$

2.1.1 Loss function

Since the number of entities in the sentences in the dataset is very small and there are a large number of negative samples, we do not use binary classification in our method but designed a multi-label loss function. For identifying entities of a specific class α, the fragments with $s_\alpha(i,j) > 0$ are regarded as the output of entities of type α. The loss function is:

$$log(1+\sum_{(i,j)\in P_\alpha} e^{-s_\alpha}(i,j))+log(1+\sum_{(i,j)\in Q_\alpha} e^{s_\alpha}(i,j))$$

Where P_α is a set of spans with entity type α in the dataset, Q_α is a set of spans that are not entities or whose entity type is not α in the sample, we only need to consider the combination of $i \leq j$, which is the upper triangular matrix in the blue area in Figure 2.

$$\omega = \{(i,j)|1 \leq i \leq j \leq n\}$$

$$P_\alpha = \left\{(i,j)|t_{[i:j]} \in \alpha\right\}$$

$$Q_\alpha = \Omega - P_\alpha$$

Due to the low accuracy in the entity extraction stage, we increase the loss weight of positive samples and decrease the loss weight of negative samples, which can increase F1 by about one percentage point. However, slot filling cannot effectively improve the model accuracy through different loss weights.

2.1.2 How to use the dev data

In view of the large difference in the distribution of training data, dev data, and test data, how to use dev data is also a key factor to ensure that the model can perform well in test data. First, we locate the position of the slot value of the official dev data. However, some position tags are difficult to capture, so we eliminate them in the training phase. Then we will merge and disarrange dev data and training data, and divide them into four folds. Finally, we will apply the split data to each stage of the pipeline.

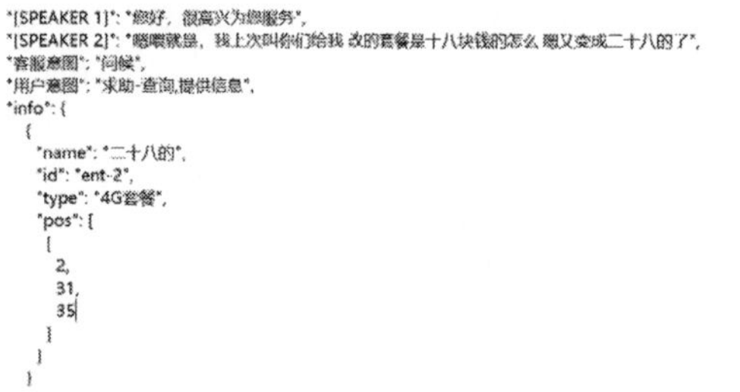

Figure 4: The data sample from challenge data.

2.1.3 The addition of global context information

In the challenge data, the information obtained by simply concatenating **[SPEAKER1]**, and **[SPEAKER2]** cannot accurately identify the entity type. As shown in Figure 4, only by adding context information, we can make it clear that the name value "二十八的" refers to "套餐" or "4G套餐". During the optimisation process, we show that adding global context information can improve a single model by about 2 percentage points.

Since we take the current dialogue content and the global context concatenating as input, we mask the concatenated tokens through attention_mask. However, the global context information is only used as enhancement content and does not participate in the calculation of loss, so we mask the context information to calculate the effective loss, as shown in Figure 5.

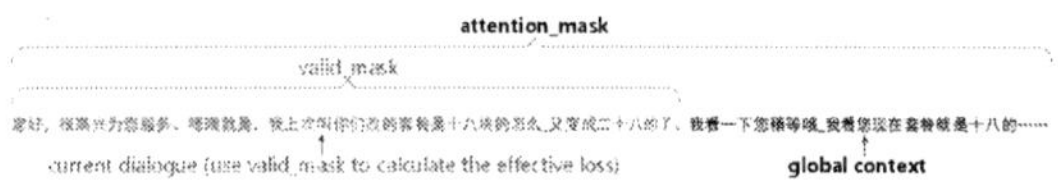

Figure 5: Attention_mask based on the global context and valid_mask for the current conversation.

2.1.4 Break down context by character

There are many phonetic expressions related to place names and special terms in the training and dev data of the challenge data. As shown in Figure 6, according to the Chinese BERT (Devlin et al., 2018) tokenizer, the Chinese pinyin may be split into words that have nothing to do with semantics, so we first split the paragraphs into single characters and then send them to the BERT tokenizer.

Figure 6: The sample data of place names with pinyin expressions and result of segmentation.

2.1.5 Pre-trained Masked Language Model (MLM)

We add training data and dev data to the Pre-trained Masked Language Model, and use the pre-trained model for entity extraction and slot filling, which increases by about 1 percentage point.

2.1.6 Entity slot alignment task optimisation

In the Baseline (Liu et al., 2022) given by the challenge, when calculating the similarity between any entity (ent) and any slot value (triple), there is some noise affecting the model training, For example, when calculating the similarity between **ent1** and **triple1**, such as **<entity>ent1<entity>... <entity>ent2<entity>... <slot>triple1<slot>**. In this case, other types of entities appear in the text between **ent1** and **triple1** will also be labelled, which will cause interference in training and dev. Therefore, in the face of this situation, we remove the entity tag **<entity>** related to **ent2**, which can directly improve the model verification result by 9 percentage points.

2.1.7 Post-processing

In the post-processing stage, there are many overlapping entities in our entity extraction part. In this case, we choose the one with the highest probability as the optimal choice. For example, in the following cases shown in Figure 7, we will remove ent1 and select ent2:

```
ent1:{"pos": [[1,20,25]],"type": "附加套餐","name": "十块钱套餐",prob:0.6}
ent2:{"pos": [[1,20,25]],"type": "套餐","name": "十块钱套餐",prob:0.9}
```

Figure 7: An example case for post-processing.

3 Model fusion

In terms of data selection and split-folding strategy, we merge the original training data and dev data, and split them into four folds for training through k-fold. In Table 1 and Table 2, the score is calculated on the out-of-fold of the combination of training and dev data.

3.1 Entity extraction

In the entity extraction subtask, we selected five models of Roformer (Su et al., 2021), DeBERTa (He et al., 2020), RoBERTa (Liu et al., 2019), MacBERT (Cui et al., 2020), and NEZHA (Wei et al., 2019) for probability average fusion, and found that the fusion of models with different token lengths can achieve better results. We chose models with a maximum token length of 256, 280, and 384 for fusion; at the same time, we also chose to add Efficient GlobalPointer (Su et al., 2022) to the fusion to increase the difference. The final fusion result (mean average of probability) is 1.3 percentage points higher than the highest single model. The result is shown in Table 1.

Backbone	Head	Max Length	4 fold F1	Ensemble F1
roformer	Efficient_GlobalPointer	384	0.557	0.570
deberta	GlobalPointer	280	0.556	
nezha	GlobalPointer	256	0.547	
roberta	GlobalPointer	256	0.547	
macbert	GlobalPointer	256	0.549	

Table 1: The model fusion result of entity extraction.

3.2 Slot filling

In the slot filling subtask, we selected four models of Roformer (Su et al., 2021), RoBERTa (Liu et al., 2019), MacBERT (Cui et al., 2020), and NEZHA (Wei et al., 2019) for probability average fusion. The final fusion result is 0.9 percentage points higher than the highest single model. The result is shown in Table 2.

Backbone	Head	Max Length	4 fold F1	Ensemble F1
roformer	GlobalPointer	256	0.607	0.616
nezha	GlobalPointer	256	0.605	
roberta	GlobalPointer	256	0.600	
macbert	GlobalPointer	256	0.602	

Table 2: The model fusion result of slot filling.

3.3 Entity coreference resolution and entity slot alignment

Due to the time limit of the challenge, the 4-fold and 5-fold models were not trained for these two tasks. First, we cut the original data into 4 folds, and merge three fold data and dev data as training data to obtain model 1. Then we cut the original data into 5 folds, and merge four fold data and dev data as training data to obtain model 2. The final submission is a probability average fusion of model1 and model2. The scores are in Table3.

Entity Coreference Resolution	
4-fold	*5-fold*
0.887	0.891
Entity Slot Alignment	
4-fold	*5-fold*
0.884	0.891

Table 3: The 4-fold and 5-fold result for resolution and alignment.

3.4 GlobalPointer fusion matrix optimisation

In the GlobalPointer fusion stage, a four-dimensional $(sample\_num \times type\_num \times L \times L)$ matrix is generated. The last two dimensions are the maximum token length of 256. Since the final matrix is too large and there are many models, the memory cost of Numpy storage and calculation is too high, especially in the slot filling stage. Therefore, we first initialise a Numpy matrix $(sample\_num \times type\_num \times L \times max\_lengh\_entity)$, in which max_lengh_entity is the maximum entity length, which is 20 or 50, which is much smaller than 256. This dimension data is obtained by truncating the matrix. And through the calculation of the model, the probability matrix is continuously filled, reducing the number of variables in the memory, and finally obtaining the final result. One example is shown in Figure 8.

4 Conclusion

In this challenge, we use the GlobalPointer-based structure and probabilistic average fusion of Roformer, DeBERTa, RoBERTa, MacBERT, and NEZHA as the main solution. At the same time, we adopted tricks such as adding global context information and breaking down context by character in the following step to further optimise the results. Finally, we end up with an entity F1 of 60.73, an entity-slot-value triple F1 of 56, and an average F1 of 58.37, and got the highest average F1 score in the challenge of SereTOD 2022 Workshop.

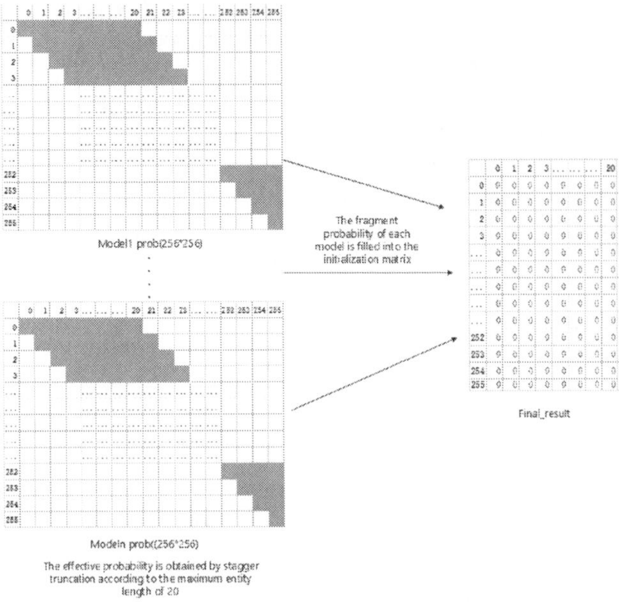

Figure 8: EntityExtraction task probability fusion – get effective probability by stagger truncation with maximum entity length of 20.

References

Yiming Cui, Wanxiang Che, Ting Liu, Bing Qin, Shijin Wang, and Guoping Hu. 2020. Revisiting pre-trained models for chinese natural language processing. *arXiv preprint arXiv:2004.13922*.

Jacob Devlin, Ming-Wei Chang, Kenton Lee, and Kristina Toutanova. 2018. Bert: Pre-training of deep bidirectional transformers for language understanding. *arXiv preprint arXiv:1810.04805*.

Jianfeng Gao, Michel Galley, and Lihong Li. 2019. *Neural approaches to conversational AI: Question answering, task-oriented dialogues and social chatbots*. Now Foundations and Trends.

Pengcheng He, Xiaodong Liu, Jianfeng Gao, and Weizhu Chen. 2020. Deberta: Decoding-enhanced bert with disentangled attention. *arXiv preprint arXiv:2006.03654*.

Hong Liu, Hao Peng, Zhijian Ou, Juanzi Li, Yi Huang, and Junlan Feng. 2022. Information extraction and human-robot dialogue towards real-life tasks: A baseline study with the mobilecs dataset. *arXiv preprint arXiv:2209.13464*.

Yinhan Liu, Myle Ott, Naman Goyal, Jingfei Du, Mandar Joshi, Danqi Chen, Omer Levy, Mike Lewis, Luke Zettlemoyer, and Veselin Stoyanov. 2019. Roberta: A robustly optimized bert pretraining approach. *arXiv preprint arXiv:1907.11692*.

Michael F McTear. 2004. *Spoken dialogue technology: toward the conversational user interface*. Springer Science & Business Media.

Zhijian Ou, Junlan Feng, Juanzi Li, Yakun Li, Hong Liu, Hao Peng, Yi Huang, and Jiangjiang Zhao. 2022. A challenge on semi-supervised and reinforced task-oriented dialog systems. *arXiv preprint arXiv:2207.02657*.

Jianlin Su, Yu Lu, Shengfeng Pan, Bo Wen, and Yunfeng Liu. 2021. Roformer: Enhanced transformer with rotary position embedding. *arXiv preprint arXiv:2104.09864*.

Jianlin Su, Ahmed Murtadha, Shengfeng Pan, Jing Hou, Jun Sun, Wanwei Huang, Bo Wen, and Yunfeng Liu. 2022. Global pointer: Novel efficient span-based approach for named entity recognition. *arXiv preprint arXiv:2208.03054*.

Junqiu Wei, Xiaozhe Ren, Xiaoguang Li, Wenyong Huang, Yi Liao, Yasheng Wang, Jiashu Lin, Xin Jiang, Xiao Chen, and Qun Liu. 2019. Nezha: Neural contextualized representation for chinese language understanding. *arXiv preprint arXiv:1909.00204*.

Zheng Zhang, Ryuichi Takanobu, Qi Zhu, MinLie Huang, and XiaoYan Zhu. 2020. Recent advances and challenges in task-oriented dialog systems. *Science China Technological Sciences*, 63(10):2011–2027.

Tiancheng Zhao and Maxine Eskenazi. 2016. Towards end-to-end learning for dialog state tracking and management using deep reinforcement learning. *arXiv preprint arXiv:1606.02560*.

A Token-pair Framework for Information Extraction from Dialog Transcripts in SereTOD Challenge

Chenyue Wang[1,2], Xiangxing Kong[2], Mengzuo Huang[2], Feng Li[2], Jian Xing[2], Weidong Zhang[2], and Wuhe Zou[2]

[1]Peking University, Beijing, China
[2]NetEase Games AI Lab, Hangzhou, China

Abstract

This paper describes our solution for SereTOD Challenge Track 1: Information extraction from dialog transcripts. We propose a token-pair framework to simultaneously identify entity and value mentions and link them into corresponding triples. As entity mentions are usually coreferent, we adopt a baseline model for coreference resolution. We exploit both annotated transcripts and unsupervised dialogs for training. With model ensemble and post-processing strategies, our system significantly outperforms the baseline solution and ranks first in triple f1 and third in entity f1.

1 Introduction

Task-oriented dialogs cover a wide range of daily application, such as ordering food, booking tickets, and querying services. With the development of deep learning and natural language processing, AI assistants start to replace human operators in a few basic scenarios. However, correctly extracting key information in complicated contexts and generating human-like yet informative responses remain a challenge for both academia and industry.

The SereTOD 2022 Workshop introduces a challenge on mobile customer-service scenario with real-world dialog dataset (Ou et al., 2022). We mainly participate in Track 1: Information extraction from dialog transcripts, and present our token-pair framework based solution in this paper.

2 Background

The challenge provides around 100k dialog transcripts between mobile service users and staff, titled as MobileCS dataset, of which 10k are annotated while the rest are unlabeled. The annotation includes service entities and the attributes or values of the service (e.g. package price) or the user (e.g. account balance) mentioned in the dialog. As the dialogs are generally colloquial, co-references are required to be resolved for entity mentions. Moreover, values for an entity may scatter in multi-turn dialogs or nested inside the verbal expression of entities.

Track 1 is mainly formulated as an information extraction problem and contains two sub-tasks: (1) entity extraction, i.e., to extract entity mentions with their corresponding entity types as defined in the schema; (2) slot filling, i.e., to extract values for entity attributes and to match the slot-value pairs with the corresponding entity concepts. F1 score is the metric for system evaluation.

3 System Overview

3.1 Model Design

The submitted system consists of two models: an information extractor for both entity extraction and slot filling, and a co-reference resolution model for value-entity assignment.

3.1.1 Information Extractor

Recent works (Wang et al., 2020; Su et al., 2022; Li et al., 2022) on named entity recognition and information extraction shift from the conventional sequence labeling method into the token-pair approach. A token-pair based model outputs logits in the shape of $c \times n \times n$, where c denotes the number of types and n denotes sequence length, predicting over possible spans in the sequence for all the types.

Compared with previous methods, the token-pair approach has the following advantages. First and foremost, it supports nested and multilabel entities. In the MobileCS dataset, target entities are often nested due to the colloquial references. For example, the price entity *38-yuan* is nested inside the package entity *that 38-yuan package*. In addition, an entity may belong to multiple types, as defined in the schema. Such cases cannot be properly handled by sequence labeling method as a token-level classification task. Secondly, the token-pair

Proceedings of the Towards Semi-Supervised and Reinforced Task-Oriented Dialog Systems (SereTOD), pages 19 - 23
December 7, 2022

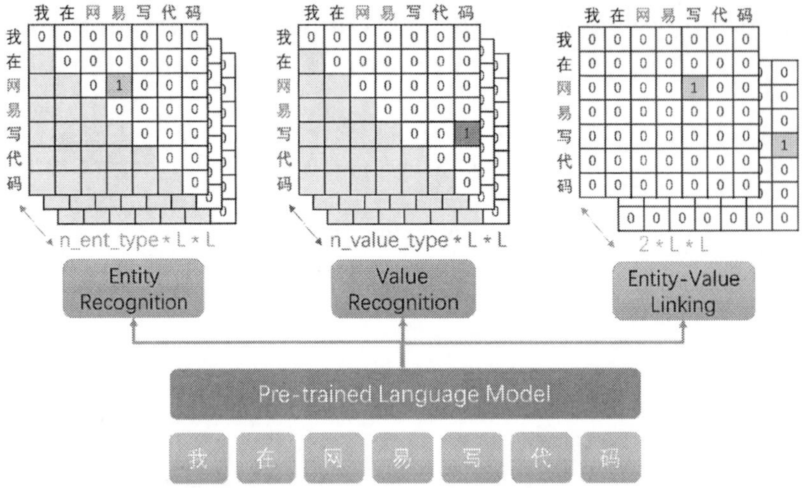

Figure 1: illustration of information extractor model, composed of an entity recognition module, a value recognition model, and an entity-value linking module. Each module is a token-pair based structure that consider all the possible spans in the input text and identify the types or relations for the recognized spans.

method directly optimizes the span-level metric and outputs straightforward result, while previous methods only focus on the token-level and require extra decoding modules such as CRF. Last but not least, the token-pair method is more versatile and flexible. Apart from NER task, it can be applied to joint information extraction and potentially other related tasks with simple modification. However, for token-pair framework, its output logits are large in quantity and extremely sparse, raising issues in model training and ensemble. Fortunately, this drawback could be alleviated.

Su et al. (2022) proposes GlobalPointer, a model structured on the token-pair framework. The encoder outputs, denoted as $[\mathbf{h}_1, \mathbf{h}_2, ..., \mathbf{h}_n]$, are transformed into queries and keys as $\mathbf{q}_i = \mathbf{W}_q\mathbf{h}_i$ and $\mathbf{k}_i = \mathbf{W}_k\mathbf{h}_i$. The score for span from i to j for type t is calculated as:

$$s_t(i, j) = \mathbf{q}_i^\mathsf{T}\mathbf{k}_j + \mathbf{w}_t^\mathsf{T}[\mathbf{q}_i; \mathbf{k}_i; \mathbf{q}_j; \mathbf{k}_j]$$

where $\mathbf{w}_t$ is a type-specific transformation.

A multi-label class-imbalance loss is proposed for countering severe class imbalance issue in the token-pair setting, where Ω_{neg} and Ω_{neg} are negative samples and positive samples, s_i and s_j are the scores for negative and positive sample:

$$\log\left(1 + \sum_{i\in\Omega_{neg}} e^{s_i}\right) + \log\left(1 + \sum_{j\in\Omega_{pos}} e^{-s_j}\right)$$

We adopt both the structure and loss design in our information extractor model.

Previous token-pair based IE models, such as GPLinker (Su, 2022) and TPLinker (Wang et al., 2020), formulate joint extraction as a token pair linking problem and introduce tagging schemes that align the boundary tokens of entity pairs under each relation type. However, entity types are not considered in the schemes.

Alternatively, we decompose the extractor model into three modules to simultaneously extract and link the entity and value mention together with their types: (1) entity recognition, (2) value recognition, and (3) entity-value linking, as illustrated in Figure 1. For a candidate span, denoted by the its start and end positions as [*i, j*], the first two modules predict whether the span text is an entity or value that belongs to the current type, while the linking module predicts the head-to-head (and tail-to-tail) matching for an entity and a value mention that starts (and ends) at position *i* and *j*, respectively. The entity and triple results can be obtained by combining the outputs of the three modules.

The extractor model is trained with a multitask loss, where $\mathcal{L}_{ent}$, $\mathcal{L}_{val}$, and $\mathcal{L}_{link}$ are the multi-label class-imbalance loss for each module:

$$\mathcal{L}_{total} = \lambda_1\mathcal{L}_{ent} + \lambda_2\mathcal{L}_{val} + \lambda_3\mathcal{L}_{link}$$

For simplicity, we set $\lambda_1 = \lambda_2 = \lambda_3 = 1$ without further tuning.

3.1.2 Co-reference Resolution Model

As is required, each value should match a resolved entity concept. We adopt the entity co-reference model from the baseline solution (Liu et al., 2022). The model transforms the embedding of the predicted entity tokens into corresponding representations by average pooling, scores candidate entity pairs, and groups them into concept clusters.

In the predicted triples, a value may correspond to multiple entity mentions. Once the concept groups for the entities are determined, we select the most matched entity's concept for each value.

We also attempt other approaches for value-entity resolution. One solution is to group the entity mentions that correspond to the same value into the same concept group. By using disjoint set, we can connect local groups into the global ones. However, this process is significantly affected by mismatched triples and achieves relatively low triple metric.

The co-reference resolution model could be integrated into the IE model and share the same encoder. Nonetheless, the co-reference resolution metrics are not stable during training and the valid result is much lower. How to integrate the co-reference resolution into the token-pair based framework remains further investigation.

3.2 Training

Our system is mainly trained on the annotated dialogs with exploitation of the unlabeled data.

3.2.1 Labeled Data

As the triple annotation only marks the value mention without detailed positions, we directly match all the value mentions in the turn utterances and add position information. Dialogs are then split into segments every 3 turns, since a majority of values have their entity mentions appear in this range. In each segment, we further supplement triples by matching values and entities that belong to the same entity group. Utterances are joined by the [SEP] token as input texts. We add specific user tokens at the beginning of each text segment, which serve as the head entity for user-attribute values. The positions and types of the entity and value spans are used as supervised signals for training the IE model.

For the co-reference resolution model, we segment the sessions with a token length of 512 and consider the inter-segment entity co-references. The details are the same as the baseline solution.

3.2.2 Unlabeled Data

We conduct domain adaptive pretraining (Gururangan et al., 2020) on the unlabeled dialog utterances to further fit the language model into the mobile service scenarios. In addition, we infer on the first 10k unlabeled dialogs with models trained on labeled data and adopt the predictions as pseudo annotations. These pseudo-labeled dialogs are then used as training data for a part of the ensemble models.

3.3 Inferring

Different from the data construction strategies in training stage, we infer on each dialog in a sliding window manner with a size of 3 turns. For the predicted triples, which are in the format of *(entity, prop, value)*, we record all distinct value mentions and their matched entities. The predicted entities are fed into the co-reference resolution model and assigned with group ids. Finally, each distinct value mention shares the same group id as its most matched entity.

In our submitted system, we ensemble a dozen of models of different pretraining methods (RoBERTa by Liu et al., 2019, MacBERT by Cui et al., 2020, etc., with or without DAPT), model scale (base or large), and training data (with or without pseudo-labels), by averaging their logits during inference. Invalid and repeated predictions are filtered during this process.

4 Discussions

4.1 Experiments and Results

We present key experiment results on validation set in Table 1 and briefly discuss the effects of the proposed strategies. Our scores and rankings in the official evaluation result are reported in Table 2. The triple-f1 ranks first among all the teams while the ent-f1 ranks third. Our averaged f1 only keeps a minor gap with the top-2 solutions.

4.1.1 Token-pair Framework

Compared with the baseline solution, our system obtains 19.48 percent absolute improvement in entity f1 and 17.06 percent in triple f1 using the same backbone model. This result proves the effectiveness of our token-pair framework. We argue that the improvement derives from better NER result, particularly for the nested and multilabel entities, as well as the joint extraction, alleviating error accumulation as in the pipeline solution. Moreover, our system is more efficient than the baseline, since we integrate three steps (i.e., named entity recognition, slot recognition, and entity slot alignment) into one IE module that shares the same encoder.

methods	entity metrics (p/r/f1)	triple metrics (p/r/f1)	#entity	#triple
RoBERTa$_{large}$ Baseline	- / - / 33.45	- / - / 34.94	-	-
RoBERTa$_{base}$ TPIE	52.87 / 53.37 / 53.12	47.88 / 38.25 / 42.53	6550	8535
w/ coref	52.87 / 53.37 / 53.12	55.07 / 44.00 / 48.92	6550	8535
w/ coref + *DAPT*	55.99 / 51.84 / 53.83	55.04 / 43.08 / 48.33	6000	8362
w/ coref + *pseudo*	57.22 / 53.42 / 55.26	58.93 / 45.15 / 51.13	6048	8185
RoBERTa$_{large}$ TPIE	53.47 / 52.39 / 52.93	52.68 / 40.79 / 45.98	6356	8272
w/ coref	53.47 / 52.39 / 52.93	59.58 / 46.13 / 52.00	6356	8272
w/ coref + *DAPT*	51.35 / 54.33 / 52.80	60.72 / 45.99 / 52.34	6887	8093
w/ coref + *pseudo*	53.81 / 53.36 / 53.58	61.37 / 44.58 / 51.65	6457	7759
Ensemble	**63.27** / 49.67 / 55.65	63.31 / 36.74 / 46.50	5083	6467
w/ coref	**63.27** / 49.67 / 55.65	**70.80** / 41.08 / 51.99	5083	6467
w/ coref + *lower thres.*	56.51 / **56.83** / **56.67**	58.55 / **53.16** / **55.72**	6527	9701

Table 1: evaluation results on dev set. The baseline result is reported in the official implementation. TPIE is our token-pair based information extractor. *DAPT* indicates domain adaptive pretraining on the LM, *pseudo* indicates training with 10k pseudo-labeled dialogs, *lower thres.* indicates adjusting threshold when inferring.

entity f1	entity ranking	triple f1	triple ranking	avg. f1	avg. ranking
55.17	3	56.07	1	55.62	3

Table 2: official evaluation result

4.1.2 Co-reference Resolution Model

As the challenge requires extracted values to be related with an entity concept, it is necessary to train a task-specific co-reference resolution model in place of the error-prone merging strategy solely based on the IE triple results. Experiment results show that better co-reference resolution results improve the triple metric by more than 5 percents.

4.1.3 Training with Unsupervised Data

Domain adaptive pretraining and pseudo labeling are the two methods for exploiting unsupervised data. As the mobile service domain differs from the general pretraining corpus, we expect DAPT to yield considerable benefit. However, the results suggest otherwise. To our surprise, training with pseudo-labeled data improves entity recognition task. Notably, the triple f1 for RoBERTa base model is significantly boosted with pseudo-labels.

4.1.4 Large Pretrained Model

Using larger pretrained model improves triple f1, which relies more on the entity-value linking module. Compared with named entity and value recognition, entity-value linking task is more complex and challenging. We argue that larger models are capable of solving such harder tasks and contribute to better performance.

4.1.5 Model Ensemble

Directly adopting model ensemble only yields marginal or even negative gains. The numbers of predicted entities and triples drop by a large portion, resulting in higher precision but lower recall. This suggests model ensemble suppresses the averaged logits and the default threshold is no longer suitable. We empirically lower the thresholds for entity and value recognition to balance precision and recall for higher f-scores.

4.2 Noisy Labels

In the initially released dataset, there exist a number of noisy entity type labels. Some clearly defined items are marked with different types. For example, the item *Two City, One Family*, is partially marked as *Long-distance Plan* and partially *Plan*, an ancestor for the former in the entity type hierarchy. Classifying an item as its ancestor type, though not perfect, is somehow acceptable. Therefore, we propose type smoothing to counter type label noise by assigning soft label weight instead of hard one-hot for entity types:

$$label_i^j = \begin{cases} w_1, & \text{if } j \text{ in ancestor types} \\ w_2, & \text{if } j \text{ is annotated type} \\ 0, & \text{otherwise} \end{cases}$$

Type label discrepancies are mostly corrected

by rule-based filtering in the later released dataset during the challenge, thus we do not adopt this strategy in our submitted system.

Span boundary issues also prevail in the annotated transcript as the entity and value mentions are typically colloquial. For example, for the expression *that 38-yuan package*, annotators may neglect *that*. Determiners and attributes as such are tricky for uniform annotations. Some value types, e.g. user demands, package rules, are too flexible to uniformly determine the mention spans.

Boundary smoothing (Zhu and Li, 2022) is a recently proposed technique to handle boundary issues for span-based models. It assigns a portion of probability ϵ from the target span $[i, j]$ to its neighboring spans whose Manhattan distances are within the smoothing size D. However, we discover a large portion of boundary noise also exist in the dev set and urge for cleaner validation samples to verify the effects of label denoising strategies.

5 Conclusion and Further Work

We present our solution for information extraction from dialog transcripts in SereTOD Challenge. The system is trained on both annotated transcripts and unsupervised dialogs. Various strategies and tricks are employed to further boost system performance, with their effects analyzed and discussed. Compared with the baseline implementation, our token-pair solution not only integrates multiple modules into a unified model framework, but also significantly outperforms the baseline result by more than 20 percent. In the official evaluation results, our system ranks first in triple-f1 and third in ent-f1.

For further work, we plan to integrate the coreference resolution model into the token-pair framework. We will evaluate the proposed label denoising methods and expect a well-anotated dataset. Detailed settings, such as multi-task weighting, shall also be tuned for better performance.

References

Yiming Cui, Wanxiang Che, Ting Liu, Bing Qin, Shijin Wang, and Guoping Hu. 2020. Revisiting pretrained models for chinese natural language processing. *arXiv preprint arXiv:2004.13922*.

Suchin Gururangan, Ana Marasović, Swabha Swayamdipta, Kyle Lo, Iz Beltagy, Doug Downey, and Noah A Smith. 2020. Don't stop pretraining: Adapt language models to domains and tasks. In *Proceedings of the 58th Annual Meeting of the Association for Computational Linguistics*, pages 8342–8360.

Jingye Li, Hao Fei, Jiang Liu, Shengqiong Wu, Meishan Zhang, Chong Teng, Donghong Ji, and Fei Li. 2022. Unified named entity recognition as word-word relation classification. In *Proceedings of the AAAI Conference on Artificial Intelligence*, volume 36, pages 10965–10973.

Hong Liu, Hao Peng, Zhijian Ou, Juanzi Li, Yi Huang, and Junlan Feng. 2022. Information extraction and human-robot dialogue towards real-life tasks: A baseline study with the mobilecs dataset. *arXiv preprint arXiv:2209.13464*.

Yinhan Liu, Myle Ott, Naman Goyal, Jingfei Du, Mandar Joshi, Danqi Chen, Omer Levy, Mike Lewis, Luke Zettlemoyer, and Veselin Stoyanov. 2019. Roberta: A robustly optimized bert pretraining approach. *arXiv preprint arXiv:1907.11692*.

Zhijian Ou, Junlan Feng, Juanzi Li, Yakun Li, Hong Liu, Hao Peng, Yi Huang, and Jiangjiang Zhao. 2022. A challenge on semi-supervised and reinforced task-oriented dialog systems. *arXiv preprint arXiv:2207.02657*.

Jianlin Su. 2022. GPLinker: A joint extraction of entities and relations based on GlobalPointer.

Jianlin Su, Ahmed Murtadha, Shengfeng Pan, Jing Hou, Jun Sun, Wanwei Huang, Bo Wen, and Yunfeng Liu. 2022. Global pointer: Novel efficient span-based approach for named entity recognition. *arXiv preprint arXiv:2208.03054*.

Yucheng Wang, Bowen Yu, Yueyang Zhang, Tingwen Liu, Hongsong Zhu, and Limin Sun. 2020. TPLinker: Single-stage joint extraction of entities and relations through token pair linking. In *Proceedings of the 28th International Conference on Computational Linguistics*, pages 1572–1582, Barcelona, Spain (Online). International Committee on Computational Linguistics.

Enwei Zhu and Jinpeng Li. 2022. Boundary smoothing for named entity recognition. *arXiv preprint arXiv:2204.12031*.

Prompt Learning for Domain Adaptation in Task-Oriented Dialogue

Makesh Narsimhan Sreedhar
University of Wisconsin - Madison *
msreedhar@wisc.edu

Christopher Parisien
NVIDIA
cparisien@nvidia.com

Abstract

Conversation designers continue to face significant obstacles when creating production-quality task-oriented dialogue systems. The complexity and cost involved in schema development and data collection is often a major barrier for such designers, limiting their ability to create natural, user-friendly experiences. We frame the classification of user intent as the generation of a *canonical form*, a lightweight semantic representation using natural language. We show that canonical forms offer a promising alternative to traditional methods for intent classification. By tuning soft prompts for a frozen large language model, we show that canonical forms generalize very well to new, unseen domains in a zero- or few-shot setting. The method is also sample-efficient, reducing the complexity and effort of developing new task-oriented dialogue domains.

1 Introduction

Task-oriented dialogue systems in Conversational AI are challenging for developers to create. The current generation of dialogue frameworks requires developers to define actions (*intents*) and parameters (*slots*) that the natural language understanding (NLU) module accepts. This is then used to populate API service calls that operate in the backend to fulfill the user request. Casting natural language utterances from the user to a discrete set of intents and slots is often not very intuitive. This in turn leads to a situation where developers rely on hand-crafted rule-based grammars or a large annotated set of training samples for machine learning models to implement a given design. Any change to the design of the dialogue system would then require the developers to revisit and modify the implementation which is very often a time-consuming process. In this work, we aim to make dialogue system design easier and more intuitive.

The tremendous success of pre-trained language models such as BERT (Devlin et al., 2019) have made them the de facto standard for most intent classification and slot-filling tasks. However, these models are not immune to the challenge of adapting and extending existing models to new domains. One adaptation approach that has exploded in popularity in recent times is the usage of prompts with these language models. With a task description and few samples showing the input-output pairs, these language models become extremely effective at solving these tasks, especially at larger model sizes.

Manually specifying prompts suffers from sensitivity to phrasing; we get widely varying results based on how we frame the prompt. Prompt tuning (Lester et al., 2021) and p-tuning (Liu et al., 2021) have emerged as strong alternatives to manual prompt designing and they help optimize task-specific prompt tokens to get the best performance while keeping the language model itself frozen. In this work, we explore the task of intent classification using these large language models and p-tuning. Generative methods for classification tasks have not been widely adopted because generation is inherently difficult to control and utilize for further downstream tasks. Using our experiments on the Schema Guided Dialogue (Rastogi et al., 2019) dataset and the Virtual Assistant Benchmark (Liu et al., 2019), we show that with p-tuning we can achieve promising zero-shot and few-shot generalization capabilities to unseen domains.

In the task of intent classification, the intent labels provided as part of the dataset are usually terse and rigid. Generative models generalize better when intent labels are more descriptive but structured at the same. We borrow some aspects and terminology from semantic parsing to cast the intent labels to a more compositional format, known as *canonical forms*. In the traditional sense, canonical forms are paraphrases of the user utterances to

* Work done as part of an internship with NVIDIA

Proceedings of the Towards Semi-Supervised and Reinforced Task-Oriented Dialog Systems (SereTOD), pages 24 - 30
December 7, 2022 ©2022 Association for Computational Linguistics

convert them to a form that the semantic parser can operate on to output logical representations. In our use case, we loosely use the term, *canonical forms*, to refer to intent labels that are more descriptive than the discrete ones but are not too verbose, *e.g.*, "transfer_money" → "transfer money to bank account". We manually frame these canonical forms and do not rely on any grammar, simplifying the approach.

We observe that using such *canonical forms* as labels for the intent classification task allows the model to generalize better to domains that are adjacent, but not seen at train time (*e.g.*, *Flight Reservations* → *Bus Bookings*). We also find that it is beneficial to do a two-stage P-tuning for domain adaption, *i.e.*, once we have a p-tuned large language model on a wide set of domains, we can continue p-tuning this model on a small set of labelled samples from the target domain to allow the model to generalize better. We find that this few-shot approach works very well and this has promising implications for developers for dialogue systems; with minimal effort it would be feasible to adapt an existing model pre-trained on multiple domains to a new domain. In summary, our contributions are:

- We cast the problem of intent classification into a generative approach and rewrite intent labels in a more descriptive format (*canonical forms*).
- When using such canonical forms, generative approaches with Large Language Models(LLMs) show promising results when compared with traditional methods for intent classification.
- Generative models generalize very well to unseen domains in zero-shot and few-shot settings when compared with BERT-style approaches.
- We demonstrate the sample efficiency of p-tuning LLMs where we can achieve close to full dataset performance with a fraction of the data.

2 Method

In this section, we describe the creation of canonical forms and the prompt tuning technique we adopt for intent classification in the task-oriented dialogue setting.

2.1 Canonical Forms

Canonical forms are usually paraphrases of the user utterance to a standardized form that can be utilized by downstream systems. These forms are traditionally obtained by using a set of grammar rules written by experts. The output of this process is a natural language sequence, but structured in a form that makes it better suited for a semantic parser. Different semantic parsers employ different canonical forms and thus transfer across datasets is quite challenging.

Utterance	Canonical Form
what is the newest published article?	article that has the largest publication date
who has published the most articles?	person that is author of the most number of article

Table 1: Examples of canonical forms corresponding to user utterances from the Overnight (Wang et al., 2015) semantic parsing dataset.

Our work uses canonical forms as a method of obtaining the intent of a user utterance. Traditionally, intent labels tend to be terse, which makes it difficult for models to generalize to unseen domains. The expressive and compositional nature of language models can be exploited if the intent labels are more verbose, allowing them to extrapolate the generated intents to capture even novel domains. At the same time, if the intent labels tend to be very long and riddled with descriptions, the language models become susceptible to hallucinations. Our work proposes the use of canonical forms as a way of establishing a balance between being terse and too verbose. We map intent labels to short descriptive phrases, *e.g.*, "*check_balance*" → "*check balance in bank account*". Unlike traditional canonical forms, we do not use any formal grammar to perform this mapping and the phrases are manually specified. We believe that such an approach would reduce the burden on developers and designers of conversational systems.

2.2 P-tuning

Large Language Models (LLMs) have exhibited remarkable generalization capability when queried using *prompts* that contain examples of the task to be performed. However, the performance of LLMs varies widely depending on how such prompts are constructed. In order to overcome this issue of LLM sensitivity to the format of the prompt, multiple studies have come up with methods for automated prompt construction using discrete tokens (Lester et al., 2021) as well as soft tokens (Liu et al.,

2021).

In this work, we utilize the p-tuning approach that appends learnt *soft* tokens into the prompt that is fed to the LLM. The soft tokens traditionally do not have a mapping to words/subwords in the model vocabulary and are simply vectors optimized using gradient descent. Following the setup proposed by Liu et al. (2021), we use an LSTM model to learn and predict these soft tokens. The parameters of the LLM are frozen and only the parameters of this LSTM model are updated during p-tuning. We initialize the LSTM with random weights at the beginning of the p-tuning process and then update it during the training stage to output the optimal soft tokens. At the end of the training phase, we store these soft tokens and append them with the prompt to the LLM to get its prediction. The advantage of p-tuning is that we freeze the LM weights and update only the weights of the LSTM (14M parameters). This results in modifying only a very small fraction of the weights compared to traditional fine-tuning where all of the weights are updated.

The LM of choice in our experiments are the Megatron-GPT (Narayanan et al., 2021) models that are *decoder-only* transformers.

3 Experimental Setting

In this section, we describe the datasets used, the baselines we use for comparison and the evaluation metrics.

3.1 Datasets

We consider two widely known datasets in the dialogue community, the Schema Guided Dialogue (SGD) dataset (Rastogi et al., 2019) and the Virtual Assistant dataset (Liu et al., 2019).

Schema Guided Dialogue - This dataset covers 16 domains and has over 16k annotated conversations. The domains span a variety of user actions, including setting calendars and alarms, travel booking (car rentals, flights, buses and trains), music, weather, movies, and more. The dataset also contains *multi-domain* dialogues where the utterances switch between domains. For the purpose of our experiments, we consider only the *single-domain* dialogues with 37 intents across all utterances.

Virtual Assistant Dataset - This dataset covers 21 domains with 64 intents across all utterances. As the name suggests, the domains relate to user queries over a wide range of topics, including operating smart-home devices, media consumption, weather and travel. It has over 25k annotated user utterances that identify intents and slot values.

3.2 Prompt Template

The prompts that we use for intent classification have the following format

$<v_1..v_n> \quad utterance \quad intent: canonical$

where $< v_1, v_2, .., v_n >$ indicate the virtual tokens.

During the training stage of p-tuning, the model is shown the entire sequence, but the loss is computed only on the *answer* which in this case is the predicted canonical form. During inference, the context to the model includes the sequence until the word *"intent:"* and the model completes the sequence with its prediction for the intent. We use 100 virtual tokens with our prompt-encoder being an LSTM model with 2 layers.

3.3 Evaluation Method

Intent Classification Evaluating generative models for a classification task is not straightforward. This is further complicated by the fact that our model generates a canonical form identifying the intent of a given user utterance. We propose two methods to cast this generation problem to a classification setting. The difficulty arises from the fact that generated sequences very often differ from the exact gold truth sequence that the model sees as part of training. We utilize two approaches based on associating the generated canonical form to its closest label, *i.e.*, a nearest neighbor search. Once the canonical form label has been identified as the prediction, it becomes trivial to compute the classification accuracy. Since we already have a one-to-one mapping between canonical form labels and the discrete intent label, we can easily measure the performance of our model.

- Using Fasttext Embeddings (Bojanowski et al., 2016): We take the mean of all the embedding vectors of the generated canonical form and consider the vector obtained to be the representation of the whole sequence. We compute similar vectors for all the canonical form labels and consider the canonical form label that has the maximum cosine similarity with the generated one as the model's prediction.

- Using Sentence Transformers (Reimers and Gurevych, 2019): We use the *miniLM-QA* (Wang et al., 2020) transformer model that has been pretrained on multiple datasets on the text entailment/semantic search task, *i.e.*, given a query and a set of keys (documents/labels), it ranks the keys in order of relevance. We give as input to the model the generated canonical form (query) and the list of canonical form labels (keys). The model then returns the closest canonical form label to the generated canonical form which we consider as the prediction.

3.4 Baselines

We consider the following baselines for the intent classification task.

- **BERT-based finetuned model** (Intent Classification): We finetune BERT models on the datasets described in section 3.1. While some of the Megatron-GPT models we use are larger than the BERT model in terms of number of parameters, it should be noted that the LM parameters are frozen during the training stage of p-tuning and only the weights of the LSTM (14M parameters) are updated.

3.5 Evaluation Settings

We evaluate the performance of our model in two settings: in-domain and out-of-domain.

3.5.1 In-Domain

This setting corresponds to the traditional dataset splits where the train and test sets come from similar distributions. We p-tune the Megatron-GPT models on the train set and evaluate them on the test set for intent classification.

3.5.2 Out-of-Domain

In this setting, we aim to explore the generalization capability of LLMs. We hold out certain domains from the train set and use utterances from the held out domains as our test. This helps us understand how well these LLMs can generalize to unseen domains. The held out sets that we consider are:

- **Schema Guided Dialogue** (SGD): We hold out utterances corresponding to *bus bookings* and *hotel reservations* to form our test set. The train set includes utterances from adjacent domains: flight booking and restaurant reservations. This should be a relatively easy setting for the language model to generalize to.

- **Virtual Assistant**: To make things more challenging, we hold out utterances corresponding to *operating IOT devices* and *media consumption commands* (*e.g.*, commands that are variants of "play" - play movie, play audiobook). The train set does not have utterances from similar domains and this setting is more challenging for the model.

We consider the generalization capability of the model in two modes:

- **Zero-shot**: P-tune the model on the train set and evaluate zero-shot on the unseen domain test set.

- **Few-shot**: After p-tuning on the train set, we do a second stage p-tuning on a set of k samples from the target domain. Unless otherwise noted, k here is 5, 10, 50 or 100 samples.

The few-shot paradigm may be very useful for dialogue system developers in a limited-resource setting. Developers can implement new domains using existing language models and a small set of curated examples, without the burden and expense of retraining or providing a large number of labelled samples.

4 Results

In this section, we review the quantitative performance of the models for intent classification.

4.1 Intent Classification

We compute and list the accuracy of the baselines and our p-tuned GPT model in identifying the intent given the user utterance.

4.1.1 In-domain

We find that both the p-tuned GPT model as well as the BERT baseline perform very well on the standard in-domain split where both the train and test set come from the same distribution (Table 2). The classification accuracy of Megatron-GPT increases as we increase the model size. The trend of results remains consistent for both the SGD and Assistant datasets.

Model	SGD	Assistant
BERT-Large	0.88	0.91
Megatron-GPT - 345M	0.87	0.88
Megatron-GPT - 1.3B	0.91	0.92
Megatron-GPT - 5B	0.95	0.94

Table 2: Classification Accuracy on test sets of the SGD and Assistant datasets

4.1.2 Out-of-Domain

The out-of-domain setting is where the advantage of using a LLM becomes apparent. It is not feasible to expect a finetuned BERT model to generalize to an unseen domain not present in the train set. Such models continue to predict that the intent belongs to one of the intent labels they see during training. The p-tuned Megatron-GPT models, on the other hand, show impressive zero-shot and few-shot generalization capabilities on the SGD dataset (Table 3). For instance, having seen intents such as *"buy flight roundtrip tickets"* when presented with utterances for *Flight Reservations* in training, we can expect the model to reasonably generalize to utterances from *Bus Reservations* with utterances like "Get me a return trip on the bus" with the model's prediction for the intent being *"buy bus roundtrip tickets"*.

Mode	Bus Booking			Hotel Reservation		
	345M	1.3B	5B	345M	1.3B	5B
Zero Shot	0.755	0.762	0.787	0.379	0.448	0.467
FS - 10 samples	0.907	0.789	0.942	0.793	0.720	0.939
FS - 50 samples	0.953	0.965	0.975	0.957	0.968	0.970

Table 3: Zero-shot and Few Shot (FS) performance on the held out domains of the SGD dataset. The columns indicate the size of the Megatron-GPT model.

In the Assistant dataset, the p-tuned models face the same issue as the BERT models: they struggle to generalize to completely unseen domains and the performance is close to random (Table 4). Unlike in SGD, the held-out domains do not have sufficiently similar domains in training from which to generalize. However, the few-shot setting holds promise as the performance of the models improves with few samples. Since the held out domains have far more intents compared to the held out domains from the SGD dataset, we employ stratified sampling to ensure that the few-shot examples are representative of all intents in the domain.

Mode	IOT devices			Media Consumption		
	345M	1.3B	5B	345M	1.3B	5B
Zero Shot	0.096	0.011	0.022	0.037	0.008	0.012
FS - 10 samples	0.62	0.71	0.75	0.58	0.62	0.68
FS - 50 samples	0.69	0.83	0.87	0.67	0.86	0.89

Table 4: Zero-shot and Few Shot (FS) performance on the held out domains of the Assistant dataset. The columns indicate the size of the Megatron-GPT model.

5 Discussion

The results on zero-shot and few-shot settings for unseen domains demonstrate that p-tuning a LLM to have intents that are more verbose than discrete labels can be very helpful.

In this section, we analyze the impact of the structure of canonical forms, what helps the language model generalize, how sample efficient are these language models and what all this means for a developer of chatbots and dialogue systems.

5.1 How important is framing the right canonical form?

The phrasing of canonical forms has a significant impact on zero-shot cross domain generalization. In our initial experiments, we observed that the language models, especially the smaller ones, sometimes rely on spurious correlations to predict the intent. For instance, if the intent *SearchFlightOneWay* is mapped to the canonical form *search tickets for flight one way*, the model correlates the word *ticket* in both the user utterance and canonical form to identify the intent. When we use this model to predict the intent of user utterances related to *bus bookings* in a zero-shot manner, the model predicts that that the intent is related to a *flight booking* as most utterances in the *bus domain* contain the word *ticket*.

Mode	**Accuracy**		
	345M	**1.3B**	**5B**
ZS - Original	0.08	0.13	0.21
ZS - Modified	0.755	0.762	0.787

Table 5: Zero shot (ZS) performance on utterances from *Bus Bookings*. **Original** refers to having the canonical form for flight bookings as *search tickets for flight one way* which led to incorrect generalizations. **Modified** refers to having the improved canonical form for flight bookings as *search for flights one way*.

Rephrasing the canonical form for the intent

SearchFlightOneWay to *search for flights one way* helps the model to avoid making the spurious correlation and the performance in the zero-shot setting (Table 5) is significantly improved.

Mode	Accuracy	
	345M	**1.3B**
ZS - Original	0.08	0.13
FS 10 samples- Original	0.76	0.72
FS 20 samples - Original	0.84	0.87

Table 6: Zero shot (ZS) performance on utterances from *Bus Bookings*. **Original** refers to having the canonical form for flight bookings as *search tickets for flight one way* which led to incorrect generalizations. Adding a small number of examples resolves the error.

However, the few-shot setting (Table 6) alleviates this problem of sensitivity of the model to the canonical form structure. When we provide the model with a few samples from the the target domain, it learns to associate that the important words to distinguish between the domains are *flight* and *bus* and not *ticket.*

5.2 What do good canonical forms looks like?

Based on our experiments, a set of good canonical forms has the following properties:

- **Similarity in structure**: Use similar verbs for similar actions/domains, *e.g.*, **book** a flight, **book** bus tickets, **search** for hotels, **search** for restaurant reservations.
- **Compositional**: Using similar structures for canonical forms in similar domains naturally lends to compositionality. This makes it easier for the model to generalize in the zero-shot/few-shot setting while still allowing the developers to easily map the generations to a supported service on the backend.
- **Looks like natural language**: Since LLMs are pretrained on very large corpora of natural language, the benefit of pre-training is realized when the canonical forms resemble natural language rather than complex semantic forms. Making discrete intents look more like typical verb phrases brings out the expressive nature of language models.

Future work will explore and refine methods to automate the creation of canonical forms.

5.3 Do we need the entire training set for p-tuning?

We look for the fewest labelled samples for p-tuning needed to get an accuracy close to accessing the entire train set. We randomly sample k samples per intent ($k \in 5, 10, 20, 30$) to form the train set the model is p-tuned on, and evaluate on the same test set as above. The train and test sets are from the in-domain setting for both SGD (Table 7) and Assistant (Table 8) datasets.

#Samples/Intent	Train Size	Accuracy		
		345M	1.3B	5B
10	370	0.77	0.81	0.827
20	740	0.82	0.83	0.844
30	1110	0.84	0.85	0.87

Table 7: Accuracy on the SGD test set when using only k samples per intent. The columns indicate the size of the Megatron-GPT model used.

#Samples/Intent	Train Size	Accuracy		
		345M	1.3B	5B
10	640	0.69	0.81	0.84
20	1280	0.74	0.84	0.91
30	1920	0.79	0.87	0.91

Table 8: Accuracy on the Assistant test set when using only k samples per intent. The columns indicate the size of the Megatron-GPT model used.

5.3.1 Comparison with BERT

We observe that Megatron-GPT is more sample efficient than BERT-type models, even when adjusting for the number of parameters. We use the 345M parameter version of the Megatron-GPT for a fair comparison. We finetune BERT-Large and p-tune the GPT model on the same training subset of the SGD dataset. Results are shown in Table 9.

With a small number of samples (10 per intent), both Megatron-GPT and BERT-Large have very similar performance. But with small increases in the number of labelled samples per intent in the train set, we observe that the performance of the GPT model improves faster than the BERT model.

5.4 What does this mean for dialogue system developers?

Task-oriented dialogue systems are challenging to create. Most common frameworks cast utterances

#Samples/Intent	Accuracy	
	345M	BERT
10	0.77	0.75
20	0.82	0.767
30	0.84	0.773

Table 9: Accuracy on the SGD test set when using only k samples per intent. MegatronGPT-345M is more sample efficient than BERT-Large.

into discrete intents and slots, but it is often not clear how to define these concepts for a given design. Such frameworks also employ NLU models that often require the creation of either rule-based grammars or a significantly large corpus of labelled samples. While ML-based approaches have come a long way, distributional shifts in the way utterances are structured can degrade performance. By leveraging LLMs, our approach reduces the effort involved in framing intents and training classifiers. Because of the flexibility in canonical form schemas and the sample efficiency of p-tuning, we argue that development of new task-oriented dialogues becomes simpler and faster. We envision a setting where a model publisher trains and releases a general-purpose p-tuned language model covering a broad set of cases. A conversation designer may then write a small set of example queries, submit a brief p-tuning job, and deploy a new application with minimal cost.

6 Conclusion

We explore the use of Large Language Models and p-tuning for intent classification in task-oriented dialogue systems. We show framing intent labels into more verbose forms allows LMs to exploit the underlying structure better and exhibit impressive zero-shot and few-shot generalization. We also analyze how important the phrasing of the verbose forms are and how many samples are needed to get good quantitative performance. We hope that this work on using sample efficient LLMs serves to motivate further research in making ToD systems simpler and quicker to develop.

7 Acknowledgements

The authors would like to thank Zhilin Wang, Virginia Adams, Sandeep Subramanian, Vlad Getselevich, Prasoon Varshney, and Jonathan Cohen for many useful discussions during the course of this work.

References

Piotr Bojanowski, Edouard Grave, Armand Joulin, and Tomas Mikolov. 2016. Enriching word vectors with subword information. *arXiv preprint arXiv:1607.04606*.

Jacob Devlin, Ming-Wei Chang, Kenton Lee, and Kristina Toutanova. 2019. BERT: Pre-training of deep bidirectional transformers for language understanding. In *Proceedings of the 2019 Conference of the North American Chapter of the Association for Computational Linguistics: Human Language Technologies, Volume 1 (Long and Short Papers)*, pages 4171–4186, Minneapolis, Minnesota. Association for Computational Linguistics.

Brian Lester, Rami Al-Rfou, and Noah Constant. 2021. The power of scale for parameter-efficient prompt tuning.

Xiao Liu, Yanan Zheng, Zhengxiao Du, Ming Ding, Yujie Qian, Zhilin Yang, and Jie Tang. 2021. Gpt understands, too.

Xingkun Liu, Arash Eshghi, Pawel Swietojanski, and Verena Rieser. 2019. Benchmarking natural language understanding services for building conversational agents.

Deepak Narayanan, Mohammad Shoeybi, Jared Casper, Patrick LeGresley, Mostofa Patwary, Vijay Anand Korthikanti, Dmitri Vainbrand, Prethvi Kashinkunti, Julie Bernauer, Bryan Catanzaro, Amar Phanishayee, and Matei Zaharia. 2021. Efficient large-scale language model training on gpu clusters using megatron-lm.

Abhinav Rastogi, Xiaoxue Zang, Srinivas Sunkara, Raghav Gupta, and Pranav Khaitan. 2019. Towards scalable multi-domain conversational agents: The schema-guided dialogue dataset.

Nils Reimers and Iryna Gurevych. 2019. Sentence-bert: Sentence embeddings using siamese bert-networks. In *Proceedings of the 2019 Conference on Empirical Methods in Natural Language Processing*. Association for Computational Linguistics.

Wenhui Wang, Furu Wei, Li Dong, Hangbo Bao, Nan Yang, and Ming Zhou. 2020. Minilm: Deep self-attention distillation for task-agnostic compression of pre-trained transformers.

Yushi Wang, Jonathan Berant, and Percy Liang. 2015. Building a semantic parser overnight. In *Proceedings of the 53rd Annual Meeting of the Association for Computational Linguistics and the 7th International Joint Conference on Natural Language Processing (Volume 1: Long Papers)*, pages 1332–1342, Beijing, China. Association for Computational Linguistics.

Disentangling Confidence Score Distribution for Out-of-Domain Intent Detection with Energy-Based Learning

Yanan Wu[1*], Zhiyuan Zeng[1*], Keqing He[2*], Yutao Mou[1], Pei Wang[1], Yuanmeng Yan[1], Weiran Xu[1*]

[1]Beijing University of Posts and Telecommunications, Beijing, China

[2]Meituan, Beijing, China

{yanan.wu,zengzhiyuan,myt,wangpei,
yanyuanmeng,xuweiran}@bupt.edu.cn
{hekeqing}@meituan.com

Abstract

Detecting Out-of-Domain (OOD) or unknown intents from user queries is essential in a task-oriented dialog system. Traditional softmax-based confidence scores are susceptible to the overconfidence issue. In this paper, we propose a simple but strong energy-based score function to detect OOD where the energy scores of OOD samples are higher than IND samples. Further, given a small set of labeled OOD samples, we introduce an energy-based margin objective for supervised OOD detection to explicitly distinguish OOD samples from INDs. Comprehensive experiments and analysis prove our method helps disentangle confidence score distributions of IND and OOD data.[1]

Case	Ground Truth	Softmax Pred
1. Can you give me a meal suggetion from the sourth	meal_suggetion	meal_suggetion
2. Give me a suggetion for roofers	OOD	meal_suggetion

Figure 1: IND (case 1) vs OOD sample (case 2). Softmax score recognizes OOD sample as IND intent type because of overconfidence issue.

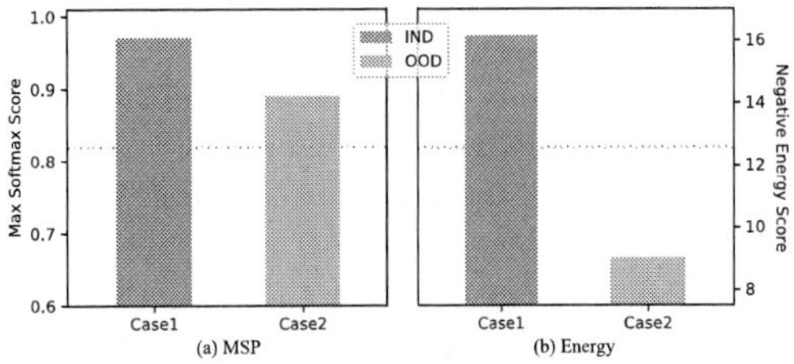

Figure 2: Softmax score from MSP vs energy score from our method. Softmax score are similar for IND and OOD (both > 0.85) but energy score are more distinguished.

1 Introduction

Detecting Out-of-Domain (OOD) or unknown intents from user queries is crucial to a task-oriented dialog system (Akasaki and Kaji, 2017; Tulshan and Dhage, 2018; Shum et al., 2018; Lin and Xu, 2019; Xu et al., 2020; Zeng et al., 2021a; Wu et al., 2022b). It can avoid performing wrong operations and provide potential directions of future development when an input query falls outside the range of predefined intents. Since the exact number of unknown intents in practical scenarios is hard to know and annotate, the lack of real OOD examples makes it challenging to identify these samples in dialog systems.

Depending on whether labeled OOD samples are available, previous OOD detection work can be generally classified into two types: unsupervised (Bendale and Boult, 2016; Hendrycks and Gimpel, 2017; Shu et al., 2017; Lee et al., 2018; Ren et al., 2019; Lin and Xu, 2019; Xu et al., 2020; Zeng et al., 2021a,b; Wu et al., 2022a) and supervised (Fei and Liu, 2016; Kim and Kim, 2018; Larson et al., 2019a; Zheng et al., 2020). The former firstly learn an in-domain (IND) intent classifier only using labeled IND data and then estimates the confidence score of a test query. For example, Maximum Softmax Probability (MSP) (Hendrycks and Gimpel, 2017) uses maximum softmax probability as the confidence score and regards an intent as OOD if the score is below a fixed threshold. The assumption is that OOD intents should produce a lower softmax probability than INDs. However, neural networks can produce arbitrarily high softmax confidence even for such abnormal OOD samples (Guo et al., 2017; Liang et al., 2018), as shown in Fig 1&2, which we call *overconfidence*. Further, another distance-based method, Gaussian discriminant analysis (GDA) (Xu et al., 2020), is proposed to use the maximum Mahalanobis distance (Mahalanobis, 1936) to all in-domain classes centroids as the confidence score. Compared to MSP, GDA gets better OOD performance but requires expensive computation for complex Mahalanobis distance.

*The first three authors contribute equally. Weiran Xu is the corresponding author.

[1]Our code is available at https://github.com/pris-nlp/EMNLP2022-energy_for_OOD/.

Proceedings of the Towards Semi-Supervised and Reinforced Task-Oriented Dialog Systems (SereTOD), pages 31 - 38
December 7, 2022 ©2022 Association for Computational Linguistics

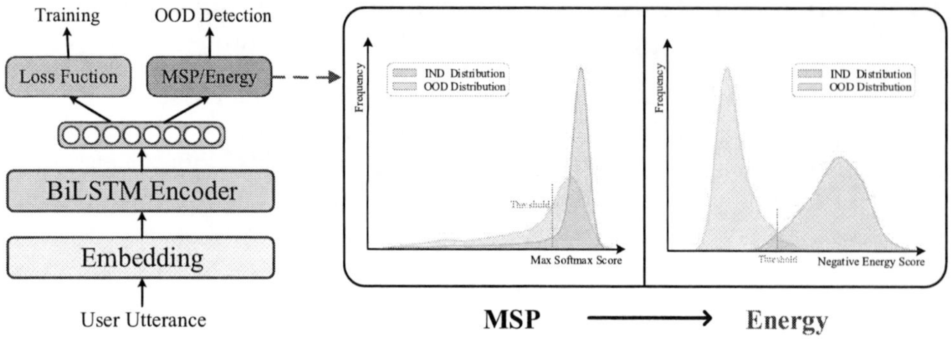

a) The overall architecture b) OOD detection

Figure 3: The overall architecture of our proposed method.

In this paper, we aim to use simple softmax confidence scores for both higher performance and efficiency. For supervised OOD detection, Fei and Liu (2016); Larson et al. (2019a), form a *(N+1)*-class classification problem where the *(N+1)*-th class represents the OOD intents. Further, Zheng et al. (2020) uses labeled OOD data to generate an entropy regularization term. But these methods require numerous labeled OOD intents to get superior results. We focus on using fewer labeled OOD data (like 20 or 30) to achieve comparable even better performance.

In this paper, we propose an energy-based score function to detect OOD in an unsupervised manner. The energy-based score function maps each query to a single energy scalar which is lower for IND samples and higher for OOD samples based on the energy theory (LeCun et al., 2006). We first train an in-domain intent classifier via IND data, then replace the original softmax layer with the energy-based score function. Our method can not only mitigate the issue of overconfident softmax probability but also reduce expensive post-processing computation. Further, given a small portion of labeled OOD samples, we propose an energy-based margin objective to explicitly distinguish OOD samples from IND samples. Our contributions are three-fold: (1) We propose an energy-based learning method for OOD intent detection to achieve higher performance and efficiency. (2) We propose an energy-based margin objective to distinguish energy distributions of OOD and IND samples. (3) Extensive experiments and analysis on two benchmarks demonstrate the effectiveness of our method.

2 Methodology

Overall Architecture Fig 3 (a) shows the overall architecture of our proposed method. We first train an in-domain intent classifier using IND data in training stage. Then in the test stage, we extract the intent feature of a test query and employ the detection algorithms MSP (Hendrycks and Gimpel, 2017) or Energy to detect OOD. Fig 3 (b) demonstrates the effectiveness of our method distinguishing OOD distributions from IND[2].

Energy-based Score Function To mitigate the issue of overconfident softmax probability in MSP, we propose an energy-based score function to push apart score distributions of OOD and IND samples. We first briefly review the energy theory (LeCun et al., 2006) then explain our proposed energy-based score function for OOD detection. The previous energy work (LeCun et al., 2006; Zhai et al., 2016; Grathwohl et al., 2020; Liu et al., 2020b; Kaur et al., 2021) aims to build a function $E(\mathbf{x}) : R^D \to R$ which maps a sample $\mathbf{x}$ to a single scalar called the *energy*. Given a data point $\mathbf{x} \in R^D$, the energy function can be defined as follows:

$$E(\mathbf{x}) = -T \cdot \log \int_{y'} e^{-E(\mathbf{x},y')/T} \tag{1}$$

where T is the temperature parameter and $E(\mathbf{x}, y')$ is the marginal energy over label y'. Essentially, energy scores can be transfered to the likelihood probability:

$$p(y \mid \mathbf{x}) = \frac{e^{-E(\mathbf{x},y)/T}}{\int_{y'} e^{-E(\mathbf{x},y')/T}} = \frac{e^{-E(\mathbf{x},y)/T}}{e^{-E(\mathbf{x})/T}} \tag{2}$$

For OOD detection, since we focus on the detection algorithms for the test stage in this paper, we train the same BiLSTM in-domain intent classifier

[2]Because the max softmax score is higher for IND samples and lower for OOD samples, we use the negative energy score to align with the conventional definition where positive (IND) samples get higher scores.

Models		CLINC-Full				CLINC-Small			
		IND		OOD		IND		OOD	
		Acc	F1	Recall	F1	Acc	F1	Recall	F1
Unsupervised OOD	MSP (Hendrycks and Gimpel, 2017)	87.16	87.64	41.40	44.86	85.02	85.18	35.81	36.60
	LOF (Lin and Xu, 2019)	85.87	86.08	58.32	59.28	82.83	82.98	53.96	54.63
	GDA (Xu et al., 2020)	86.83	87.90	64.14	65.79	84.46	84.87	60.72	61.89
	SCL (Zeng et al., 2021a)	87.01	88.28	66.80	67.68	85.73	86.61	63.96	64.44
	Energy (Ours)	**88.71**	**89.17**	**68.10**	**69.64**	**86.42**	**86.48**	**65.78**	**66.52**
Supervised OOD	N+1	**91.24**	85.29	24.51	31.08	**90.13**	83.23	21.50	29.17
	MSP+Entropy (Zheng et al., 2020)	87.48	87.81	49.90	53.93	85.24	85.31	45.90	48.57
	MSP+Bound (Liu et al., 2020a)	88.03	87.26	45.21	56.86	86.16	83.04	42.38	51.43
	MSP+Margin (Ours)	88.31	87.98	**57.27**	**59.96**	85.33	85.37	**54.90**	**55.37**
	LOF+Entropy	85.98	86.37	61.10	61.13	83.49	83.86	57.70	57.79
	LOF+Bound	86.36	85.66	57.83	60.15	81.36	82.88	64.41	59.30
	LOF+Margin (Ours)	86.13	86.59	**65.70**	**65.59**	83.57	83.97	63.60	**63.18**
	GDA+Entropy	87.27	88.14	68.53	68.82	85.01	85.53	65.22	65.65
	GDA+Bound	87.09	86.86	67.32	66.41	84.44	84.75	65.19	64.14
	GDA+Margin (Ours)	87.54	88.23	68.42	68.73	85.51	85.81	65.13	65.68
	Energy+Margin (Ours, Full Model)	**89.75**	**89.46**	**73.92**	**74.06**	**87.84**	**87.53**	**72.76**	**72.98**

Table 1: Performance comparison on CLINC-Full and CLINC-Small datasets ($p < 0.01$ under t-test).

$f(\mathbf{x})$ via IND data as Lin and Xu (2019) in the training stage. Then given a test query, we simply use the logits from the intent classifier to represent $E(\mathbf{x}, y')$. Therefore, the energy score function Eq 1 can be formulated as:

$$E(\mathbf{x}; f) = -T \cdot \log \sum_{i}^{K} e^{f_i(\mathbf{x})/T} \quad (3)$$

where K is the size of IND intent classes and $f_i(\mathbf{x})$ is the logit of $\mathbf{x}$ belonging to i-th class. We simply use a threshold on the energy score to consider whether a test query belongs to OOD. Intuitively, the reason why the energy score works for OOD detection is that higher energy represents a lower likelihood of occurrence according to LeCun et al. (2006). Therefore, unobserved OOD samples in the training stage should get lower likelihoods as well as higher energy scores than observed IND samples. In Appendix C, we provide a detailed theoretical derivation of why the energy function can alleviate the overconfidence problem. Besides, Experiment 4.1 also proves energy scores better distinguish confidence distribution of OOD data from IND data than softmax probabilities.

Energy-guided Margin Objective To further distinguish OOD from IND, we propose an energy-guided margin objective for few-shot supervised OOD detection. Different from Liu et al. (2020a), our approach directly models the energy boundary by pushing apart the samples from IND and OOD, which helps recognize OOD intents near the decision boundary and is easier to tune and less sensitive to the noise. Specifically, we use an energy-based max-margin loss as well as the standard cross-entropy loss to explicitly set an energy

CLINC	Full	Small
Avg utterance length	9	9
Intents	150	150
Training set size	15100	7600
Training samples per class	100	50
Training OOD samples amount	100	100
Development set size	3100	3100
Development samples per class	20	20
Development OOD samples amount	100	100
Testing Set Size	5500	5500
Testing samples per class	30	30
Development OOD samples amount	1000	1000

Table 2: Statistics of the CLINC datasets.

gap between OOD and IND. We aim to learn more discriminative representations for energy score distributions in the training stage. The energy margin loss is formulated as:

$$\mathcal{L} = \mathbb{E}_{(\mathbf{x}_{\text{ind}}, \mathbf{x}_{\text{ood}}) \sim \mathcal{D}} \max(0, m + E(\mathbf{x}_{\text{ind}}) - E(\mathbf{x}_{\text{ood}})) \quad (4)$$

where m is the energy margin and E is the energy score of IND or OOD samples in train set. Then in the test stage, we still use the energy score to detect OOD. Analysis 4.1 displays the effectiveness of the margin loss over unsupervised OOD.

3 Experiments

3.1 Datasets

We use two public benchmark OOD datasets[3], CLINC-Full and CLINC-Small (Larson et al., 2019b). We show the detailed statistic of these

[3]https://github.com/clinc/oos-eval

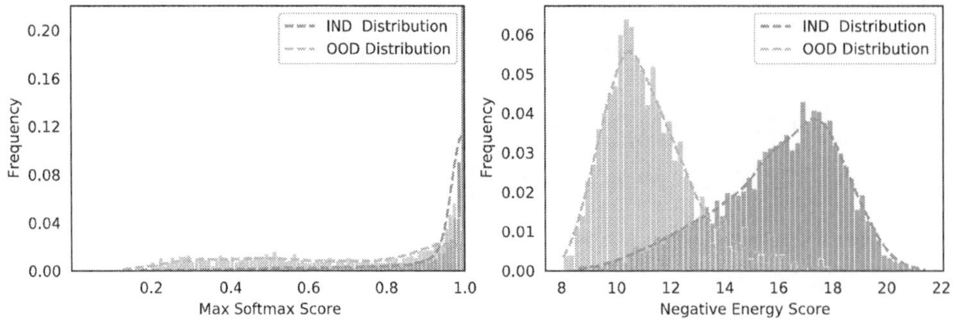

Figure 4: Distribution of softmax scores vs energy scores.

datasets in Table 2. They both contain 150 in-domain intents across 10 domains. The difference is that CLINC-Small has fewer in-domain training examples than CLINC-Full. Note that all the datasets we used have a fixed set of labeled OOD data but we don't use it for training.

3.2 Metrics

We report both OOD metrics: Recall and F1-score (F1) and in-domain metrics: F1-score (F1) and Accuracy (ACC). Since we aim to improve the performance of detecting out-of-domain intents from user queries, OOD Recall and F1 are the main evaluation metrics in this paper.

3.3 Baselines

For detection algorithms, we use MSP, LOF and GDA as baselines. For training objectives, we use N+1, entropy and bound as baselines. We present dataset statistics, baselines and implementation details in the appendix. We will release our code after blind review.

3.4 Main Results

Table 1 shows the main results. (1) For unsupervised OOD detection, using the energy function achieves 24.78, 10.36, 3.85, 1.96 OOD F1 improvements over MSP, LOF, GDA and SCL on CLINC-Full. The results prove the effectiveness of energy score function for OOD detection. Besides, for IND metrics, energy function also outperforms SCL by 0.89% (F1), which reflects energy scores can better distinguish OOD from IND samples without sacrificing IND performance. (2) For supervised OOD detection, we compare different pre-training losses under the same detection score function. We find our Margin approach achieve consistent improvements under different detection functions on both datasets. It demonstrates that

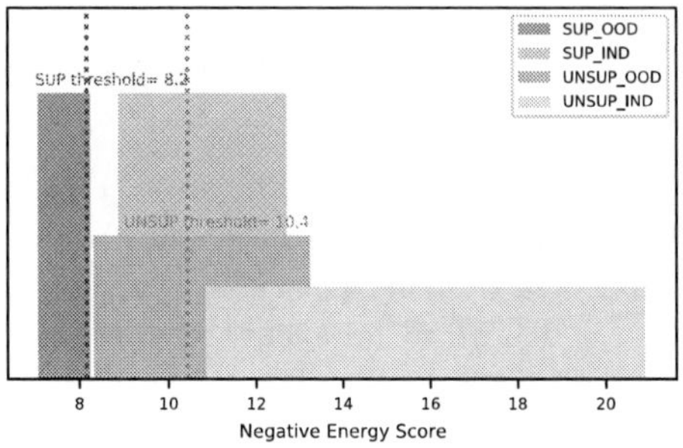

Figure 5: Unsupervised vs supervised OOD detection.

Margin objective can stably improve the representation space by directly pushing apart the samples from IND and OOD. We also observe under MSP, our proposed Margin objective outperforms Entropy by 6.03% and Bound by 3.10% on CLINC-Full. But on GDA we find no significant performance difference. We argue the energy-based learning may not always fit in generative distance-based detection methods like GDA. Overall, combining energy score function and margin objective achieve the best performance over the previous state-of-the-art by 5.24%.

4 Analysis

4.1 Distribution of softmax scores vs energy scores

To figure out why energy scores outperform softmax scores, we compare the score histogram distributions for IND and OOD data in Fig 4. We use the same pre-trained intent classifier to compute scores on the test set. We find softmax scores for both IND and OOD data concentrate on high values, resulting in severe overconfidence. By contrast, energy scores better distinguish score distribution of OOD data from IND data. And energy distribu-

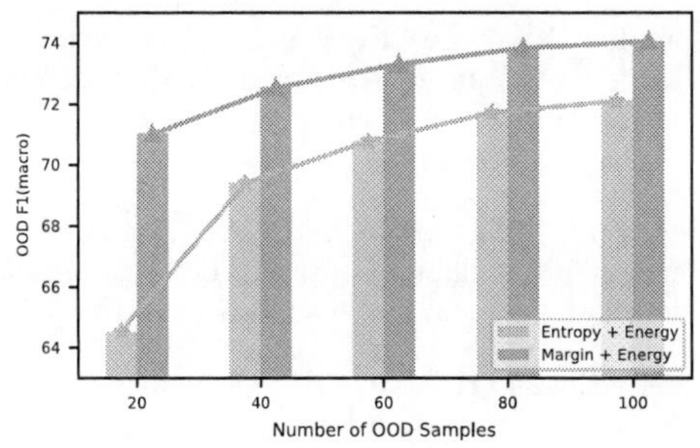

Figure 6: Effect of number of labeled OOD samples.

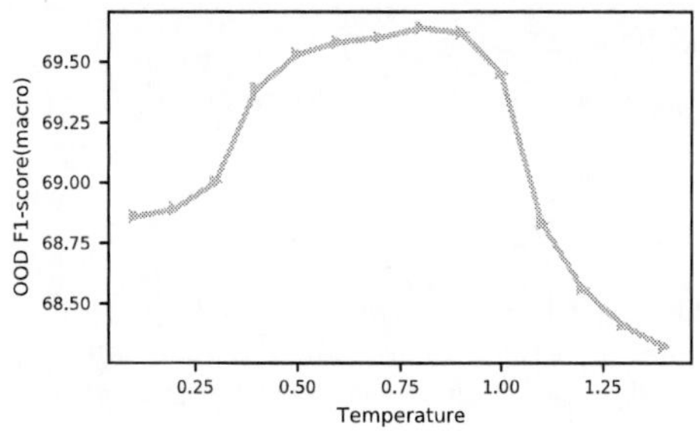

Figure 7: Effect of energy temperature T

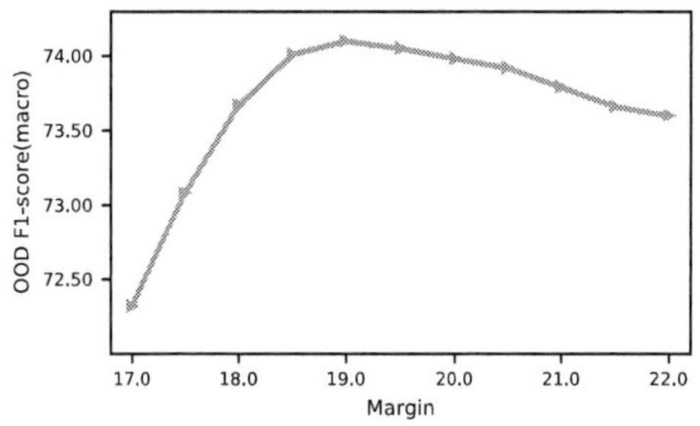

Figure 8: Effect of energy margin m

tions are smoother than softmax score distributions. Overall, our proposed energy-based score function can disentangle confidence score distributions for IND and OOD data.

4.2 Unsupervised vs supervised OOD detection

To verify the effectiveness of our proposed energy-based margin objective, we compare the energy score statistics of unsupervised (Energy) and supervised (Margin+Energy) OOD detection in Fig 5. Each rectangle in Fig 5 represents the energy distribution of IND or OOD data, where the middle of the rectangle is energy mean and the width of the rectangle is energy variance. Results show that compared to Energy, Margin+Energy makes negative energy scores of both OOD and IND data smaller. Further, the supervised Margin objective can significantly decrease the variance of both OOD ($1.86 \downarrow$) and IND ($3.11 \downarrow$) data. Therefore, Margin can push apart energy score distributions for OOD detection by shrinking its variance to avoid overlapping. Besides, combined with the energy threshold (dot line in Fig 5), unsupervised (Energy) still gets a portion of OOD samples above the threshold which are misclassified into IND, but supervised (Margin+Energy) on the opposite. It proves that Margin can further mitigate the issue of overconfidence.

4.3 Effect of number of labeled OOD samples

Fig 6 shows the effect of labeled OOD training data size for supervised OOD detection. We find Margin+Energy consistently outperforms Entropy+Energy, especially in the few-shot supervised OOD scenario, which demonstrates strong robustness and generalization of our proposed energy-based margin objective for OOD detection.

4.4 Effect of Parameters

Temperature T**.** Fig 7 shows the effect of different energy temperature T. We conduct the experiments on the CLINC-Full dataset, using Energy for unsupervised OOD. The X-axis denotes the value of temperature T. In general, $T \in (0.5, 1.0)$ achieves relatively better performances and has a broad range.

Margin m**.** Fig 8 shows the effect of different energy margin m. We conduct the experiments on the CLINC-Full dataset, using Margin+Energy for supervised OOD. The X-axis denotes the value of margin m. Results show that $m = 19.0$ achieves the best performance and is robust to minor changes.

5 Conclusion

Traditional softmax-based OOD detection methods are susceptible to the overconfidence issue. Therefore, we propose a novel energy-based score function to mitigate the issue of softmax overconfidence. To use labeled OOD data, we further introduce an energy-based margin objective to explicitly distinguish energy score distributions of OOD from IND. Experiments and analysis confirm the effectiveness of our energy-based method for OOD detection. For future work, we hope to explore theoretical concepts of energy and provide new guidance.

References

Satoshi Akasaki and Nobuhiro Kaji. 2017. Chat detection in an intelligent assistant: Combining task-oriented and non-task-oriented spoken dialogue systems. *ArXiv*, abs/1705.00746.

Abhijit Bendale and Terrance E. Boult. 2016. Towards open set deep networks. *2016 IEEE Conference on Computer Vision and Pattern Recognition (CVPR)*, pages 1563–1572.

Geli Fei and Bing Liu. 2016. Breaking the closed world assumption in text classification. In *Proceedings of the 2016 Conference of the North American Chapter of the Association for Computational Linguistics: Human Language Technologies*, pages 506–514.

Will Grathwohl, Kuan-Chieh Wang, Jörn-Henrik Jacobsen, David Duvenaud, Mohammad Norouzi, and Kevin Swersky. 2020. Your classifier is secretly an energy based model and you should treat it like one. *ArXiv*, abs/1912.03263.

Chuan Guo, Geoff Pleiss, Yu Sun, and Kilian Q Weinberger. 2017. On calibration of modern neural networks. In *International Conference on Machine Learning*, pages 1321–1330. PMLR.

Dan Hendrycks and Kevin Gimpel. 2017. A baseline for detecting misclassified and out-of-distribution examples in neural networks. *ArXiv*, abs/1610.02136.

Ramneet Kaur, Susmit Jha, Anirban Roy, O. Sokolsky, and Insup Lee. 2021. Are all outliers alike? on understanding the diversity of outliers for detecting oods. *ArXiv*, abs/2103.12628.

Joo-Kyung Kim and Young-Bum Kim. 2018. Joint learning of domain classification and out-of-domain detection with dynamic class weighting for satisficing false acceptance rates. *ArXiv*, abs/1807.00072.

Diederik P Kingma and Jimmy Ba. 2014. Adam: A method for stochastic optimization. *arXiv preprint arXiv:1412.6980*.

Stefan Larson, Anish Mahendran, Joseph Peper, Christopher Clarke, Andrew Lee, Parker Hill, Jonathan K. Kummerfeld, Kevin Leach, Michael Laurenzano, Lingjia Tang, and Jason Mars. 2019a. An evaluation dataset for intent classification and out-of-scope prediction. In *EMNLP/IJCNLP*.

Stefan Larson, Anish Mahendran, Joseph J. Peper, Christopher Clarke, Andrew Lee, Parker Hill, Jonathan K. Kummerfeld, Kevin Leach, Michael A. Laurenzano, Lingjia Tang, and Jason Mars. 2019b. An evaluation dataset for intent classification and out-of-scope prediction. In *EMNLP-IJCNLP*.

Yann LeCun, Sumit Chopra, Raia Hadsell, M Ranzato, and F Huang. 2006. A tutorial on energy-based learning. volume 1.

Kimin Lee, Kibok Lee, Honglak Lee, and Jinwoo Shin. 2018. A simple unified framework for detecting out-of-distribution samples and adversarial attacks. *ArXiv*, abs/1807.03888.

Shiyu Liang, Yixuan Li, and R. Srikant. 2018. Enhancing the reliability of out-of-distribution image detection in neural networks. *arXiv: Learning*.

Ting-En Lin and Hua Xu. 2019. Deep unknown intent detection with margin loss. In *Proceedings of the 57th Annual Meeting of the Association for Computational Linguistics*, pages 5491–5496.

Weitang Liu, Xiaoyun Wang, John Owens, and Yixuan Li. 2020a. Energy-based out-of-distribution detection. *Advances in Neural Information Processing Systems*.

Weitang Liu, Xiaoyun Wang, John Douglas Owens, and Yixuan Li. 2020b. Energy-based out-of-distribution detection. *ArXiv*, abs/2010.03759.

Prasanta Chandra Mahalanobis. 1936. On the generalized distance in statistics. National Institute of Science of India.

Jeffrey Pennington, Richard Socher, and Christopher D Manning. 2014. Glove: Global vectors for word representation. In *Proceedings of the 2014 conference on empirical methods in natural language processing (EMNLP)*, pages 1532–1543.

Jie Ren, Peter J. Liu, Emily Fertig, Jasper Snoek, Ryan Poplin, Mark A. DePristo, Joshua V. Dillon, and Balaji Lakshminarayanan. 2019. Likelihood ratios for out-of-distribution detection. *ArXiv*, abs/1906.02845.

Lei Shu, Hu Xu, and Bing Liu. 2017. Doc: Deep open classification of text documents. In *Proceedings of the 2017 Conference on Empirical Methods in Natural Language Processing*, pages 2911–2916.

H. Shum, X. He, and Di Li. 2018. From eliza to xiaoice: challenges and opportunities with social chatbots. *Frontiers of Information Technology & Electronic Engineering*, 19:10–26.

Amrita S Tulshan and Sudhir Namdeorao Dhage. 2018. Survey on virtual assistant: Google assistant, siri, cortana, alexa. In *International symposium on signal processing and intelligent recognition systems*, pages 190–201.

Yanan Wu, Keqing He, Yuanmeng Yan, QiXiang Gao, Zhiyuan Zeng, Fujia Zheng, Lulu Zhao, Huixing Jiang, Wei Wu, and Weiran Xu. 2022a. Revisit overconfidence for ood detection: Reassigned contrastive learning with adaptive class-dependent threshold. In *NAACL*.

Yanan Wu, Zhiyuan Zeng, Keqing He, Yutao Mou, Pei Wang, and Weiran Xu. 2022b. Distribution calibration for out-of-domain detection with bayesian approximation. In *COLING*.

Hong Xu, Keqing He, Yuanmeng Yan, Sihong Liu, Zijun Liu, and Weiran Xu. 2020. A deep generative distance-based classifier for out-of-domain detection with mahalanobis space. In *Proceedings of the 28th International Conference on Computational Linguistics*, pages 1452–1460, Barcelona, Spain (Online). International Committee on Computational Linguistics.

Zhiyuan Zeng, Keqing He, Yuanmeng Yan, Zijun Liu, Yanan Wu, Hong Xu, Huixing Jiang, and Weiran Xu. 2021a. Modeling discriminative representations for out-of-domain detection with supervised contrastive learning. In *Proceedings of the 59th Annual Meeting of the Association for Computational Linguistics and the 11th International Joint Conference on Natural Language Processing (Volume 2: Short Papers)*, pages 870–878, Online. Association for Computational Linguistics.

Zhiyuan Zeng, Keqing He, Yuanmeng Yan, Hong Xu, and Weiran Xu. 2021b. Adversarial self-supervised learning for out-of-domain detection. In *NAACL*.

Shuangfei Zhai, Yu Cheng, W. Lu, and Zhongfei Zhang. 2016. Deep structured energy based models for anomaly detection. In *ICML*.

Yinhe Zheng, Guanyi Chen, and Minlie Huang. 2020. Out-of-domain detection for natural language understanding in dialog systems. *IEEE/ACM Transactions on Audio, Speech, and Language Processing*, 28:1198–1209.

A Baseline Details

We perform main experiments based on two different settings, unsupervised OOD and supervised OOD detection. For unsupervised OOD detection, we compare our proposed energy detection algorithm with other methods, MSP (Maximum Softmax Probability) (Hendrycks and Gimpel, 2017), LOF (Local Outlier Factor) (Lin and Xu, 2019), GDA (Gaussian Discriminant Analysis) (Xu et al., 2020). For supervised OOD detection, we also compare our proposed energy-based margin objective with entropy (Zheng et al., 2020) and N+1 (Fei and Liu, 2016; Larson et al., 2019a). Note that margin and entropy objectives are used in the training stage, we still need detection algorithms MSP, GDA or Energy to detect in the test stage. We supplement the relevant baseline details as follows:

MSP (Maximum Softmax Probability) (Hendrycks and Gimpel, 2017) uses maximum softmax probability as the confidence score and regards an intent as OOD if the score is below a fixed threshold.

LOF (Local Outlier Factor) (Lin and Xu, 2019) uses the local outlier factor to detect unknown intents. The motivation is that if an example's local density is significantly lower than its k-nearest neighbor's, it is more likely to be considered as the unknown intents.

GDA (Gaussian Discriminant Analysis) (Xu et al., 2020) is a generative distance-based classifier for out-of-domain detection with Euclidean space. They estimate the class-conditional distribution on feature spaces of DNNs via Gaussian discriminant analysis (GDA) to avoid over-confidence problems and use Mahalanobis distance to measure the confidence score of whether a test sample belongs to OOD. GDA is the state-of-the-art detection method till now, our proposed energy score still significantly outperforms GDA.

Note that LOF and GDA both require additional post-processing modules to estimate density or distance, which induces expensive computation. We conduct a performance comparison for inference time in Table 3. Since SCL only adds a pre-training loss along with CE and also uses GDA for detection, the inference time is equal to GDA.

Detect Method	Inference time
MSP	1.00x
Energy (Ours)	1.00x
GDA/SCL	30.63x
LOF	30.89x

Table 3: Inference time comparison between different methods.

SCL (Zeng et al., 2021a) uses a supervised contrastive learning objective to minimize intra-class variance by pulling together in-domain intents belonging to the same class and maximize inter-class variance by pushing apart samples from different classes. Note that SCL still needs a confidence score function. To keep fair comparison, we follow the original paper using GDA detection method.

N+1 (Fei and Liu (2016); Larson et al. (2019a)) is an N+1 classification model which simply considers OOD samples as a new class.

Entropy (Zheng et al. (2020)) uses labeled OOD data to generate an entropy regularization term to enforce the predicted distribution of OOD inputs closer to the uniform distribution:

$$\mathcal{L} = \mathbb{E}_{(\mathbf{x_{ood}})\sim\mathcal{D}}[-H(p_\theta(y|x_{ood}))] \quad (5)$$

where H is the Shannon entropy of the predicted distribution. $p_\theta(y|x_{ood})$ is the predicted distribution of the input OOD utterance x_{ood}.

Bound (Liu et al. (2020b)) uses a regularization loss defined in terms of energy to further widen the energy gap:

$$\mathcal{L} = \mathbb{E}_{(\mathbf{x}_{\text{ind}})\sim\mathcal{D}} \max(0, E(\mathbf{x}_{\text{ind}}) - \text{m}_{\text{ind}}))^2 + \mathbb{E}_{(\mathbf{x}_{\text{ood}})\sim\mathcal{D}} \max(0, \text{m}_{\text{ood}} - E(\mathbf{x}_{\text{ood}})))^2 \quad (6)$$

where E is the energy score of IND or OOD samples in the train set. This learning objective using two squared hinge loss with two hyper-parameters m_{ind} and m_{ood}. Note that **Bound** aims at OOD image classification and replies on two independent energy bounds. Instead, our proposed Margin constructs a contrastive energy margin between IND intents and OOD intents to better disentangle energy distributions.

B Implementation Details

We use the public pre-trained 300 dimensions GloVe embeddings (Pennington et al., 2014)[4] to embed tokens. We use a two-layer BiLSTM as a feature extractor and set the dimension of hidden states to 128. The dropout value is fixed at 0.5. We use Adam optimizer (Kingma and Ba, 2014) to train our model. We set the learning rate to 1E-03. In the training stage, we use standard cross-entropy loss for unsupervised OOD and cross-entropy+energy-guided margin loss for supervised OOD. Besides, in supervised OOD scenario, we employ restriction-oriented random sampling. Specifically, we guarantee that IND and OOD samples are both included in each batch to facilitate calculation of margin loss. We both set the training epoch up to 200 with a early stop of patience 15. For our proposed energy-guided margin loss, we set the margin m to 19.0 and the temperature T to 0.8. We use the best OOD F1 scores on the validation set to calculate the threshold adaptively. Each result of the experiments is tested 5 times under the same setting and gets the average value. The training stage of our models lasts about 2 minutes for unsupervised OOD and 4 minutes for supervised OOD both on a single Tesla T4 GPU (16 GB of memory). The average value of the trainable model parameters is 3.05M. We will release our code after blind review.

C A Theoretical Proof of Energy Score vs Softmax Score

In this section, we give a theoretical proof of why energy score outperforms softmax score. Supposing we get the output logits from the intent classifier, we represent MSP as follows:

$$\begin{aligned} log\,\mathbf{MSP}(logits) &= log\ max\ softmax(logits) \\ &= log\ max \frac{exp(logits_i)}{\sum_i exp(logits_i)} \\ &= log\ \frac{exp\ max(logits)}{\sum_i exp(logits_i)} \\ &= max(logits) - log\ sum\ exp(logits) \end{aligned} \quad (7)$$

where $logits_i$ represents the i-th value in the vector $logits$. Recap the energy defination:

$$E(\mathbf{x}; f) = -T \cdot \log \sum_i^K e^{f_i(\mathbf{x})/T} \quad (8)$$

Here we set T to 1. Therefore, we get the following equation:

$$log\,\mathbf{MSP}(logits) = \underbrace{max(logits)}_{regularization\ item} + \mathbf{Energy}(logits) \quad (9)$$

If the output logits get a high max value, then $max(logits)$ performs as a regularization item to avoid energy score increasing. Therefore, energy score can better mitigate the overconfidence issue than softmax score.

[4]https://github.com/stanfordnlp/GloVe

Semi-Supervised Knowledge-Grounded Pre-training for Task-Oriented Dialog Systems

Weihao Zeng[1*], Keqing He[2*], Zechen Wang[1*], Dayuan Fu[1], Guanting Dong[1]
Ruotong Geng[1], Pei Wang[1], Jingang Wang[2], Chaobo Sun[2], Wei Wu[2], Weiran Xu[1*]
[1]Beijing University of Posts and Telecommunications, Beijing, China
[2]Meituan, Beijing, China
{zengwh,zechen_wang,fdy,dongguanting,ruotonggeng,wangpei,xuweiran}@bupt.edu.cn
{hekeqing,wangjingang,sunchaobo,wuwei}@meituan.com

Abstract

Recent advances in neural approaches greatly improve task-oriented dialogue (TOD) systems which assist users to accomplish their goals. However, such systems rely on costly manually labeled dialogs which are not available in practical scenarios. In this paper, we present our models for Track 2 of the SereTOD 2022 challenge, which is the first challenge of building semi-supervised and reinforced TOD systems on a large-scale real-world Chinese TOD dataset MobileCS. We build a knowledge-grounded dialog model to formulate dialog history and local KB as input and predict the system response. And we perform semi-supervised pre-training both on the labeled and unlabeled data. Our system achieves the first place both in the automatic evaluation and human interaction, especially with higher BLEU (+7.64) and Success (+13.6%) than the second place.[1]

1 Introduction

Task-oriented dialogue (TOD) systems assist users to accomplish their goals like booking a ticket and make an effect on everyone's lives with recent advances in neural approaches (Gao et al., 2018). A typical TOD system consists of three sub-modules: (1) natural language understanding (NLU) for recognizing the user's intent and slots (Goo et al., 2018; Qin et al., 2019; He et al., 2020a; Xu et al., 2020; He et al., 2020b); (2) dialog management (DM) for tracking dialog states (Wu et al., 2019; Gao et al., 2019) and deciding which system action to take (Peng et al., 2018; Liu et al., 2021); (3) natural language generation (NLG) for generating dialogue response corresponding to the predicted system action (Peng et al., 2020). Traditional modular methods (Goo et al., 2018; Wu et al., 2019; Peng et al., 2020) and recent end-to-end modeling methods (Peng et al., 2021; Su et al., 2022; Liu et al., 2022a) achieve decent performance in several or all modules. However, such systems rely on costly manually labeled dialogs which are not available in practical scenarios. It's valuable to explore semi-supervised learning (SSL) (Zhu, 2005) for TOD, which aims to leverage both labeled and unlabeled data.

To facilitate relevant research, SereTOD 2022 Workshop [2] proposes the first challenge of building semi-supervised and reinforced TOD systems by releasing a large-scale Chinese TOD dataset MobileCS from real-world dialog transcripts between real users and customer-service staffs from China Mobile. MobileCS contains 10,000 labeled dialogs and 90,000 unlabeled dialogs. There are two tracks: (1) Information extraction (Track 1) aims to extract entities together with their slot values. (2) Task-oriented dialog system (Track 2) aims to build a complete TOD system, including predicting the user intent, querying the local KB, and generating appropriate system intent and response according to the given dialog history. The core challenge is how to combine a small labeled dataset and a large unlabeled dataset.

In this paper, we present our system for Track 2 of the SereTOD 2022 challenge. The main intuition behind our system comes from semi-supervised knowledge-grounded pre-training on both labeled and unlabeled datasets. We divide Track 2 into two task groups, classification (user intent and system intent) and generation (system response). For the classification tasks, we employ Roberta-large [3] and build two separate classification models. We also perform continual pre-training on all the dialog data. For the generation task, we build a knowledge-grounded dialog model, which is the key point of this paper. Specifically, we firstly use

*The first three authors contribute equally. Weiran Xu is the corresponding author.

[1]Our code, models and other related resources are publicly available at https://github.com/Zeng-WH/S2KG.

[2]http://seretod.org/

[3]https://huggingface.co/hfl/chinese-roberta-wwm-ext-large

Proceedings of the Towards Semi-Supervised and Reinforced Task-Oriented Dialog Systems (SereTOD), pages 39 - 47
December 7, 2022

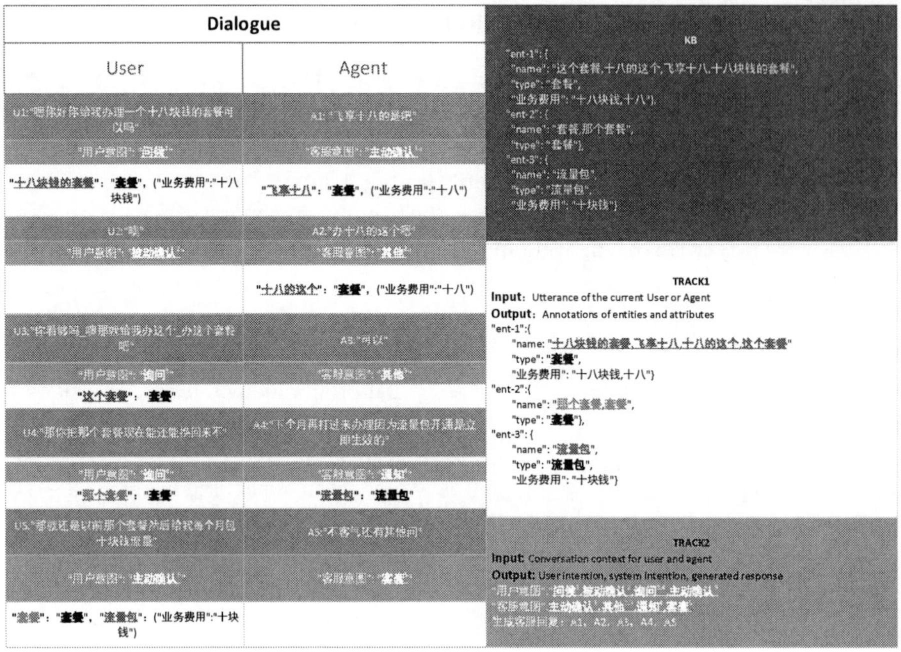

Figure 1: An example from MobileCS.

pre-trained language models (e.g. T5 [4] and UFA (He et al., 2022)) as our backbone. Then, we take the dialog history and serialized local KB [5] as input and output system response. Here, we simply concatenate each key-value pair in the local KB as *key: value* to build a string input. We only use response generation as the learning objective. For the labeled dataset, we use the golden KB annotations as our input. For the unlabeled dataset, we obtain the predicted KB results using our model in Track 1. Finally, we mix up all the data to train a knowledge-grounded dialog model.

We summarize the main contributions of our system S2KG (**S**emi **S**upervised **K**nowledge-**G**rounded pre-training) as follows:

- We build a knowledge-grounded dialog model to formulate dialog history and local KB as input and predict the system response.
- We perform semi-supervised pre-training both on the labeled and unlabeled data.

Our system achieves the first place both in the automatic evaluation and human interaction, especially with higher BLEU (+7.64) and Success (+13.6%) than the second place.

Metric	labeled	unlabeled
Dialogs	8,975	87,933
Turns	100,139	972,573
Tokens	3,991,197	39,491,883
Avg.turns per dialog	11.16	11.06
Avg.tokens per turn	39.86	40.61
Slots	26	-
Values	14,623	-

Table 1: Training dataset statistics of MobileCS. The challenge also provides another 1,000 labeled dialogs as evaluation data (dev set).

2 Task Description

MobileCS is a large Chinese TOD dataset collected from real-world dialog transcripts between real users and customer-service staffs. Different from the simulated MultiWOZ dataset (Budzianowski et al., 2018), it consists of real-life data and large unlabeled dialogs. Specifically, MobileCS contains 10,000 labeled dialogs and 90,000 unlabeled dialogs. The full data statistics are shown in Table 1. The challenge has two tracks. Track 1 (information extraction) aims to extract entities and attributes to

[4] https://github.com/ZhuiyiTechnology/t5-pegasus

[5] A local KB for a dialog could be viewed as being composed of the relevant snapshots from the global KB. Please see more details in Ou et al. (2022).

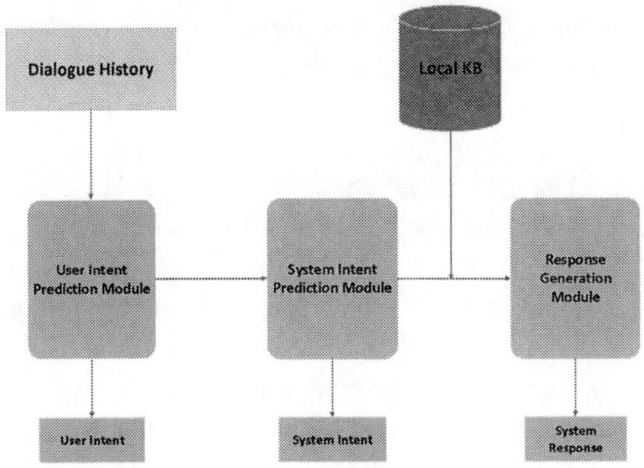

Figure 2: Overall architecture of our knowledge-grounded task-oriented dialogue system.

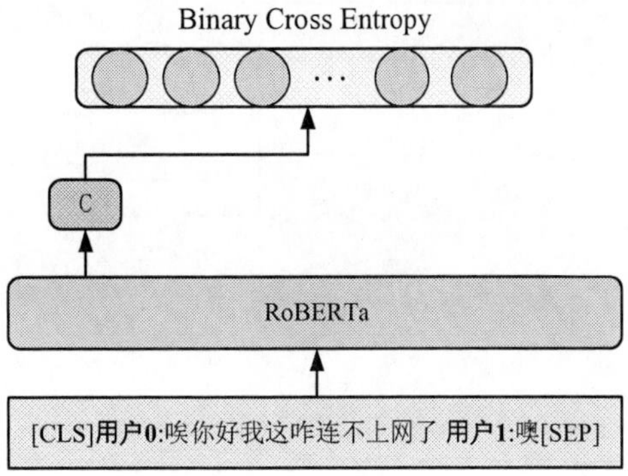

Figure 3: The architecture of the classification models.

build a local knowledge base (KB). And Track 2 uses the KB and raw dialogs to train a complete TOD system. We provide a real annotated dialog in Figure 1. In this paper, we focus on Track 2. Here, we elaborate on the task details. Track 2 for the TOD system is, for each dialog turn, given the dialog history, the user utterance and the local KB, to predict the user intent, query the local KB and generate appropriate system intent and response according to the queried information. For every labeled dialog, the annotations consist of user intents, system intents and a local KB. The local KB is obtained by collecting the entities and triples annotated for Track 1. For unlabeled dialogs, there are no such annotations.

To measure the performance of TOD systems, both automatic evaluation and human evaluation will be conducted. For automatic evaluation, metrics include Precision/Recall/F1 score, Success rate and BLEU (Papineni et al., 2002) score. P/R/F1 are calculated for both predicted user intents and system intents. Success rate is the percentage of generated dialogs that achieve user goals. BLEU score evaluates the fluency of generated responses[6]. For human evaluation for different TOD systems, real users will interact with those systems according to randomly given goals. For each dialog, the user will score the system on a 5-point scale (1-5) by the following 3 metrics. 5 denotes the best and 1 denotes the worst, respectively.

- **Success**. This metric measures if the system successfully completes the user goal by interacting with the user;
- **Coherency**. This metric measures whether the system's response is logically coherent with the dialogue context;
- **Fluency**. The metric measures the fluency of the system's response.

The average score from automatic evaluation and human evaluation is the main ranking basis on the leaderboard.

3 Methodology

3.1 Overall Architecture

Figure 2 shows the overall system architecture for Track 2. Track 2 contains three tasks: user intent, system intent, and system response. For the user intent and system intent tasks, we use Roberta-large and build two separate classification models. For the system response task, we build a knowledge-grounded dialog model and perform semi-supervised pre-training both on the labeled and unlabeled data.

3.2 Subtask 1: Classification

Given a dialog history, the user intent and system intent tasks aim to predict the user intent or system intent(act) respectively. Considering both the tasks are multi-label, we formulate the tasks as multi-label text classification questions. As Figure 3 displays, we adopt Roberta as our backbone and use the dialog history as input. For the user intent task, we concatenate two user utterances as input. We find too many turns bring no further improvements and introducing system responses has a side effect. We suppose the gap between training and prediction affects the model performance. For the system intent task, we concatenate three

[6]The challenge adopts BLEU-4.

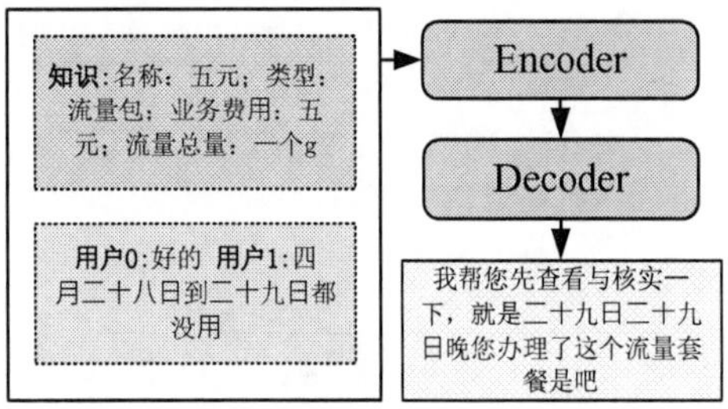

Figure 4: The architecture of the generation model.

user utterances as input.[7] Then, we use the hidden state of the [CLS] token to predict the results. Binary cross entropy is the learning objective. Section 4.3 proves classification models outperform GPT-based end-to-end models. Besides, we also introduce some augmentation strategies as follows:

- **Continual Pre-training**. We pre-train Roberta on the labeled and unlabeled dialogs using MLM objective like BERT (Devlin et al., 2019). We pre-train 20 epochs using a learning rate of 5e-4 and 15% mask rate. MLM continual pre-training brings large improvements of 1.68% on User Intent F1 and 1.86% on System Intent F1.

- **Class-wise Threshold**. We adaptively select the best threshold for each intent type based on the performance on the dev set. This strategy brings improvements of 1.23% on User Intent F1 and 1.48% on System Intent F1.

- **Adversarial Training**. We adopt FGM (Goodfellow et al., 2015) as our adversarial training strategy. This strategy brings improvements of 0.64% on User Intent F1 and 0.46% on System Intent F1.

3.3 Subtask 2: Generation

For the generation task, we build a knowledge-grounded dialog model, S2KG in Figure 4. Specifically, we firstly use pre-trained language models (e.g. T5 [8] and UFA (He et al., 2022)) as our backbone. Then, we take the dialog history and serialized local KB as input and output system response. Here, we simply concatenate each key-value pair in the local KB as *key: value* to build a string input. We only use response generation as the learning objective. We find KB grounding has a large improvement over baselines (see Section 4.4).

The SereTOD challenge gives a large-scale (90,000) unlabeled dataset that doesn't contain KB annotations and a relatively small (10,000) labeled dataset. So we perform semi-supervised pre-training to utilize all these dialogs. For the labeled dataset, we use the golden KB annotations as our input. For the unlabeled dataset, we obtain the predicted KB results using our model in Track 1. We implement our system of Track 1 mainly based on the official baseline (Liu et al., 2022b). Finally, we mix up all the data to train a knowledge-grounded dialog model. We find only using unsupervised pre-training gets an improvement of 1.91 BLEU, but drops by 14.6 on Success, because raw response generation pre-training makes the model memorize similar dialogs but predict unfaithful responses without grounding ability. Therefore, it's necessary to obtain pseudo KB annotations to perform pre-training. Note that the performance of the Track 1 system is relatively poor so we argue the quality of pseudo KB makes no significant effect on the final results. We leave more discussion to future work.

4 Experiment

4.1 Setup

We train our models on the training set and report our results on the dev set. The final leaderboard results are evaluated on the test set. Since the test set is not released until the end of the challenge, we perform ablation studies only on the dev set. We conduct our experiments using Huggingface[9] and computation platform JiuTian[10].

4.2 Main Results

Table 2 shows the final automatic results on the test set of the top 5 teams[11]. Our system (Team 11) achieves the state-of-the-art on all metrics, especially for generation task, demonstrating the effectiveness of our proposed S2KG. Specifically, our method outperforms the second place (Team 5) by 1.4% on User Intent F1 and 0.6% on System Intent F1. The improvements mainly come from better pre-trained LM, continual pre-training, class-wise threshold, and adversarial training. We will dive

[7] The system intent task also requires intent arguments. We use heuristic rules based on the local KB to match the entities.

[8] https://github.com/ZhuiyiTechnology/t5-pegasus

[9] https://huggingface.co/

[10] https://jiutian.10086.cn/edu/#/home

[11] See all the results in the official leaderboard.

Team ID	Automatic Evaluation				
	User Intent F1	System Intent F1	BLEU	Success	Combined
Team-11 (Ours)	**0.728**	**0.595**	**14.430**	**0.780**	**2.392**
Team-5	0.714	0.589	6.790	0.432	1.871
Team-13	0.706	0.587	5.526	0.251	1.655
Team-10	0.664	0.504	3.629	0.217	1.458
Team-8	0.699	0.550	6.440	0.644	2.022
official baseline	0.644	0.394	4.170	0.315	1.436

Table 2: Final automatic results on the test set of the top 5 teams released by the officials. User Intent F1 denotes the performance of classifying the input user query and System Intent F1 denotes the predicted system acts. Success rate is the percentage of generated dialogs that achieve user goals. Combined score is the overall result which is calculated as follows: Combined score = User intent F1 + System intent F1 + Success + BLEU/50.

Methods	User Intent F1	System Intent F1
GPT-2 (baseline)	0.6488	0.4012
Roberta	0.7448	0.5158
Roberta+FGM	0.7512	0.5204
Roberta+FGM+Threshold	0.7635	0.5352
Roberta+FGM+Threshold+MLM	**0.7803**	**0.5538**

Table 3: Comparison of different user intent and system intent models on the dev set.

into details in Section 4.3. For generation metrics, our S2KG model significantly outperforms the second place with a large margin of 7.640 on BLEU and 34.8% on Success. The improvements are mainly attributed to knowledge-grounded dialog model and semi-supervised pre-training, which are the key points of this paper. We leave the discussion to Section 4.4.

4.3 Classification

To verify the effect of our proposed models, we perform an ablation study of different user intent and system intent models on the dev set in Table 3. GPT-2 is the official baseline (Liu et al., 2022a) which is an end-to-end generative model based on Chinese GPT-2[12]. For pre-trained language models, we find Roberta-based classification models get better performance with improvements of 9.60% on User Intent F1 and 11.46% on System Intent F1. Based on Roberta, we also introduce some training or inference strategies, including adversarial training FGM, class-wise threshold, and MLM continual pre-training. All the strategies show advantages. MLM continual pre-training brings the largest improvements of 1.68% on User Intent F1 and 1.86% on System Intent F1, demonstrating the effectiveness of pre-training on domain corpus. Other strategies also get 0.5-1% improvements.

[12]https://huggingface.co/uer/gpt2-chinese-cluecorpussmall

4.4 Generation

Table 5 displays the ablation study of our S2KG system for the response generation task. We analyze the results from the following perspectives.

Knowledge Grounding GPT2-FT (finetune) denotes the official baseline. GPT2-KGFT is our proposed knowledge grounding finetuning method which uses the serialized KB as knowledge. The first two lines in Table 5 show GPT2-KGFT significantly outperforms GPT2-FT by 3.09 BLEU and 34.8% Success, demonstrating the effectiveness of knowledge grounding based on local KB. We also find knowledge grounding improves the factual consistency of generated responses. We give examples in Section 5.1.

Semi-Supervised Pre-training The SereTOD challenge gives a large-scale unlabeled dataset that doesn't contain KB annotations. So we perform different pre-training settings to utilize these unlabeled dialogs. T5-KGFT is our proposed knowledge grounding model which replaces GPT2 with T5. Based on T5-KGFT, T5-Unsup-KGFT first performs an unsupervised response generation pre-training without KB input and then adopts knowledge grounding finetuning. Results show unsupervised pre-training gets an improvement of 1.91 BLEU, but drops by 14.6 on Success. We argue it's because raw response generation pre-training makes the model memorize similar dialogs but predict unfaithful responses without grounding ability. T5-Semi replaces unsupervised pre-training with semi-supervised pre-training which uses Track 1 system to generate the pseudo local KB for these unlabeled dialogs. T5-Semi outperforms T5-Unsup-KGFT by 1.16 BLEU and 17.2% Success, demonstrating the effectiveness of semi-supervised pre-training. We also find continual knowledge grounding finetuning on labeled data (T5-Semi-

Team ID	Human Evaluation				Final Score
	Fluency	Coherency	Success	Average	
Team-11 (Ours)	**4.23**	**3.73**	**3.47**	**3.81**	**3.10**
Team-5	4.06	3.14	3.40	3.53	2.70
Team-13	3.55	3.03	2.77	3.12	2.39
Team-10	3.20	2.98	3.11	3.10	2.28
Team-8	2.39	2.29	2.03	2.24	2.13

Table 4: Final human evaluation results on the test set of the top 5 teams released by the officials. Final score is the average of Combined score from automatic evaluation and averaged human evaluation score. It's the main ranking basis on the Track 2 leaderboard.

Methods	BLEU	Success
GPT2-FT (baseline)	4.39	0.344
GPT2-KGFT	7.48	0.692
T5-KGFT	11.32	0.741
T5-Unsup-KGFT	13.23	0.595
T5-Semi	14.39	0.767
T5-Semi-KGFT	12.30	0.761
UFA-Semi	14.51	0.789

Table 5: Comparison of different system response generation models on the dev set.

KGFT) can't bring further improvements upon T5-Semi because of knowledge forgetting.

Pre-trained Language Model We also compare different PLMs. We find that T5 consistently achieves better results than GPT-2. Besides, we experiment with a large PLM specified for customer service, UFA-large (He et al., 2022), which has 1.2B parameters compared to 220M T5 and 117M GPT-2. UFA-large further outperforms T5 by 0.12 BLEU and 2.2% Success.[13]

4.5 Human Evaluation

SereTOD performs human evaluation for different TOD systems, where real users interact with those systems according to randomly given goals. Table 4 shows the results of human evaluation and final scores. Our system also achieves state-of-the-art on all the metrics. Specifically, our method outperforms the second place (Team 5) by 0.17 on Fluency, 0.59 on Coherency, and 0.07 on Success.

5 Analysis

5.1 Case Study

Figure 5 shows three examples from the baseline model and the S2KG model, respectively, proving the advantages of S2KG model from the three dimensions of Success, Fluency, and Coherency.

Success In example one, the local KB includes the user's mobile package balance and information about the data package plan currently held by the user. The user's utterance is "Could you please check my data package for me?", which means the user asks the system to query the mobile package balance. The baseline system misidentified the user's intent and mistakenly believed that the user was querying the information of the data package plan, so it retrieved the wrong knowledge "ten yuan data package plan", thereby generating a reply wrongly. The S2KG model correctly identified the user's request, retrieved the correct result based on local KB, and successfully answered that the current mobile package balance was 295M in the reply. It proves that knowledge-grounded semi-supervised pre-training can greatly improve the accuracy of knowledge selection.

Fluency In example two, the user's second round of utterance is intended to query the date when the data package cap is exceeded. Since there is no corresponding information in the current local KB, the system cannot retrieve the knowledge. In this scenario, the baseline system repeated meaninglessly and failed to generate fluent responses. Due to the large-scale pre-training, the S2KG model can explain the situation to the user, guide the user correctly, and provide the user with a reasonable solution.

Consistency In example three, the user's dialogue history is mainly related to the data package given by the activity, while the baseline model mainly answers the user's current data package in the second round of replies, which cannot be consistent with the dialogue history. The S2KG model has good modeling of the dialogue history through pre-training, so it can explain the activity rules to the

[13]Considering the inference efficiency and hardware limit, we submit our final results on T5.

Dialogue		
Example 1	**Example 2**	**Example 3**
KB		

"NA": {
"用户需求":"查一下我的流量",
"流量余额": "二百九十五兆" },
"ent-1": {
"name": "十块钱一百兆",
"type": "流量包",
"业务费用": "十块钱",
"流量总量": "一个G"}}
	"NA": {
	"欠费": "欠费了六十多块钱" },
	"ent-1": {
	"name": "二十的",
	"type": "流量包",
	"业务费用":"二十,三百兆",
	"套餐外流量计费":"一兆按两毛九收费的,一兆按两毛九扣费"}}
		"ent-1": {
		"name": "活动",
		"type": "业务",
		"业务规则":"十二点到二十一点
		每整点开始,前一千名首次登陆用户
		可获三十兆,首次注册并登陆
		10086app的新用户成功注册登陆后即有机会获流量奖励
		,每天八点开始前两百名首次登陆可以获一个g,二百零一到六百名获五百兆"}}

"用户":"麻烦你帮我查一下我的流量吧"	"用户":"哦_嗯，不是上网，不是那个，嗯_流量不是开通了吗，七月份的"	"用户":"噢我问一下我刚才下载了一下客户端么你看我这个手机现在是不是送流量了"
"Golden客服": "好的请稍等一下", "Base客服":"好的请您稍等我帮您查询" "S2KG客服":"好的,请您稍等,我帮您查询"	"Golden客服": "先生您好，流量的话，我这边给您查了一下是_流量，我这边查了一下，有一个二十的，三百兆，_但是你已经，你们家的孩子呢，已经用超了六十块钱" "Base客服":"嗯，您稍等，我帮您查一下" "S2KG客服":"您七月份开的是二十的,三百兆的流量,已经用完了"	"Golden客服":"刚刚下载了客户端" "Base客服":"嗯我看一下您稍等" "S2KG客服":"刚刚下载了客户端"
"用户": "嗯好"	"用户":"啊，哟哟哟哟_什么时候用超的啥"	"用户":"噢"
"Golden客服":"流量呢已经超出扣了二百九十五兆", "Base客服":"您好感谢您的耐心等待, 我这边查看了一下您的这个手机上面的话，有一个呃，一个十块钱的流量包_然后有" "S2KG客服":"您好,感谢您的耐心等待,我这边查询到您的流量现在剩了二百九十五兆"	"Golden客服":"具体时间，我这边看不到的，就是今天上网的，超出的", "Base客服":"您这个月的话，您这个月的话，您这个月的话，您这个月的话" "S2KG客服":"具体时间我这边没有显示,先生,您要查一下详单,我把详单查询方式给您发过来,好吧"	"Golden客服":"现在上面没有看到有赠送的流量呀", "Base客服":"嗯_那您这个月的话呢 是有一个一百块钱的流量包_然后呢" "S2KG客服":"刚刚下载了客户端是给您送流量了它是说在十二点到二十一点每个整点开始新用户成功注册登陆后即有机会获得流量奖励每天的八点开始前两百名首次登陆是可以获一个g"
"用户": "二十九十五兆，那那个啥_我开通了多少兆"	"用户":"哦，哦_哎，它怎么要，这么多来呢，刚开"	"用户":"噢他说我下载客户端要送要赠送流量是我怎么操作我自己操作还是你们那给我弄"
"Golden客服": "十块钱一百兆" "Base客服":"二十九十五兆" "S2KG客服": "十块钱一百兆"	"Golden客服":"它是一兆按两毛九收费的，先生" "Base客服":"嗯，这个是您的基本套餐，然后您的流量的话，是有一个g的，然后的话呢，是有一个g的流量的" "S2KG客服":"一兆按两毛九收费的"	"Golden客服":"嗯这个是您下载客户端的时候赠送的流量" "Base客服":"您告我一下您下载了什么是10086那个app还是什么呢" "S2KG客服":"呃这个活动的话呢是在十二点到二十一点 每个整点开始 然后前一千名首次登陆的用户可获得三十兆"

Figure 5: Case study for three examples from Baseline and S2KG system. We present the local KB, the user utterances, golden response, baseline predictions, and prediction of S2KG system.

user in detail, to meet the user's intent, and the generated replies are consistent with the dialogue history.

5.2 Challenge

Although the S2KG model has achieved SOTA in the three dimensions of Success, Fluency and Coherency, there are still issues unresolved as showed in Figure 6: (1) **Response Diversity**: As shown in example 1, the user wants to figure out the rules for the user points redemption activity. Although the system provides the retrieved plan rules, the user still cannot understand these rules. So the user asks a question again, then the system repeats the business rules in the KB, resulting in a decrease in the diversity of the response and the user's engagement. (2) **Knowledge Redundancy**: As shown in example 2, the user asks the system about the data packages the user hold, the S2KG model not only provides the name of the packages in the reply, but also retrieves other information associated with the packages, such as fees, etc. As a result, there is knowledge redundancy in the system's reply, which is not conducive to the user's ability to grasp the key points.

6 Conclusion

In this paper, we present our models for Track 2 of the SereTOD 2022 challenge aiming to build semi-supervised and reinforced TOD systems. We divide Track 2 into two task groups, classification (user intent and system intent) and generation (system response). For the classification tasks, we employ Roberta-large and build two separate classification models. We also perform continual pre-training, class-wise threshold, and adversarial training strate-

Dialogue	
Example 1	Example 2
KB	

"NA":{
"账户余额": "两千二百积分" 、
},
"ent-1":{
"name": "活动",
"type": "业务",
"业务规则":"关注山西移动10086关注成功以后在上面积分的话享三折打三折然后兑换流量,七百五六的积分您就能兑换五百兆的省内流量"
}
	"NA":{
	"用户状态": "欠费",
	"持有套餐":
	"咪咕视频,家校通,二十八元的基本套餐,两块钱语音包,流量安心包,校讯通,qq会员,和留言,咪咕视频会员"
	}
	"ent-5":{
	"name": "qq会员",
	"type": "业务",
	"业务费用": "十五",
	"业务规则": "取消立即失效"
	},
	"ent-7":{
	"name": "流量安心包",
	"type": "流量包",
	"业务规则": "不使用不收费"
	}

"用户":"唉你帮我查一下我这个_这张卡_呃积分有多少呢"	"用户":"你好? "
"S2KG客服":"积分现在有两千二百积分"	"S2KG客服":"您好请问什么可以帮您?"
"用户": "嗯这个能换流量吗"	"用户": "我想请问下我当前的持有套餐? "
"S2KG客服":"兑换流量的话现在有个活动关注山西移动10086微信关注成功以后在上面积分的话享三折打三折然后兑换流量"	"S2KG客服":"您现在的套餐是二十八元的基本套餐, 两块钱语音包, 和校园家校互动a包, 咪咕视频会员,流量安心包不使用不收费一个qq会员十五一个
"用户": "那个如果我现在这个没没有网能能_能弄吗"	"用户": "那我现在是欠费了? "
"S2KG客服":"手机上得关注山西移动10086关注成功以后在上面积分的话享三折打三折然后兑换流量"	"S2KG客服":" 欠费金额属于您个人隐私人工台查询不了先生 您可以拨打10086按一号键再转三号键查询一下好吧"

Figure 6: Case study for two examples from S2KG system. We present the local KB, the user utterances and prediction of S2KG system.

gies. For the generation task, we build a knowledge-grounded dialog model S2KG and perform semi-supervised pre-training both on labeled data and unlabeled data. Our system achieves first place both in the automatic evaluation and human interaction. We also discuss the advantages and challenges of our system to provide a guideline for future work.

Acknowledgements

We thank all anonymous reviewers for their helpful comments and suggestions. We are also grateful to the track organizers for their valuable work. This work was partially supported by National Key R&D Program of China No. 2019YFF0303300 and Subject II No. 2019YFF0303302, DOCOMO Beijing Communications Laboratories Co., Ltd, MoE-CMCC "Artifical Intelligence" Project No. MCM20190701.

References

Paweł Budzianowski, Tsung-Hsien Wen, Bo-Hsiang Tseng, Iñigo Casanueva, Stefan Ultes, Osman Ramadan, and Milica Gasic. 2018. Multiwoz - a large-scale multi-domain wizard-of-oz dataset for task-oriented dialogue modelling. In *EMNLP*.

Jacob Devlin, Ming-Wei Chang, Kenton Lee, and Kristina Toutanova. 2019. BERT: Pre-training of deep bidirectional transformers for language understanding. In *Proceedings of the 2019 Conference of the North American Chapter of the Association for Computational Linguistics: Human Language Technologies, Volume 1 (Long and Short Papers)*, pages 4171–4186, Minneapolis, Minnesota. Association for Computational Linguistics.

Jianfeng Gao, Michel Galley, and Lihong Li. 2018. Neural approaches to conversational AI. In *Proceedings of the 56th Annual Meeting of the Association for Computational Linguistics: Tutorial Abstracts*, pages 2–7, Melbourne, Australia. Association for Computational Linguistics.

Shuyang Gao, Abhishek Sethi, Sanchit Agarwal, Tagyoung Chung, and Dilek Z. Hakkani-Tür. 2019. Dialog state tracking: A neural reading comprehension approach. In *SIGdial*.

Chih-Wen Goo, Guang-Lai Gao, Yun-Kai Hsu, Chih-Li Huo, Tsung-Chieh Chen, Keng-Wei Hsu, and Yun-Nung (Vivian) Chen. 2018. Slot-gated modeling for joint slot filling and intent prediction. In *NAACL*.

Ian J. Goodfellow, Jonathon Shlens, and Christian Szegedy. 2015. Explaining and harnessing adversarial examples. *CoRR*, abs/1412.6572.

Keqing He, Jingang Wang, Chaobo Sun, and Wei Wu. 2022. Unified knowledge prompt pre-training for customer service dialogues. *ArXiv*, abs/2208.14652.

Keqing He, Yuanmeng Yan, and Weiran Xu. 2020a. Learning to tag oov tokens by integrating contextual representation and background knowledge. In *ACL*.

Keqing He, Jinchao Zhang, Yuanmeng Yan, Weiran Xu, Cheng Niu, and Jie Zhou. 2020b. Contrastive zero-shot learning for cross-domain slot filling with adversarial attack. In *COLING*.

Hong Liu, Yucheng Cai, Zhijian Ou, Yi Huang, and Junlan Feng. 2022a. Revisiting markovian generative architectures for efficient task-oriented dialog systems. *ArXiv*, abs/2204.06452.

Hong Liu, Hao Peng, Zhijian Ou, Juan-Zi Li, Yi Huang, and Junlan Feng. 2022b. Information extraction and human-robot dialogue towards real-life tasks: A baseline study with the mobilecs dataset. *ArXiv*, abs/2209.13464.

Sihong Liu, Jinchao Zhang, Keqing He, Weiran Xu, and Jie Zhou. 2021. Scheduled dialog policy learning: An automatic curriculum learning framework for task-oriented dialog system. In *FINDINGS*.

Zhijian Ou, Junlan Feng, Juan-Zi Li, Yakun Li, Hong Liu, Hao Peng, Yi Huang, and Jiangjiang Zhao. 2022. A challenge on semi-supervised and reinforced task-oriented dialog systems. *ArXiv*, abs/2207.02657.

Kishore Papineni, Salim Roukos, Todd Ward, and Wei-Jing Zhu. 2002. Bleu: a method for automatic evaluation of machine translation. In *ACL*.

Baolin Peng, Chunyuan Li, Jinchao Li, Shahin Shayandeh, Lars Lidén, and Jianfeng Gao. 2021. Soloist: Building task bots at scale with transfer learning and machine teaching. *Transactions of the Association for Computational Linguistics*, 9:807–824.

Baolin Peng, Xiujun Li, Jianfeng Gao, Jingjing Liu, Kam-Fai Wong, and Shang-Yu Su. 2018. Deep dyna-q: Integrating planning for task-completion dialogue policy learning. In *ACL*.

Baolin Peng, Chenguang Zhu, Chunyuan Li, Xiujun Li, Jinchao Li, Michael Zeng, and Jianfeng Gao. 2020. Few-shot natural language generation for task-oriented dialog. In *Findings of the Association for Computational Linguistics: EMNLP 2020*, pages 172–182, Online. Association for Computational Linguistics.

Libo Qin, Wanxiang Che, Yangming Li, Haoyang Wen, and Ting Liu. 2019. A stack-propagation framework with token-level intent detection for spoken language understanding. In *EMNLP*.

Yixuan Su, Lei Shu, Elman Mansimov, Arshit Gupta, Deng Cai, Yi-An Lai, and Yi Zhang. 2022. Multi-task pre-training for plug-and-play task-oriented dialogue system. In *ACL*.

Chien-Sheng Wu, Andrea Madotto, Ehsan Hosseini-Asl, Caiming Xiong, Richard Socher, and Pascale Fung. 2019. Transferable multi-domain state generator for task-oriented dialogue systems. In *Proceedings of the 57th Annual Meeting of the Association for Computational Linguistics (Volume 1: Long Papers)*. Association for Computational Linguistics.

Hong Xu, Keqing He, Yuanmeng Yan, Sihong Liu, Zijun Liu, and Weiran Xu. 2020. A deep generative distance-based classifier for out-of-domain detection with mahalanobis space. In *COLING*.

Xiaojin Zhu. 2005. Semi-supervised learning literature survey.

CMCC: A Comprehensive and Large-Scale Human-Human Dataset for Dialogue Systems

Yi Huang[1,4], Xiaoting Wu[1,4], Si Chen[1,4], Wei Hu[1,4], Qing Zhu[1,4], Junlan Feng[1,4], Chao Deng[1,4], Zhijian Ou[3,4] and Jiangjiang Zhao[2]

[1]JIUTIAN Team, China Mobile Research,[2]China Mobile Online Marketing and Services Center

[3]Speech Processing and Machine Intelligence (SPMI) Lab, Tsinghua University

[4]Tsinghua University-China Mobile Communications Group Co., Ltd. Joint Institute

[1] {huangyi,wuxiaoting,chensiyjy,huweiyjy,zhuqingai,fengjunlan,dengchao}@chinamobile.com

[3]ozj@tsinghua.edu.cn, [2]zhaojiangjiang@cmos.chinamobile.com

Abstract

Dialogue modeling problems severely limit the real-world deployment of neural conversational models and building a human-like dialogue agent is an extremely challenging task. Recently, data-driven models become more and more prevalent which need a huge amount of conversation data. In this paper, we release around 100,000 dialogue, which come from real-world dialogue transcripts between real users and customer-service staffs. We call this dataset as CMCC (China Mobile Customer Care) dataset, which differs from existing dialogue datasets in both size and nature significantly. The dataset reflects several characteristics of human-human conversations, e.g., task-driven, care-oriented, and long-term dependency among the context. It also covers various dialogue types including task-oriented, chitchat and conversational recommendation in real-world scenarios. To our knowledge, CMCC is the largest real human-human spoken dialogue dataset and has dozens of times the data scale of others, which shall significantly promote the training and evaluation of dialogue modeling methods. The results of extensive experiments indicate that CMCC is challenging and needs further effort. We hope that this resource will allow for more effective models across various dialogue sub-problems to be built in the future.

1 Introduction

Task-oriented dialogue systems (Young et al., 2013; Williams et al., 2017; Su et al., 2021; He et al., 2021; Jayanthi et al., 2021) are designed to assist user in completing daily tasks, which involve reasoning over multiple dialogue turns. Tremendous progress has been made recently, but building a human-like dialogue system is a challenging task remaining. To drive the progress of building dialogue systems using data-driven approaches, a number of conversational corpora have been released in the past. Task-oriented dialogue corpus, such as Frames (Asri et al., 2017), MultiWOZ (Budzianowski et al., 2018), CrossWOZ (Zhu et al., 2020), RiSAWOZ (Quan et al., 2020), are collected by two crowd workers playing the roles of the user and the system, which often leads to be small-scale, and can not sufficiently capture a number of challenges that arise with production scaling. More recently, some researchers construct dialogue datasets from real human-to-human scenario conversations, especially human-to-human customer service scenario, such as JDDC (Chen et al., 2020) and MobileCS (Ou et al., 2022). JDDC is collected from E-commerce scenario and annotates intent information. MobileCS is conducted from mobile customer service scenario and model the process as task-oriented conversations. Therefore, the entity information related to tasks is annotated. However, the complexity of the dialogue process is far more than TOD, in addition to task completion, it is also accompanied by emotional support that appease an angry customer and providing solutions.

Several emotional support conversation corpora (Welivita and Pu, 2020; Sharma et al., 2020; Rashkin et al., 2019; Sun et al., 2021) are designed to emotional chat or provide empathetic responding. Since the emotional supporters are not well-trained, existing datasets do not naturally exhibit examples or elements of supportive conversations. As a result, data-driven models which leverage such corpora are limited in their ability to explicitly learn how to provide effective support. ESConv (Liu et al., 2021) is collected by communication of trained individuals who play the roles of the seeker and the supporter, and guided by predefined emotional support conversation framework, however, it is more focused on alleviating the negative emotions that users encounter in their daily lives.

Despite the efforts in modeling emotional support, work that focuses specifically on modeling emotional care and support in task-oriented dia-

Proceedings of the Towards Semi-Supervised and Reinforced Task-Oriented Dialog Systems (SereTOD), pages 48 - 61
December 7, 2022 ©2022 Association for Computational Linguistics

logue system is relatively limited. To this end, we design a customer service care-oriented taxonomy, and annotate care-oriented information for MobileCS dataset, covering 9 types of emotion labels and 17 types of customer service act labels finally. This new dataset consists of two parts, 8975 dialogues which are labeled with annotations of care-oriented information and other more than 90,000 unlabeled dialogues. We call this new dataset as **CMCC** (China **M**obile **C**ustomer **C**are) dataset. To be able to explain the patterns and trends of the conversation flow, we employ visualization methods to illustrate the most frequent exchanges and reveal how they temporally vary as dialogues proceed. Finally, we explore and demonstrate the effectiveness of care-oriented information for dialogue sub-tasks.

We highlight our contributions as follows:

- We provide a customer service care-oriented taxonomy, and conduct CMCC dataset on top of MoibleCS to facilitate the dialogue research.
- We employ visualization methods to illustrate the most frequent exchanges and reveal how patterns and trends temporally vary as dialogues proceed.
- We report the benchmark models and results of two evaluation tasks on CMCC, indicating that the dataset is a challenging testbed for future work.

2 Data Annotation

2.1 Motivation

We collect the CMCC dataset from the user-customer service conversations in real-life scenarios. These dialogues are inherently rich in user and customer service acts and emotional information. Therefore, our data annotation process integrates such features in the data and concentrates on how the customer service provides caring and empathetic acts according to a dynamic in the user's emotions. We present a novel data annotation approach by adding "User Emotion", "Expanded Customer Service Caring Act", and "Satisfaction" labels to emphasize the importance of emotions and "care-oriented" in the conversations. To our best knowledge, limited datasets have demonstrated such features in previous studies.

2.2 Guideline for Annotations

Our dataset is developed in multiple ways, which are provided in detail throughout the following sections. Compared to the MobileCS dataset, three new dimensions are added in our data annotation: user emotions, expanded customer service caring acts, and satisfaction. We also redefine the user intents to clarify the differences between intents and emotions.

2.2.1 User Emotion

We notice that users express various emotions throughout the conversations with customer service representatives, which can have a large impact on data division and annotation. Limited studies were conducted to consider this factor. As a result, we capture subtle user emotions throughout the conversations to derive and divide them into 8 labels for annotations. The refined annotation is necessary because customer service can act accordingly with "care-oriented" methods. We develop the "User Intent" labels from the MobileCS dataset, and add "Propose suggestion" and "Propose criticism" labels to separate intents from emotions. We pre-define an annotation schema and an intent set consisting of the 8 user emotion labels. At each turn, if emotions are explicitly expressed, the user's utterances are allowed to be annotated with one or more labels, which is common since multiple emotions could be expressed in one sentence in real-life conversations. The annotators are instructed to determine if the user's utterances contain emotions according to the schema and common sense. For example, "上次打电话说好了好了好了谁给我开的我要投诉他" (That's fine on the last phone call. Who opened the business for me last time, I want to complain to him), the label for this sentence is "Emotionally More Agitated". "这样哦要像每个人这样扣的话，还得了" (Would it be worth it if everyone's package was deducted like this?) is labeled with "Complain About A Problem".

2.2.2 Expanded Customer Service Caring Act

It's essential that good customer service provides "care-oriented" responses for emotional support. Adopting the original customer service acts from the MobileCS dataset, we derive and pre-define an "Expanded Customer Service Caring Act" set from the conversations. At each turn, the annotators are instructed to determine if the customer service utterances contain caring and empathetic acts to respond to user emotions and intents, allowing the use of multiple labels in one sentence. In addition, we extract keywords in each customer service utterance, such as "放心" (relax), "理解" (understand)， and "别着急" (don't worry), etc., indicating different customer service caring acts. For example, "还有剩下的是基本费用请您放心好吧" (The rest is the basic fee, please rest assured.) is labeled as "comfort". "确实是您的心情我非常理解" (I really understand how you feel) is labeled as "empathy".

2.2.3 Satisfaction

The satisfaction labels are pre-defined based on the context of conversations. Each conversation is required to be annotated with one of the three labels. "3" indicates the user is satisfied; "2" indicates the user accepts the suggestion provided by the customer service representative while the problem is unsolved; "1" indicates the user is unsatisfied. The annotators are instructed to comprehend the context of the conversation and annotate each conversation with one of the three satisfaction labels. For example, customer service: "请问还有其他可以帮到您吗？ " (Is there anything else I can help you with ?) user: "没有啦谢谢" (No thanks) is labeled as "3", suggesting that the user is very satisfied with the solution and result that the customer service provided.

2.3 Annotation Results

We improve the MobileCS dataset and further develop it by incorporating user emotions, expanded customer service caring acts, and satisfaction in the dialogues. Our novel dataset not only is motivated by the inherent nature of customer service-user dialogues but also aims to emphasize a "care-oriented" focus. Also, the experiment results support that the CMCC dataset is advancing and valuable in user-customer service conversations. The label set consists of 4 expanded customer service caring acts, 13 original customer service acts, 9 user emotions, 14 user intents, and 3 satisfaction labels in total.

2.4 Quality Control

Since the annotations are conducted on several dimensions simultaneously and differently on multiple criteria, missing and incorrect labels are inevitable problems we might face. To ensure a high-quality annotation result, we review and revise the missing or incorrect annotations based on several effective strategies. First, we conduct keyword extractions to check for the missing and incorrect labels, which are manually filtered out and re-labeled by the qualified annotators. For example, "您稍等一下好吗，我这边的话肯定会站在你的角度去想" (Can you wait a moment, I will definitely think from your point of view) misses the "empathy" label during the first round of annotation, and it's added during the manual check. Based on this strategy, we review and re-label the dataset two more times, which guarantees the efficiency and completeness of our annotation. Additionally, for the satisfaction annotation, we randomly sample 10% of conversations to check for the annotation quality. For example, "唉算了算了反正还有几天就" (Oh, forget it, there are still a few days left) is labeled as "3" in the first round of annotation, but it should be "2" instead.

Upon review, the missing labels and incorrect labels from the dataset are all revised and corrected for the quality control process. As a result, this ensures the high quality of our data annotation process.

3 Data Characteristics

This section mainly introduces the characteristics of the data. In addition to showing the number of conversations and labels in the dataset, we also demonstrate the characteristics of customer service dialogue data by visualizing the transition between customer service acts and user emotion in dialogues.

3.1 Data Statistics

The basic information of the labeled part in this dataset is shown in Table 1. The labeled data contains a total of 8,975 dialogues. The maximum

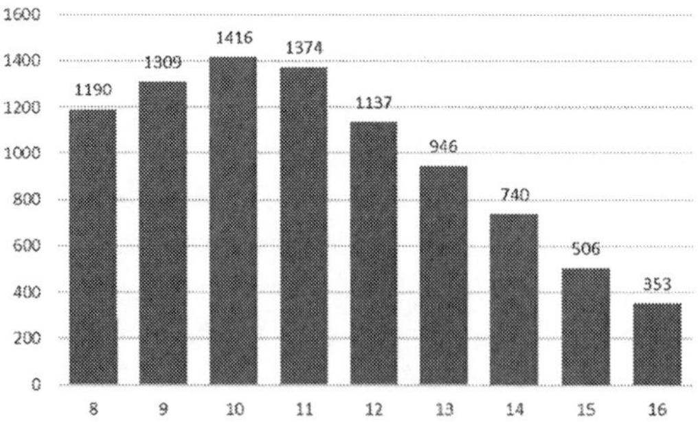

Figure 1: The histogram of dialogue turns. The horizontal axis is the number of dialogue turns, and the vertical axis is the number of dialogues, filtering the dialogues with less than 10 dialogues.

Criteria	Statistics
Total no. of dialogues	8,975
Total no. of dialogue turns	100,139
Average no. of turns per dialogue	22.31
Maximum no. of turns per dialogue	16 (353 dialogues)
Minimum no. of turns per dialogue	5 (1 dialogue)
Total no. of customer service turns	100,139
Total no. of user turns	100,138
Average no. of customer service tokens per dialogue turn	25.27
Average no. of user tokens per dialogue turn	14.58

Table 1: Dialogue statistics in the dataset.

number of dialogue turns included in the dataset is 16. Figure 1 is a histogram of dialogue turns. It can be observed that most of the dialogue turns in the dataset are concentrated between 8 and 13. This means that the dialogue between the user and the customer service typically ends in around 10 turns. If there are situations such as user's problems that are difficult to solve, the number of turns in this dialogue will increase significantly.

The histogram of user negative emotion labels is shown in Figure 2. The statistical scope is all negative emotions of users in the dialogue, excluding neutral emotions. The largest proportion of the entire user emotion label is "Complain About A Problem". This label is about the user emotion that often appears on the user side in the field of customer service dialogue. It generally occurs when users complain about networks, fees, business use, business handling, and e-commerce after-sales. The second-largest user emotion label is "Emotionally More Agitated". This label indicates that various businesses or services have seriously affected the user experience, or that customer service has not effectively helped users to solve problems.

Figure 3 is a statistical histogram of customer service intent labels. It can be seen that the labels with the largest proportion of intent are "Inform" and "Passive Confirmation". "Inform" means that the customer service informs the user of certain information, usually definite information, such as the customer service will perform a certain operation,

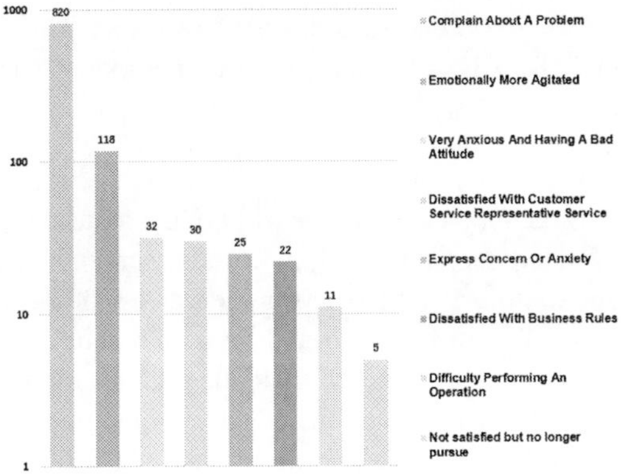

Figure 2: The histogram of user negative emotion. The horizontal axis is user emotion labels, and the vertical axis is the number of emotions.

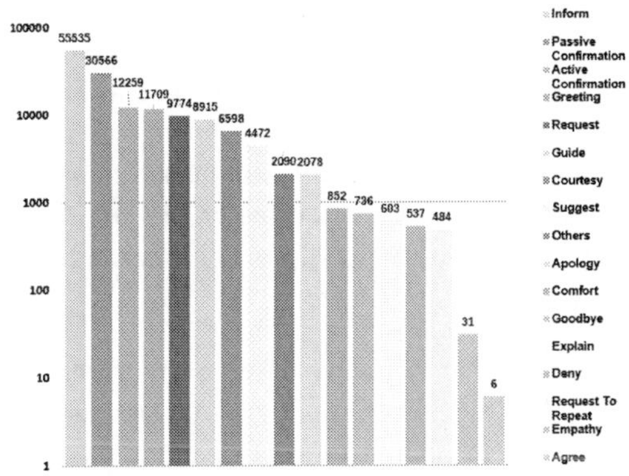

Figure 3: The histogram of customer service act. The horizontal axis is the customer service act label, and the vertical axis is the number of acts.

the problem will be solved within a certain period of time, etc. "Passive Confirmation" means the act of confirming based on the user's inquiry or information provided above. Since the common content of dialogues in the field of customer service is to solve the user's problem, the labels of "Inform" and "Passive Confirmation" will be ubiquitous in each turn of dialogue.

3.2 Data Structure

For a better understanding of the data structure, we investigate which customer service acts are frequently associated with users when responding to different emotional situations. We list the labeled instances of customer service act, user emotion, examples and the proportion of all labels, respectively (detailed in the appendix). Most conversations have multiple intent labels or emotion labels. For example, "Hello, nice to serve you, sorry to keep you waiting" includes "Apology" and "Greeting". Based on the statistics of user emotions and customer service acts, we observe the overall distribution of labels on the dataset.

In the following part, we will explore more about the conversion relationship between user emotions and customer service acts in the process of a dialogue. Figure 4 is a chord diagram of emotion-act labels. It represents the dialogue relationship between the user's emotion and the customer service act in the dialogue.The nodes and edges of the same color in the graph represent the user emotion and the customer service act corresponding to the next round of dialogue. It can be seen from the figure that the largest act dialogue is from "Complain About A Problem" to "Inform". This shows that when the user encounters a business problem, the customer service is more inclined to explain the cause or solution to the problem to the user. This phenomenon is in line with the most common scenario in the field of customer service, that is, customer service helps users solve related problems.

In order to intuitively observe the conversion relationship between user emotion and customer service act in multiple turns of dialogue, we draw a Sankey diagram of the dialogue between user emotion and customer service act in multi-turns. Figure 5 is the dialogue flow diagram of user emotions and customer service acts in four turns of dialogues. The first and third turns are user emotions, and the second and fourth turns are customer service acts. After the second turn of customer service replies to the user's dialogue with negative emotions, it can be observed that the user's emotion in the next turn, which is also the third turn, has become more "Neutral". This shows that as the customer service responds to the user's questions, the user's negative emotions will gradually disappear.

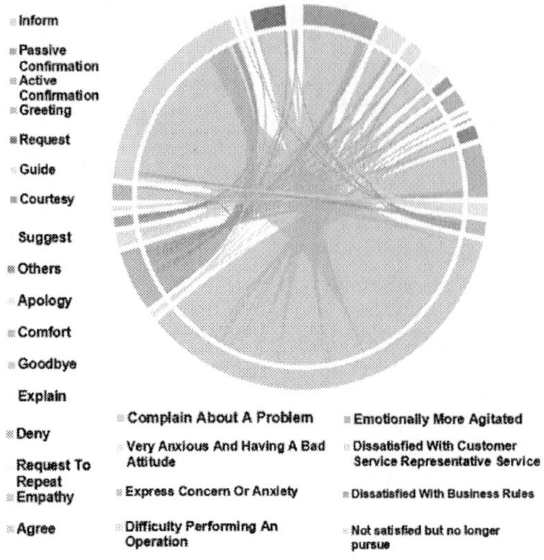

Figure 4: The chord diagram for user emotion and customer service act relationship. More details on labels can be found in the appendix. Best viewed in color.

4 Experiments

In this section, we conduct experiments on the CMCC dataset. We focus on two tasks: dialogue response generation and user emotion recognition.

4.1 Dialogue Response Generation

Our experiments in this part mainly focus on the question: Can extra care-oriented information improve the generative dialogue model?

4.1.1 Comparable Models

Similar to (Ou et al., 2022), we employ a Markovian generative architecture (MGA) (Liu et al., 2022) based on Chinese GPT-2 as baseline and build the following variant model:

Baseline The baseline model is a MGA generative model, which is designed to be $p_\theta(e_t, ui_t, a_t, r_t|e_{t-1}, u_t)$. u_t denotes the user utterance, e_t is entity names of dialogue history, ui_t is the user intent, and r_t is the customer service response, respectively, at turn $t = 1, ..., T$, for a diaogue of T turns.

Variants with care-oriented information To incorporate the care-oriented annotations into the baseline model, we add user emotion generation and expand original customer service acts to with caring acts in it. As is shown in Figure 6, for each customer service response, we append user emotion before corresponding customer service act. Then MGA generative process can ber represented as $p_\theta(e_t, ui_t, uemo_t, a_t, r_t|e_{t-1}, u_t)$, where $uemo_t$ is the user emotion at turn t. The model generates the response conditioned on the predicted user emotion and customer service act.

We study two variants that use care-oriented annotations in the experiments. (1) End2End: customer service response is generated conditioned on predicted customer service act and predicted user emotion, user emotion and customer service act are

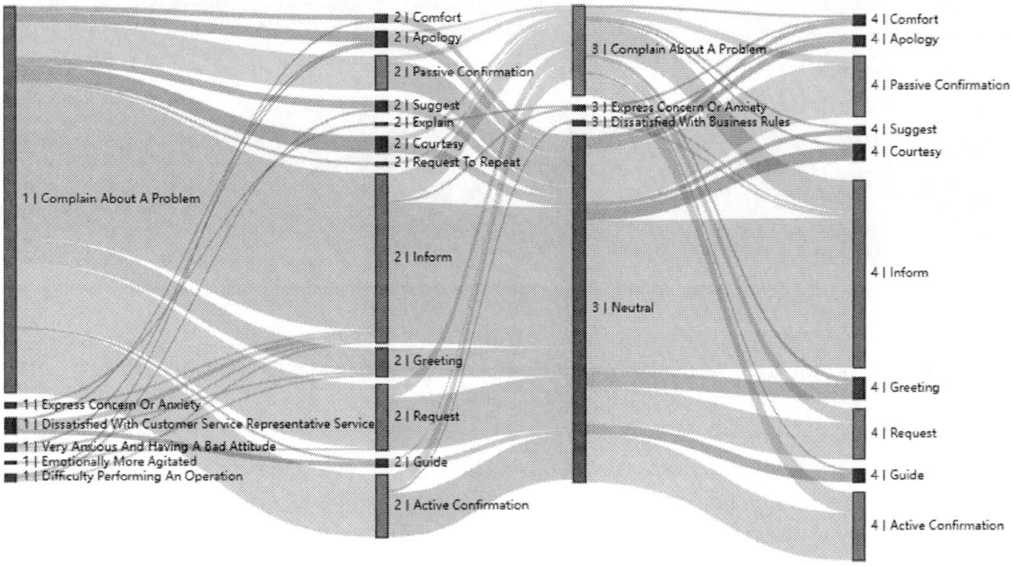

Figure 5: Dynamic transformation of user emotion vs. customer service act in the first four rounds of dialogue. Best viewed in color.

generated conditioned on KB result, KB result is queryed conditioned on predicted entity name and user intent. (2) Oracle: customer service response is generated conditioned on gold reference of customer service act, entity name, user intent and KB result.

4.1.2 Evaluation Measures

To investigate the impact of utilizing care-oriented information on the model performance with Chinese GPT-2 as backbone, we compare the performance of End2End and Oracle variants with the Baseline model. The automatic metrics include F1 score, Success rate and BLEU score. F1 is calculated for both predicted user intent and customer service act. Success rate (Budzianowski et al., 2018) is the percentage of generated dialogues that achieve user goals. BLEU-4 score (Papineni et al., 2002) evaluates the fluency of generated responses.

4.1.3 Experimental Results

The experimental results are shown in Table 2, which demonstrates the effectiveness of our model. There are 3 major findings from the experiments. (1) The Variant model has improved the Baseline model's performance of user intent F1, success rate and BLEU-4 of response, but the F1 of the customer service act has decreased slightly. It may be because the variant model expands the original cutomer service act labels, those with less data affects the overall performance. (2) Whether it is End2End or Oracle results, variant model is better than baseline model in BLEU-4 of response, we attribute it to the fact that care-oriented information matters and it enhances the dialogue generation positively. Care-oriented information includes user emotion and expanded customer service caring act, which part brings more gain will be analyzed in ablation experiments. (3) End2End results are lower than Oracle's results, because if predicted intermediate results is different from the ground truth, the generated response will be much different from the reference response.

Models	F1 for user intent	Success rate	F1 for customer service act	BLEU-4
Baseline Model (End2End)	0.642	0.315	0.575	4.137
Variant Model (End2End)	**0.656**	**0.357**	0.567	**4.669**
Baseline Model (Oracle)	–	–	–	6.230
Variant Model (Oracle)	–	–	–	**7.385**

Table 2: Results of automatic evaluation. The results in bold are better than the baseline.

4.1.4 Analysis

Our variant models consider care-oriented information, user emotion and customer service caring act. To investigate more, we conduct extra experiments and the analysis results.

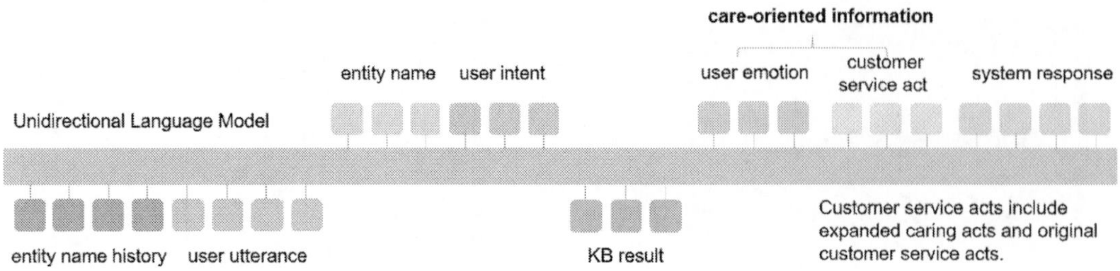

Figure 6: Variant model architecture with care-oriented information.

In order to verify the improvement brought by each added part (user emotion, expanded customer service caring act), we drop these two parts from the original variant model and check the performance changes. Results are presented in Table 3. We have the following observations: (1) In most circumstances, when user emotion is removed, BLEU-4 dropped more and success rate dropped less. (2) When expanded customer service caring act is removed, situation differs. That is, BLEU-4 dropped less and success rate dropped more. It indicates that expanded customer service caring act provides more gain for the entity-related part of the response, while user emotion plays more for the non-entity-related part (e.g., caring or empathetic responding).

Models	F1 for user intent	Success rate	F1 for customer service act	BLEU-4
Variant Model (End2End)	0.656	0.357	0.567	4.669
w/o user emotion	0.611	0.356	0.567	4.462
w/o expanded customer service caring act	0.656	0.340	0.577	4.657

Table 3: Evaluation results of ablation study.

In Table 4, examples are presented to compare the response generated by variant model and the baseline model. The first column is user utterance, the second column is the response of manual customer service, the third and fourth columns are the responses generated by variant model and baseline model respectively. In the first example, user reports that the broadband network is not working well, and accompanied by complaints. The variant model can generate the response with the soothing keyword "马上" (right now). In the second example, user's emotion is neutral and the variant model is still able to generate a more friendly response with "请您放心" (please do not worry) keyword. Intuitively, the variant model which is introduced with care-oriented information achieves better performance than the baseline model.

4.2 User Emotion Recognition

In this part, we focus on the effect of different models used in the emotion recognition task: the classification-based model and generation-based one. We will conduct experiments on the dataset CMCC and answer the question: are both models suitable to solve the emotion recognition problem?

4.2.1 Classification-based Model

We first treat the emotion recognition task as a mutli-label classification problem because a user utterance may contain multiple emotions, e.g., *complain about a problem* and *dissatisfied with buisiness rules* at the same time. Taking the pre-trained models bert-base-chinese[1] as the backbone, the classification model takes dialogue utterances X as input and predicts a binary result for each possible dialogue emotion:

$$P = Sigmoid(W(G(X))) \in R^N, \quad (1)$$

where $W \in R^{d_b*N}$ is a trainable weight matrix, d_b is the hidden size and G is used to encode the input utterance to our representation. The model is trained with binary cross-entropy loss. The task uses the threshold of 0.3 to predict whether the emotion is triggered. We evaluate micro-F1 and macro-F1 scores on our dataset for the emotion recognition task.

4.2.2 Generation-based Model

The Generation-based model is consistent with the variant model in the previous section 4.1.1. The user emotion is generated conditioned on KB result which is queryed conditioned on predicted entity name and user intent. Micro-F1 and macro-F1 are aggregation methods for the user emotion recognition task. Specifically, micro-F1 score gives equal

[1]https://huggingface.co/bert-base-chinese

User Utterance	Response of Manual Customer Service	Prediction of Variant Model	Prediction of Baseline Model
用户：每天晚上一到这个时候啊到十二点过钟连看电视都看不到 User: Every night at this time, I can't even watch TV until after twelve o'clock.	客服：嗯抱歉先生现在连我的远程系统都看不了任何状态了_这边的话请您稍后再来电正在恢复当中恢复好了请您这边再来电好吗 Customer Service: I'm sorry sir, I can't even see any status of my remote system now. Please call back later. It is recovering. Please call again when it is restored.	系统：嗯好的那我这边的话呢马上给您反映到后台去给您核实处理一下 System: Okay, I'll report it to you i mmediately to the backstage, and check it out.	系统：嗯那您这个问题的话我这边帮您记录反馈到后台去给您处理一下_然后呢我们这边的话呢会尽快的给您回 System: I will help you record the feedback and send it to the background to handle it for you, and then we will call you back as soon as possible.
用户：帮我登记一下啊安排你们师傅过来看 User: Help me register and arrange for your master to come and see.	客服：诶好的 Customer Service: Oh, okay.	系统：好的那我这边的话呢已 经为您登记好了请您放心 System: Okay, I've already registered it for you, please don't worry.	系统：好的那我这边的话就帮您登记一下然后的话呢您就可以使用了 System: Okay, I'll help you to register, then you can use it.

Table 4: Responses generated from variant model and baseline model.

importance to each observation. When the classes are imbalanced, those classes with more observations will have a larger impact on the micro-F1 score. Thus the final micro-F1 score tends to hide the performance of the minority classes and amplify the majority. On the other hand, macro-F1 score gives equal importance to each class. This means that a majority class will contribute equally along with the minority, allowing macro-F1 to still return objective results on imbalanced datasets. As shown in Table 5, our experiments show that the generation_based approach can help us improve emotion classification performance on the imbalanced classes, from a classification_based baseline performance of 30.1% macro-F1 to 39.3%, an increase of 9.2 points.

Models	micro-F1	macro-F1
Generation-based	0.832	0.393
Classification-based	0.859	0.301

Table 5: Emotion recognition performance using two different models (the generation-based model and the classification-based one).

5 Conclusion

In this paper, we present CMCC, to date the largest human-to-human real-life dataset annotated with rich care-oriented information on top of MobileCS. We not only manually label each dialogue with comprehensive user emotion, customer service act and satisfaction annotations for various sub-tasks of multi-domain dialogue systems, but also further investigate approach to facilitate the research of care-oriented way via empirical experiments. In addition, the process of data annotation and visualization is described in detail. We also report the benchmark models and results of two evaluation tasks on CMCC, indicating that the dataset is a challenging testbed for future work. We will enrich the dataset annotations (e.g., solutions, external knowledge and API calls) from various aspects in future work. We hope it can bring more imagination and benefit future research in dialogue systems.

References

Layla El Asri, Hannes Schulz, Shikhar Sharma, Jeremie Zumer, Justin Harris, Emery Fine, Rahul Mehrotra, and Kaheer Suleman. 2017. Frames: a corpus for adding memory to goal-oriented dialogue systems. *arXiv preprint arXiv:1704.00057*.

Paweł Budzianowski, Tsung-Hsien Wen, Bo-Hsiang Tseng, Inigo Casanueva, Stefan Ultes, Osman Ramadan, and Milica Gašić. 2018. Multiwoz–a large-scale multi-domain wizard-of-oz dataset for task-oriented dialogue modelling. *arXiv preprint arXiv:1810.00278*.

Meng Chen, Ruixue Liu, Lei Shen, Shaozu Yuan, Jingyan Zhou, Youzheng Wu, Xiaodong He, and Bowen Zhou. 2020. The JDDC corpus: A large-scale multi-turn chinese dialogue dataset for e-commerce customer service. In *Proceedings of The 12th Language Resources and Evaluation Conference, LREC 2020, Marseille, France, May 11-16, 2020*, pages 459–466. European Language Resources Association.

Wanwei He, Yinpei Dai, Yinhe Zheng, Yuchuan Wu, Zheng Cao, Dermot Liu, Peng Jiang, Min Yang, Fei Huang, Luo Si, et al. 2021. Galaxy: A generative pre-trained model for task-oriented dialog with semi-supervised learning and explicit policy injection. *arXiv preprint arXiv:2111.14592*.

Sai Muralidhar Jayanthi, Varsha Embar, and Karthik Raghunathan. 2021. Evaluating pretrained transformer models for entity linking in task-oriented dialog. *arXiv preprint arXiv:2112.08327*.

Hong Liu, Yucheng Cai, Zhijian Ou, Yi Huang, and Junlan Feng. 2022. Revisiting markovian generative architectures for efficient task-oriented dialog systems. *arXiv preprint arXiv:2204.06452*.

Siyang Liu, Chujie Zheng, Orianna Demasi, Sahand Sabour, Yu Li, Zhou Yu, Yong Jiang, and Minlie Huang. 2021. Towards emotional support dialog systems. In *Proceedings of the 59th Annual Meeting of the Association for Computational Linguistics and the 11th International Joint Conference on Natural Language Processing, ACL/IJCNLP 2021, (Volume 1: Long Papers), Virtual Event, August 1-6, 2021*, pages 3469–3483. Association for Computational Linguistics.

Zhijian Ou, Junlan Feng, Juanzi Li, Yakun Li, Hong Liu, Hao Peng, Yi Huang, and Jiangjiang Zhao. 2022. A challenge on semi-supervised and reinforced task-oriented dialog systems. *arXiv preprint arXiv:2207.02657*.

Kishore Papineni, Salim Roukos, Todd Ward, and Wei-Jing Zhu. 2002. Bleu: a method for automatic evaluation of machine translation. In *Proceedings of the 40th annual meeting of the Association for Computational Linguistics*, pages 311–318.

Libo Qin, Wanxiang Che, Yangming Li, Haoyang Wen, and Ting Liu. 2019. A stack-propagation framework with token-level intent detection for spoken language understanding. *arXiv preprint arXiv:1909.02188*.

Jun Quan, Shian Zhang, Qian Cao, Zizhong Li, and Deyi Xiong. 2020. Risawoz: A large-scale multi-domain wizard-of-oz dataset with rich semantic annotations for task-oriented dialogue modeling. In *Proceedings of the 2020 Conference on Empirical Methods in Natural Language Processing, EMNLP 2020, Online, November 16-20, 2020*, pages 930–940. Association for Computational Linguistics.

Hannah Rashkin, Eric Michael Smith, Margaret Li, and Y-Lan Boureau. 2019. Towards empathetic open-domain conversation models: A new benchmark and dataset. In *Proceedings of the 57th Conference of the Association for Computational Linguistics, ACL 2019, Florence, Italy, July 28- August 2, 2019, Volume 1: Long Papers*, pages 5370–5381. Association for Computational Linguistics.

Ashish Sharma, Adam S. Miner, David C. Atkins, and Tim Althoff. 2020. A computational approach to understanding empathy expressed in text-based mental health support. In *Proceedings of the 2020 Conference on Empirical Methods in Natural Language Processing, EMNLP 2020, Online, November 16-20, 2020*, pages 5263–5276. Association for Computational Linguistics.

Yixuan Su, Lei Shu, Elman Mansimov, Arshit Gupta, Deng Cai, Yi-An Lai, and Yi Zhang. 2021. Multi-task pre-training for plug-and-play task-oriented dialogue system. *arXiv preprint arXiv:2109.14739*.

Hao Sun, Zhenru Lin, Chujie Zheng, Siyang Liu, and Minlie Huang. 2021. Psyqa: A chinese dataset for generating long counseling text for mental health support. In *Findings of the Association for Computational Linguistics: ACL/IJCNLP 2021, Online Event, August 1-6, 2021*, volume ACL/IJCNLP 2021 of *Findings of ACL*, pages 1489–1503. Association for Computational Linguistics.

Anuradha Welivita and Pearl Pu. 2020. A taxonomy of empathetic response intents in human social conversations. In *Proceedings of the 28th International Conference on Computational Linguistics, COLING 2020, Barcelona, Spain (Online), December 8-13, 2020*, pages 4886–4899. International Committee on Computational Linguistics.

Jason D. Williams, Kavosh Asadi, and Geoffrey Zweig. 2017. Hybrid code networks: practical and efficient end-to-end dialog control with supervised and reinforcement learning. In *Proceedings of the 55th Annual Meeting of the Association for Computational Linguistics, ACL 2017, Vancouver, Canada, July 30 - August 4, Volume 1: Long Papers*, pages 665–677. Association for Computational Linguistics.

Steve J. Young, Milica Gasic, Blaise Thomson, and Jason D. Williams. 2013. Pomdp-based statistical spoken dialog systems: A review. *Proc. IEEE*, 101(5):1160–1179.

Qi Zhu, Kaili Huang, Zheng Zhang, Xiaoyan Zhu, and Minlie Huang. 2020. Crosswoz: A large-scale chinese cross-domain task-oriented dialogue dataset. *Trans. Assoc. Comput. Linguistics*, 8:281–295.

Category	Examples	Frequency
通知(Inform)	嗯，我帮您看看您的手机有没有开通业务了，我先帮你查一查 Well, let me help you to see if your mobile phone has been opened for business, let me check for you first	37.72%
被动确认(passive confirmation)	对咱们这面办不了 Yeah, we can't do it here	20.76%
问候(Greeting)	您好很高兴为您服务 Hello, glad to serve you	8.33%
主动确认(Active Confirmation)	您好感谢您耐心等待，有一个十元一百兆的安心包确定要取消是吗 Hello, thank you for your patience, there is a peace of mind package of ten yuan and one hundred trillion, are you sure you want to cancel it?	7.95%
询问(request)	二十四小时之内先生，一般都很快的，那个您是主要在省内用吗 Within 24 hours, sir, i t's usually very fast. A re you mainly using it in the province?	6.64%
引导(Guide)	嗯请问什么其他可帮你吗先生 Well, what else can I help you with, sir?	6.05%
客套(Courtesy)	不客气已经帮您改好了稍后查看一下 You're welcome, I've fixed it for you, check it out later	4.48%
建议(Suggest)	那建议您测试一下好吗 I suggest you test it	3.04%
其他(Other)	嗯 Um	1.42%

Table 6: Types, instances, and proportions of customer service acts.

Category	Examples	Frequency
抱歉(Apology)	您好，很高兴为您服务， 抱歉让您久等了 Hello, nice to serve you, sorry to keep you waiting	1.41%
安抚(Comfort)	哦，这个的话是可以使用的 ，这您放心 Oh, this one can be used, don't worry	0.58%
再见(Goodbye)	好，麻烦了，感谢来电再见 Okay, sorry for your troubles, thanks for calling, bye	0.50%
解释(Explain)	它是每天早上八点到晚上六点 之间办公的_就说现在已经下班 了明天早上八点以后才可以拨打 It works between 8:00 am and 6:00 pm every day. It means that it is already off work now and can only be called after 8:00 am tomorrow.	0.41%
否认(Deny)	不好意思，不是，那个假日流量 只是三天时间_并且_时候才可 以的 Sorry, no, that holiday traffic is only available for three days _ and _	0.36%
请求重复(Request To Repeat)	呃我没听清 uh i didn't hear	0.33%
同理心(Empathy)	你这个心情，我非常理解， 给您带来不便，是向您致 一下歉 I understand your feelings very much. I apologize for the inconvenience caused to you.	0.02%
赞同(Agree)	嗯对是的，那您说的没错 Yes, then you are right	0.004%

Table 7: Types, instances, and proportions of customer service acts.

Category	Examples	Frequency
抱怨某问题(Complain About A Problem)	就是在那个上网的时间网络老是出现那个网络异常怎么回事儿 It's the time when the Internet is online, the network always has that network abnormality,what's the matter?	77.14%
情绪较为激动(Emotionally More Agitated)	因为我觉得我这个要求不是很高的他们确实有有点做的过分 Because I don't think my requirements are very high, they are indeed overdoing it.	11.10%
非常着急且态度恶劣(Very Anxious And Having A Bad Attitude)	没有啊_打电话了他给我说我办下，还什么办了个三十G的咋了，我说你这些人[UNK]你说话怎么这么_嘴里跑火车着呢 No, _ called and he told me that I would do it, and even a 30G package . why are you full of crap?	3.01%
对客服代表服务不满(Dissatisfied With Customer Service Representative Service)	尽快呀，快到什么时候啊_对呀，我想问下快到什么，四五天了耶，然后重点是我报修也报了三天之后也没个人给我打个电话啊 As soon as possible, it's been four or fiv e days, and the point is that I appl ied for repairs for three days and no one called me.	2.82%
表示担忧或焦虑(Express Concern Or Anxiety)	六十多岁了我能不着急吗我这个 I'm in my sixties, can I be in a hurry?	2.35%
对业务规定不满(Dissatisfied With Business Rules)	不可能吧哪有这种霸王条款我不想用我_我取掉的话它为啥不让取 Impossible, how can there be such an overlord clause, I don't want to use it, I'll jus t cancel it, why not let me cancel	2.07%
执行某项操作有困难(Difficulty Performing An Operation)	咋咋个下载法我也搞不清楚 i don't know how to download	1.03%
不太满意但不再追究(Not Satisfied But No Longer Pursue)	可以我希望你们后台人员无论处理出怎样怎么样的结果_可以在最短的时间内告知我 Yes, I hope that no matter what the result is from your backstage staff, you can let me know in the shortest possible time.	0.47%

Table 8: Types, instances, and proportions of user negative emotions.

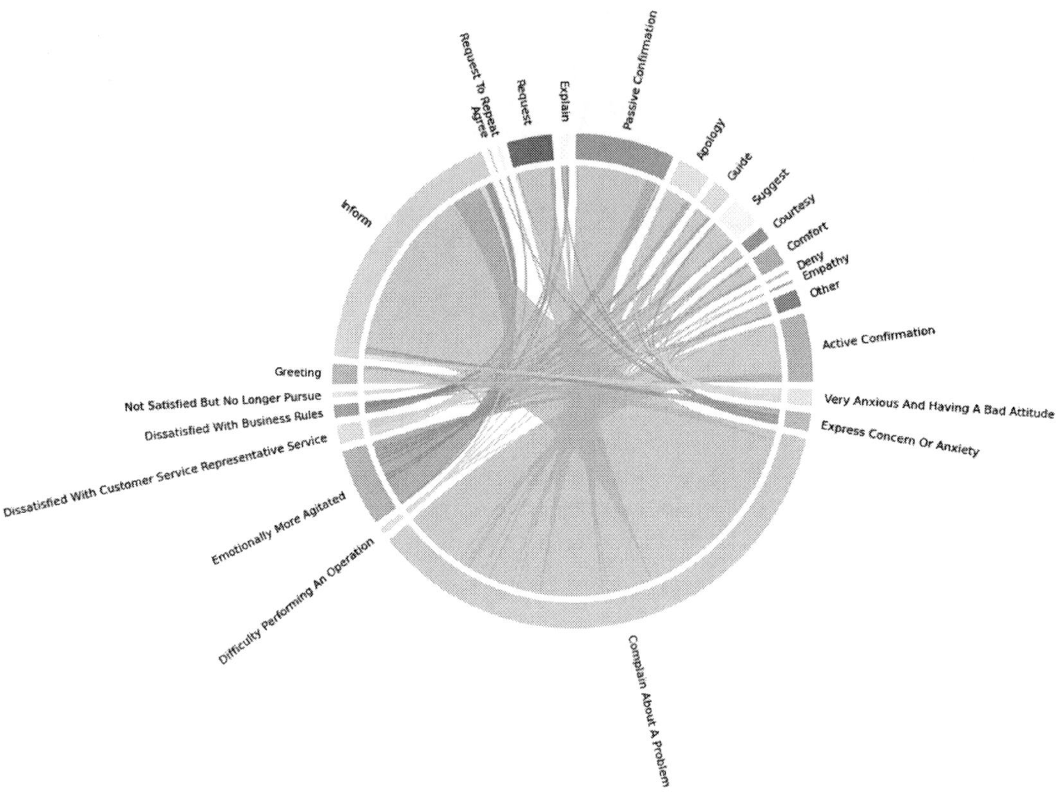

Figure 7: User emotion-customer service act conversion relationship chord diagram

Model	entity (F1)	emotion (Acc)
Stack-propagation Model	0.525	0.989
w/o user emotion	0.524	-
Baseline Model	0.382	-

Table 9: The joint performance on the stack-propagation model (Qin et al., 2019) using the CMCC dataset with or without emotion labeling.

Table 9 gives the result of the experiment comparison for entity extraction task. From results of the first two rows, we observe that without the emotion labels, simply incorporating the sequence labeling information, the entity extraction performance (micro-F1) drops slightly, which demonstrates that directly leveraging the emotion information can slightly improve the performance of the entity extraction task.

State-Aware Adversarial Training for Utterance-Level Dialogue Generation

Yi Huang, Xiaoting Wu, Wei Hu , Junlan Feng , Chao Deng
JIUTIAN Team, China Mobile Research
{huangyi,wuxiaoting,huweiyjy,fengjunlan,dengchao}@chinamobile.com

Abstract

Dialogue generation is a challenging problem because it not only requires us to model the context in a conversation but also to exploit it to generate a coherent and fluent utterance. This paper, aiming for a specific topic of this field, proposes an adversarial training based framework for utterance-level dialogue generation. Technically, we train an encoder-decoder generator simultaneously with a discriminative classifier that make the utterance approximate to the state-aware inputs. Experiments on MultiWoZ 2.0 and MultiWoZ 2.1 datasets show that our method achieves advanced improvements on both automatic and human evaluations, and on the effectiveness of our framework facing low-resource. We further explore the effect of fine-grained augmentations for downstream dialogue state tracking (DST) tasks. Experimental results demonstrate the high-quality data generated by our proposed framework improves the performance over state-of-the-art models.

1 Introduction

Task-oriented dialogue systems (Young et al., 2013; Williams et al., 2016; Wu et al., 2020; Su et al., 2021) are designed to assist user in completing daily tasks, which involve reasoning over multiple dialogue turns. User goals expressed during conversation are important for the dialogue system and often encoded as a compact set of dialogue states, which is often expressed as a collection of slot-value pairs.

Nowadays generative conversational models are drawing an increasing amount of interest and becoming a more popular trend of task-oriented dialogue generation. Most existing generative conversational models (Shang et al., 2015; Vinyals and Le, 2015; Li et al., 2016; Yao, 2015; Luan et al., 2016; Zhang et al., 2019b) predict the next dialogue utterance given the dialogue history using the maximum likelihood estimation (MLE) objective, considering conversation history to learn to generate responses via optimizing the query-response pairs, as illustrated in Figure 1. Despite its success, this over-simplified training objective leads to problems: when generating dialogue responses from these models by iteratively sampling the next token, we do not have much control over attributes of the output text, such as the topic, the style, the sentiment, etc.

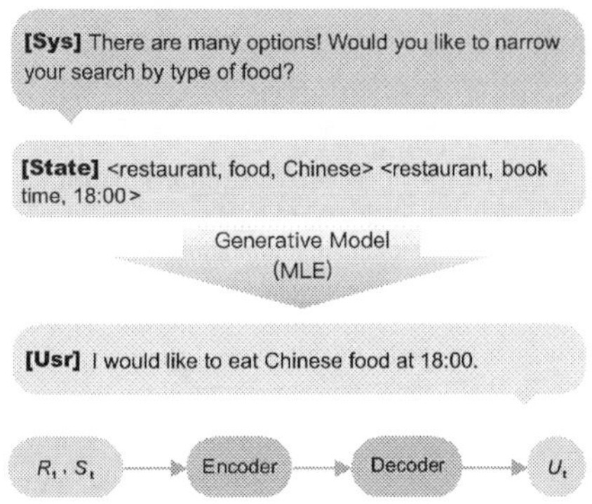

Figure 1: Dialogue generation via MLE training.

Solutions to these problems require answering a fundamental question: how to steer a powerful unconditioned dialogue model to generate content with desired attributes? Some existing studies have tackled this problem to control responses by using extended labels, however, these models still had some limitations (Wen et al., 2015; Li et al., 2016; Zhao et al., 2017; Huang et al., 2018; Zhou et al., 2018). One crucial issue was that they do not have explicit dialogue state guiding to guarantee that a controllable generation has a discriminability for a given condition.

Inspired by the success of adversarial training in computer vision (Denton et al., 2015) and natural language generation (Li et al., 2017), we delve into the challenge and propose our approach for state-aware dialogue generation with adversarial

Proceedings of the Towards Semi-Supervised and Reinforced Task-Oriented Dialog Systems (SereTOD), pages 62 - 74
December 7, 2022 ©2022 Association for Computational Linguistics

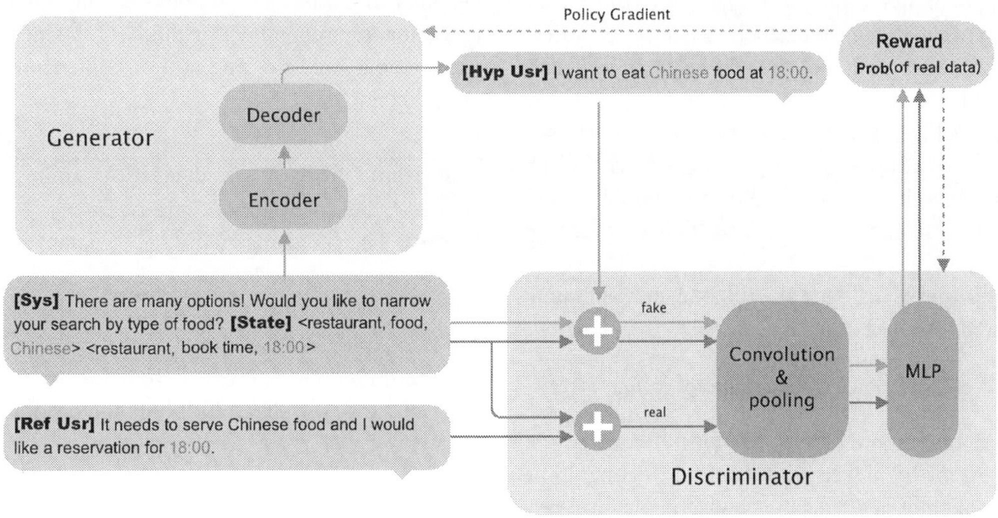

Figure 2: An overview of state-aware adversarial training. Different flow directions are marked with obviously distinguished arrows, blue and purple represent the training process of generator and discriminator, respectively. There are two cycles. The blue cycle is for generator learning, updating the model parameters of generator. The purple cycle is for discriminator learning, updating the discriminator model of periodic epoch. The learning of generator and discriminator is conducted in an alternate manner. Best viewed in color.

training. We focus on controlling the utterances by using dialogue state labels as conditions. We extend a framework of the generative adversarial network (Yu et al., 2017) for the task of generating conditional utterances on the basis of actual dialogue state constraints, alternatively training between a generator and a discriminator. The experimental results show that our proposed method has higher controllability for state-aware dialogue even though it has higher or comparable naturalness to existing methods, and improves the discriminability of generation. Furthermore, we investigate the effectiveness of our approach via downstream dialogue state tracking (DST) tasks. Experimental results demonstrate the high-quality data generated by our proposed framework improves the performance over state-of-the-art models.

The contributions of this paper are summarized as follows:

- We propose a novel adversarial training based framework for utterance-level dialogue generation, which generates more coherence and fluency utterances.

- For the downstream DST task, the high-quality data generated by our proposed framework improves the performance over state-of-the-art models.

- To our best knowledge, this is the first study of state-aware utterance generation via adversarial training with promising results.

2 Approach

In this section, we introduce the utterance-level dialogue generation of adversarial training. As shown in Figure 2, our framework consists of two main components: a generator and a discriminator. Different from the traditional generative dialogue model trained by MLE, we view the process of utterance generation as a sequence of actions that are taken according to a policy defined by the generator here. It generates controllable utterances based on input conditions, and the discriminator judges the quality of the utterances generated by the generator, feeding the reward back to the generator through policy gradient. The learning of generator and discriminator is carried out alternately.

2.1 Task Formulation

Let's denote a sequence of dialogue turns as a matrix $X_T = [R_1, U_1, \ldots, R_T, U_T]$, where U is the user utterance, R represents the system response and T denotes the number of turns. At each turn, user's goal can be regarded as a certain number of domain-slot-value pairs (e.g., *(restaurant-area, west)*). The dialogue state tracking task is to track the value for each slot over X_t ($1 \leq t \leq T$). Belief states can be considered at two granularities: turn-level (S_t) and dialogue-level (B_t). S_t denotes the information introduced in the *t-th* turn and B_t represents the accumulated information from the first turn to the *t-th* turn. The task we focus on is to generate a user utterance U_t conditioned on the turn-level dialogue state S_t and corresponding system response R_t.

2.2 State-Aware Adversarial Training

To generate more human-like user utterances, we propose using adversarial training for generation: the generator is guided by the discriminator to produce utterances that are indistinguishable from the original dialogues and consistent with the belief state condition. The discriminator is trained on the dataset consisting of the utterances of original dialogues and the utterances generated by the generator. The learning of generator and discriminator is conducted in an alternate manner, which is detailed in Algorithm 1.

Generator

The generator *G* defines the policy that generates a user utterance U_t from a given dialogue history R_t and a turn-level user goal S_t. It takes a form similar to SEQ2SEQ models, which consists of an encoder and a decoder. In this paper, the GRU-based and the T5-based generators are employed to approximate $P(U_t|R_t, S_t)$, where the concatenation of R_t and S_t is used as input to the encoder and U_t is set to be the target sequence to be generated by the decoder.

Discriminator

The discriminator *D* is a binary classifier that aims to determine whether the user utterance is generated or from the original dataset. In order to make sense of belief state condition, the concatenation of turn-level belief state and user utterance is used as input to the discriminator. We follow the setting in SeqGAN to have CNN as the backbone model for the discriminator. First, the input sequence is represented as $[U_t] \bigoplus [S_t]$, where each token is represented as a k-dimensional token embedding and $\bigoplus$ is the concatenation operator to build the input matrix. Second, a kernel applies a convolutional operation to a window size of words to produce a new feature map and a max-over-time pooling operation works. Finally the output vector of a fully connected layer is fed to a 2-class sigmoid activation, returning the probability of the input utterance generated by generator or come from the original dialogue.

Algorithm 1 State-aware adversarial training

Input: A dialogue dataset $C = \{ R, U, S \}$.
Output: The parameters θ of G; The parameters ϕ of D.

Randomly initialize θ and ϕ;
Pre-train G using cross-entropy loss on C;
Generate user utterances using the pre-trained G;
Pre-train D using generated user utterances as negative samples and utterances from original dialogue as positive samples;
for each epoch **do**
  for each generator step **do**
    Generate a user utterance $U'_{1:L}=(u'_1,\ldots,u'_L)$ using the current G, where L denotes the number of tokens;
    for t in $1 : L$ **do**
      Compute $R_{u'_t}$ by Eq. (1);
    end for
    Update θ according to Eq. (3);
  end for
  for each discriminator step **do**
    Sample <R, U, S> from the dataset C;
    Concatenate S and U as a positive sample;
    Generate U' using the current G;
    Concatenate S and U' as a negative sample;
    Update ϕ according to Eq. (4);
  end for
end for
return θ and ϕ;

Adversarial Training

We cast the state-aware utterance generation as a reinforcement learning problem that backpropagate the error computed by the discriminator to the generator via the policy gradient algorithm. The generator can be seen as an agent whose parameters θ define a policy. At each time step, it takes an action by generating a token and gets a reward value from the discriminator by employing Monte-Carlo search. The estimated probability of being real by D is used to calculate the reward:

$$R_{u_l} = D_\phi(U_{1:l}|S), \quad (1)$$

where u_l is the *l-th* token in *U*, R_{u_l} represents the reward of token u_l and ϕ is the parameters of *D*.

The goal of the generator is minimize the negative expected reward of generated utterance using the REINFORCE algorithm (Williams, 1992):

$$J_G(\theta) = -E_{U \sim G}[D_\phi(U|S)], \quad (2)$$

where $U \sim G$ represents the utterance *U* is generated from *G* and θ is the parameters of *G*.

With the likelihood ratio trick (Williams, 1992), the gradient of θ can be derived as:

$$\begin{aligned} \nabla J_G(\theta) &= -E_{U \sim G}[D_\phi(U|S)] \cdot \nabla \log G_\theta(U|S) \\ &\approx -D_\phi(U|S) \cdot \nabla \log G_\theta(U|S), \end{aligned} \quad (3)$$

The goal of the discriminator is to distinguish whether a user utterance is from original dialogue or generated by the generator. It computes the probability that the user utterance is from original dialogue given the turn-level belief state. Therefore, its objective function is to minimize classification error rate:

$$\begin{aligned} \min_\phi &- E_{U \sim ground-truth} \log D_\phi(U|S) \\ &- E_{U \sim G} \log(1 - D_\phi(U|S)), \end{aligned} \quad (4)$$

where $D_\phi(U|S)$ is the probability of *U* that it comes from original dialogue, $U \sim ground-truth$ represents the utterance *U* is from the golden label.

3 Experiments and Analysis

3.1 Dataset

We take MultiWOZ 2.0 and MultiWOZ 2.1 as datasets for the experiments. MultiWOZ[1] series dataset is a fully-labeled collection of human-human written conversations spanning over multiple domains and topics. It contains 8438 multi-turn dialogues with on average 13.7 turns per dialogue. It has 30 *(domain, slot)* pairs and over 4,500 slot values. Compared to MultiWOZ 2.0, MultiWOZ 2.1 has fixed the noisy state annotations and combined user dialogue acts as well as multiple slot descriptions per dialogue state slot into the new version. To date, these two datasets are recognized as the most widely used benchmark datasets in the field of dialogue systems.

[1]https://github.com/budzianowski/multiwoz/tree/master/data

3.2 Implementation Details

For a fair comparison, we introduce tow instantiations for the proposed framework, denoted as GRU-based and T5-based, respectively.

GRU-based: The generator is an encoder-decoder text generation model consists of simple GRU network, and the network structure of the discriminator is CNN. The optimizer for the generator and discriminator is Adam (Kingma and Ba, 2014). The learning rates are 1e-3 and 1e-4 respectively. In the adversarial training phase, the parameters of the 5 epoch discriminators are updated after each update of the parameters of the generator.

T5-based: The generator is an encoder-decoder implementation on the basis of T5, which is a pre-trained model composed of transformers, and the network structure of the discriminator is CNN. The optimizer for generator and discriminator is AdamW (Loshchilov and Hutter, 2018). The learning rates are 2e-5 and 5e-5, respectively. In the adversarial training phase, the parameters of the 4 epoch discriminators are updated after each update of the parameters of the generator.

We implement all the benchmarks using Pytorch on servers equipped with Nvidia Tesla V100 GPUs, each with 32GB memory. Source codes of our work in this paper will be open-sourced on Github as soon as we clean our code.

3.3 Main Results and Evaluation

Automatic Evaluation

We measure the quality of generated utterances by BLEU scores (Papineni et al., 2002) and BERT-score (Zhang et al., 2019a). In this experiment, only the utterances of each turn of original dialogues are used as reference sentences for the calculation of BLEU instead of the entire dataset as reference sentences. This is because the generated utterance from the dialogue model only need to be relevant to the turn-level state and input utterance, not the full dataset.

Tables 1 are experiments on the full dataset. GRU-based and T5-based represent the results of training with MLE, +GAN represents the results of using adversarial training (ADV). From Table 1 we can see our adapted models surpass original MLE up to 1.09% in BLEU-5, indicating the effectiveness of the added adversarial training process. GRU-based+GAN and T5-based+GAN exceed corresponding MLE-baselines with the same trending, respectively. Based on our proposed framework,

Model	MutilWOZ2.0					MutilWOZ2.1				
	BLEU-2	BLEU-3	BLEU-4	BLEU-5	BERT-Score	BLEU-2	BLEU-3	BLEU-4	BLEU-5	BERT-Score
GRU-based	23.41%	16.43%	11.82%	**8.70%**	88.33%	25.30%	17.82%	12.54%	8.99%	88.63%
+GAN	**24.37%**	**17.03%**	**12.15%**	8.66%	**88.35%**	**26.38%**	**18.98%**	**13.64%**	**10.08%**	**88.83%**
T5-based	25.43%	19.55%	15.39%	12.35%	89.17%	25.92%	19.95%	15.70%	12.58%	90.11%
+GAN	**25.46%**	**19.58%**	**15.42%**	**12.39%**	**89.18%**	**26.31%**	**20.23%**	**15.87%**	**12.65%**	**90.12%**

Table 1: Automatic evaluation of two models trained by MLE and adversarial training on full datasets.

Model	MutilWOZ2.0					MutilWOZ2.1				
	BLEU-2	BLEU-3	BLEU-4	BLEU-5	BERT-Score	BLEU-2	BLEU-3	BLEU-4	BLEU-5	BERT-Score
GRU-based	17.20%	11.11%	7.52%	5.18%	87.09%	17.20%	11.11%	7.52%	5.18%	87.09%
+GAN	**17.77%**	**11.69%**	**7.95%**	**5.46%**	**87.28%**	**17.77%**	**11.69%**	**7.95%**	**5.46%**	**87.28%**
T5-based	21.43%	15.39%	11.42%	8.66%	88.11%	23.71%	17.48%	13.00%	9.87%	88.53%
+GAN	**21.45%**	**15.67%**	**11.76%**	**8.92%**	**88.16%**	**23.98%**	**17.72%**	**13.22%**	**10.03%**	**88.55%**

Table 2: Automatic evaluation of two models trained by MLE and adversarial training in low-resource scenario.

Table 1 shows that the effectiveness of ADV is consistent in two datasets of different metrics.

In order to further explore the performance of our framework in the case of low-resource scenario, 100 instances of full dialogues are randomly selected from the training dataset, and 50 instances of complete dialogues are randomly selected from the validation dataset. Tables 2 shows the performance of two models on MultiWOZ 2.0 and MultiWOZ 2.1 under low-resource settings. Predictably, various degrees of performance degradation occurs, especially on GRU-based model. On the other hand, the improvement under the same setting demonstrates the effectiveness of our framework facing low-resource.

Combining the experimental results of the above different settings, it can be observed that both the BLEU score and BERT-score of the results after adversarial training are better than MLE training.

Human Evaluation

We evaluate the generated data from two perspectives: *statement fluency* and turn-level *belief state correctness*. The *statement fluency* indicates whether the generated sentence is fluent and human-likely. The turn-level *belief state correctness* evaluates whether <R_t, U'_t> is consistent with S'_t.

There are two corresponding evaluation metrics, *Sentence fluency* and *Slot accuracy*. (1) *Sentence fluency* represents whether the generated sentence conforms to the natural expression of human beings and is suitable as an answer to a question. (2) *Slot accuracy* represents whether the generated utterance contains the dialogue state of the input utterance.

Randomly select 100 instances generated by the models and invite 3 experts to evaluate the data for human evaluation. Table 3 shows human evaluation results for naturalness and controllability of GRU-based generator in MultiWOZ 2.0 dataset. Regarding the naturalness, models used adversarial learning produced a more acceptable utterance to the dialogue context. At the same time, the adversarial-explicit model achieved the best performance among the compared ones in terms of the controllability. A same trend occurs in the evaluation of T5-based one: the results show that ADV outperforms the MLE on almost all metrics and even strengthens the performance of human reference. Notably, the performance of T5-based generator even outperforms the results of the original data (corresponding **USER** line) in Table 4. In the original MultiWOZ dataset, there are label-missing errors for dialogue states. Specifically, the turn-level belief state is not reflected in the user utterance fully. Through data inspection, we find

	Sentence Fluency		Slot accuracy
	Mean score (1-5)	$\geq 3(\%)$	
USER	4.59	96.30%	80.70%
MLE	4.00	87.70%	53.30%
ADV	**4.16**	**92.00%**	**64.00%**

Table 3: Human evaluation of GRU-based generator. Sentences are scored on a scale of 1 to 5. The average value represents the average score, and $\geq$3(%) represents the proportion of the sentence evaluation score greater than or equal to three points in all sentences.

	Sentence Fluency		Slot accuracy
	Mean score (1-5)	$\geq 3(\%)$	
USER	4.78	100.00%	71.23%
MLE	4.70	98.67%	76.50%
ADV	**4.81**	98.67%	**79.73%**

Table 4: Human evaluation of T5-based generator.

that the T5-based generator corrects the errors in the original dataset. This situation shows that the model can well use the belief state as a condition to generate the corresponding user utterance.

Experimental results demonstrate that our approach produces more interactive, relevant, and fluent utterances than standard SEQ2SEQ models trained using the MLE objective function. Beyond this, evaluation details for automatic and human ways are shown in the appendix.

3.4 Downstream Results

In this section, we conduct experiments on a suite of downstream DST tasks and present the results of applying utterance-level dialogue generation on DST data augmentation. The learning of dialogue state tracker is detailed in Algorithm 2. Here data augmentation is to generate a new user utterance U_t' conditioned on a modified S_t' derived from original turn-level belief state S_t. The modification strategy uses the value substitution method (Li et al., 2021). To overcome the de-generation and over-generation phenomenons, a data filter F is employed to filtering the generated candidates (Li et al., 2021). Then a novel sequence of dialogue turns X_t'=[R_1,U_1,...,R_t,U_t'] is formed by replacing the original user utterance U_t with U_t', and B_t' which is induced by B_t based on the difference between S_t and S_t' is the dialogue-level belief states of X_t'. We use the resulting set of <X_t',B_t'> to do DST data augmentation. In the following, two known typical DST models are selected for further experiments.

- **TRADE**: TRAnsferable Dialogue statE generator (TRADE) (Wu et al., 2019) generates dialogue states from utterances using a copy mechanism, facilitating knowledge transfer between domains. The prominent difference from previous one-domain DST models is that TRADE is based on a generation approach instead of a close-set classification approach.

- **TripPy**: TripPy (Heck et al., 2020) presents a new SOTA approach which makes use of various copy mechanisms to fill slots with values to avoid the use of value picklists altogether. This model has no need to maintain a list of candidate values. Instead, all values are extracted from the dialogue context on-the-fly.

We train each DST model on the mixing of MultiWOZ 2.0 training data and augmented data.

Algorithm 2 The DST data augmentation

Input: A dialogue dataset C, the randomly initialized Generator G, data filter F, belief state modification strategy π, the dialogue state tracker with parameters ρ.
Output: Trained tracker.

Train G using Algorithm 1 on dataset C;
Train F with cross-entropy loss on dataset C;
Modify turn-level belief state from S_t to $S_t^{'}$ according to π;
Obtain new data C' according to $S_t^{'}$ by the trained G;
Obtain new data $C_F^{'}$ by filtering de-generation and over-generation data;
Train the tracker on C+$C_F^{'}$, update ρ;
Save the tracker with ρ;

Trained DST models are then evaluated on original test set. Results are shown in Table 5. Both training with augmentation of TRADE and TripPy outperform the original models. The joint goal accuracy improves to 49.76% and 59.09% respectively, and TripPy reaches the state-of-the-art performance on MultiWOZ 2.0 dateset. This shows the effectiveness of our adversarial utterance-level dialogue generation for DST data augmentation.

Model	Joint Goal Accuracy(%)
TRADE	48.62
+ Augmentation	**49.76**
TripPy	58.01
+ Augmentation	**59.09**

Table 5: Joint goal accuracy results on MultiWOZ 2.0.

3.5 Analysis and Discussion

Case study from Table 6 has displayed three typical errors in our experiments of dialogue generation tasks: (1) The slot value is wrong. (2) The slot is missing. (3) The slot type is wrong. Specifically, **System+State** stands for inputs, and **USER** represents references. Last two columns are the output results of MLE training and ADV training. The results show that the above-mentioned errors can be alleviated via our proposed framework, and the model after adversarial training can better adapt to the input conditions in the dialogue, achieving more appropriate utterance-level dialogue generation.

System+State	USER	MLE	ADV
system: tr0275 will leave at 13:29 and arrive by 14:07 . would you like to buy tickets ? **state: train book people 3**	yes , could you make a booking **for 3 people** ?	yes , i 'll need the train for 7 people . can you book the reference number ?	yes , i need book for **3 people** please .
system: i love the fez club , their phone number is 01223519224 .can i help you with anything else today ? **state: train destination ely , train day Thursday**	i would love some information on a train to get me to **ely** on **thursday** .	i also i also need a train to train leaving on **thursday**. (miss ely)	i also need a train to **ely** to leave on **thursday**.
system: would you like me to book it for you ? **state: train book people 7**	yes , for **7 people** .	yes , please . i need 7 tickets .	yes , please book it for **7 people** .

Table 6: Case study. **System+State** stands for inputs, and **USER** represents references. Last two columns are the output results of **MLE** and **ADV**. The black-lined font is the dialogue state of the current turn. We expect the generated utterances exactly correspond to the inputs. The red font are typical errors generated by MLE model.

Model	Confusion matrix			Acc(%)
MLE	Real \ Pre.	**N**	**P**	97.12
	N	594	32	
	P	4	622	
ADV	Real \ Pre.	**N**	**P**	**81.39**
	N	397	229	
	P	4	622	

Table 7: Confusion matrix for MLE and ADV. The results show that the pre-trained discriminator will misjudge the fake text after adversarial training.

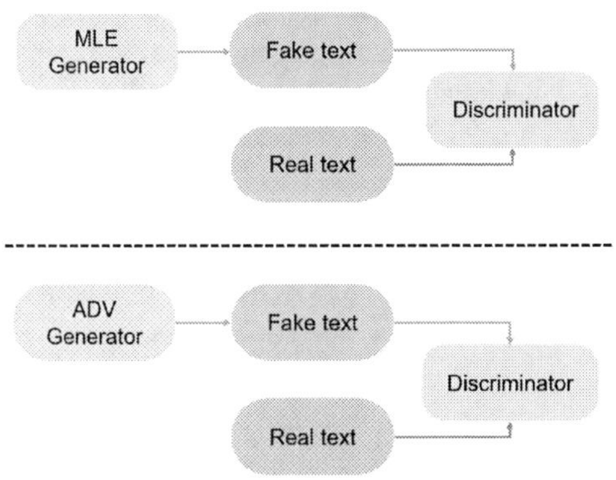

Figure 3: Contrast experiment for the quality judgment of generated utterances by two models.

To analyze the results quantitatively, we verify the effectiveness of utilizing adversarial training under the control variable method, that is, a same pre-trained discriminator is applied for both generators. We use the pre-trained discriminator to evaluate the utterances generated by the model of adversarial training (real text) and the utterances of original dialogues (fake text) as shown in Figure 3.

Table 7 shows the confusion matrix of predicting results via discriminator's classification, where negative samples (**N**) represent utterances generated by the generator and positive samples (**P**) represent utterances of original dialogues. The accuracy (Acc) is calculated as follow:

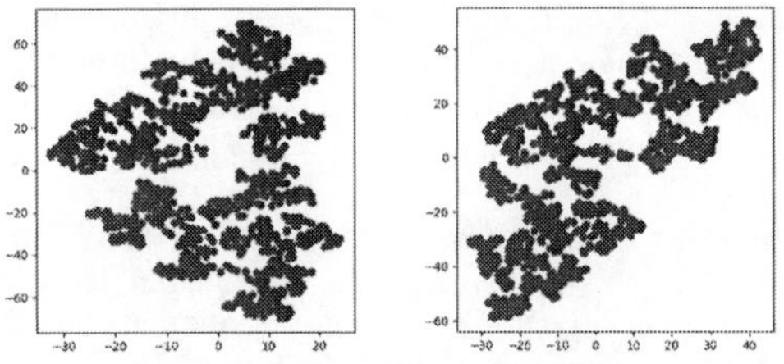

(a) Visualization of MLE. (b) Visualization of ADV.

Figure 4: Feature visualization of generative spaces for two models' comparison.

$$Accuracy = \frac{TP + TN}{TP + TN + FP + FN}, \quad (5)$$

where TP and TN represent the number of correct predictions for real text and generated text, respectively. FP and FN represent the number of incorrect predictions for real text and generated text, respectively.

It can be seen the text generated by adversarial training makes it more difficult for the pre-trained discriminator to distinguish the authenticity of the inputs. The results further support this point of view can be seen in the confusion matrix. Comparing MLE model and ADV model, the discriminator's judgment result for real samples maintains, but the judgment on generated text differs. It can be confirmed the accuracy's drop of the discriminator is affected by the decline in the generator's ability to judge more realistic generated samples.

In order to present the classification results more intuitively, dimensionality reduction of the features after the convolutional layer in the discriminator is visualized using the t-SNE algorithm (Van der Maaten and Hinton, 2008). The visual features are shown in the Figure 4. The red dots represent the real text, and the blue dots represent the generated text. Comparing (a) and (b), it can be observed that boundary becomes unrecognizable and overlapping after adversarial training, which adds a layer of complexity to the discriminator and brings new challenges.

4 Related Work

The idea of generative adversarial networks (Goodfellow et al., 2014) has enjoyed great success in computer vision (Radford et al., 2015; Chen et al., 2016; Brock et al., 2018; Karras et al., 2020). Training is formalized as a game in which the generative model is trained to generate outputs to fool the discriminator; the technique has been successfully applied to image generation. However, to the best of our knowledge, this idea has not achieved comparable success in NLP. This is due to the fact that unlike in vision, text generation is discrete, which makes the error outputted from the discriminator hard to back-propagate to the generator. Some recent work has begun to address this issue: Lamb et al. (2016) propose providing the discriminator with the intermediate hidden vectors of the generator rather than its sequence outputs. Such a strategy makes the system differentiable and achieves promising results in tasks like character-level language modeling and handwriting generation. Yu et al. (2017) use policy gradient reinforcement learning to back-propagate the error from the discriminator, showing improvement in multiple generation tasks such as poem generation, speech language generation and music generation. Outside of sequence generation, Chen et al. (2018) apply the idea of adversarial training to sentiment analysis and Zhang et al. (2017) apply the idea to domain adaptation tasks. Cui et al. (2019) proposed Dual Adversarial Learning (DAL), which uses adversarial learning to mimic human judges and guides the system to generate natural responses. To improve the diversity of responses, Xu et al. (2018) proposed a Diversity-Promoting Generative Adversarial Network (DP-GAN). This method encourages the generation of highly diverse texts by assigning low rewards to repeated texts and high rewards to new texts, and a new discriminator structure is proposed to determine repeated texts.

Our work is related to recent work that formalizes sequence generation as an action-taking problem in reinforcement learning (Sutton and Barto, 2018). Ranzato et al. (2015) train RNN decoders in a SEQ2SEQ model using policy gradient to obtain competitive machine translation results. Bahdanau et al. (2016) take this a step further by training an actor-critic RL model for machine translation. Also related is recent work (Shen et al., 2015; Wiseman and Rush, 2016) to address the issues of exposure bias and loss evaluation mismatch in neural translation.

5 Conclusion

In this paper, we address the difficulty of utterance-level dialogue generation by proposing an adversarial training based framework that can generate high-quality data to improve the downstream DST performance. Specifically, our method leverages an encoder-decoder framework in terms of an adversarial training paradigm, while taking advantage of dialogue state-aware semantic representation from the reinforced generator to construct the discriminator. The two-stage training process delivers more adversarial-balance for both after iterative interactions. Experimental results on MultiWoZ 2.0 and MultiWoZ 2.1 datasets demonstrate that the proposed framework significantly improves the performance over the state-of-the-art models. Future work includes more exploration into the design of generator-discriminator architect and improvement of more dialogue tasks.

Limitations

Our work pioneers in the adversarial training based framework for utterance-level dialogue generation, which trains an encoder-decoder generator simultaneously with a discriminative classifier that make the utterance approximate to the state-aware inputs. However, our paper may have following omissions and inadequacies.

- Our focused task is limited in turn-level belief state. DST of dialogue-level is beyond the scope of this article. We believe this situation will meet new challenges and we will explore more in the next work.
- The policy gradient reinforcement learning algorithm is used to optimizing the generator during adversarial training process, which slows down the training speed of T5-based generator.
- Though we list case study in our paper, we believe it needs more rethinking and comparison work into the internal mechanism in the future.

References

Dzmitry Bahdanau, Philemon Brakel, Kelvin Xu, Anirudh Goyal, Ryan Lowe, Joelle Pineau, Aaron Courville, and Yoshua Bengio. 2016. An actor-critic algorithm for sequence prediction. *arXiv preprint arXiv:1607.07086*.

Andrew Brock, Jeff Donahue, and Karen Simonyan. 2018. Large scale gan training for high fidelity natural image synthesis. *arXiv preprint arXiv:1809.11096*.

Xi Chen, Yan Duan, Rein Houthooft, John Schulman, Ilya Sutskever, and Pieter Abbeel. 2016. Infogan: Interpretable representation learning by information maximizing generative adversarial nets. *Advances in neural information processing systems*, 29.

Xilun Chen, Yu Sun, Ben Athiwaratkun, Claire Cardie, and Kilian Weinberger. 2018. Adversarial deep averaging networks for cross-lingual sentiment classification. *Transactions of the Association for Computational Linguistics*, 6:557–570.

Shaobo Cui, Rongzhong Lian, Di Jiang, Yuanfeng Song, Siqi Bao, and Yong Jiang. 2019. Dal: Dual adversarial learning for dialogue generation. *arXiv preprint arXiv:1906.09556*.

Emily L Denton, Soumith Chintala, Rob Fergus, et al. 2015. Deep generative image models using a laplacian pyramid of adversarial networks. *Advances in neural information processing systems*, 28.

Ian Goodfellow, Jean Pouget-Abadie, Mehdi Mirza, Bing Xu, David Warde-Farley, Sherjil Ozair, Aaron Courville, and Yoshua Bengio. 2014. Generative adversarial nets. *Advances in neural information processing systems*, 27.

Michael Heck, Carel van Niekerk, Nurul Lubis, Christian Geishauser, Hsien-Chin Lin, Marco Moresi, and Milica Gašić. 2020. Trippy: A triple copy strategy for value independent neural dialog state tracking. *arXiv preprint arXiv:2005.02877*.

Chenyang Huang, Osmar R Zaiane, Amine Trabelsi, and Nouha Dziri. 2018. Automatic dialogue generation with expressed emotions. In *Proceedings of the 2018 Conference of the North American Chapter of the Association for Computational Linguistics: Human Language Technologies, Volume 2 (Short Papers)*, pages 49–54.

Tero Karras, Samuli Laine, Miika Aittala, Janne Hellsten, Jaakko Lehtinen, and Timo Aila. 2020. Analyzing and improving the image quality of stylegan. In *Proceedings of the IEEE/CVF conference on computer vision and pattern recognition*, pages 8110–8119.

Diederik P Kingma and Jimmy Ba. 2014. Adam: A method for stochastic optimization. *arXiv preprint arXiv:1412.6980*.

Alex M Lamb, Anirudh Goyal ALIAS PARTH GOYAL, Ying Zhang, Saizheng Zhang, Aaron C Courville, and Yoshua Bengio. 2016. Professor forcing: A new algorithm for training recurrent networks. *Advances in neural information processing systems*, 29.

Jiwei Li, Will Monroe, Alan Ritter, Michel Galley, Jianfeng Gao, and Dan Jurafsky. 2016. Deep reinforcement learning for dialogue generation. *arXiv preprint arXiv:1606.01541*.

Jiwei Li, Will Monroe, Tianlin Shi, Sébastien Jean, Alan Ritter, and Dan Jurafsky. 2017. Adversarial learning for neural dialogue generation. *arXiv preprint arXiv:1701.06547.*

Shiyang Li, Semih Yavuz, Kazuma Hashimoto, Jia Li, Tong Niu, Nazneen Rajani, Xifeng Yan, Yingbo Zhou, and Caiming Xiong. 2021. Coco: Controllable counterfactuals for evaluating dialogue state trackers. In *9th International Conference on Learning Representations, ICLR 2021, Virtual Event, Austria, May 3-7, 2021.*

Ilya Loshchilov and Frank Hutter. 2018. Fixing weight decay regularization in adam.

Yi Luan, Yangfeng Ji, and Mari Ostendorf. 2016. Lstm based conversation models. *arXiv preprint arXiv:1603.09457.*

Kishore Papineni, Salim Roukos, Todd Ward, and Wei-Jing Zhu. 2002. Bleu: a method for automatic evaluation of machine translation. In *Proceedings of the 40th annual meeting of the Association for Computational Linguistics*, pages 311–318.

Alec Radford, Luke Metz, and Soumith Chintala. 2015. Unsupervised representation learning with deep convolutional generative adversarial networks. *arXiv preprint arXiv:1511.06434.*

Marc'Aurelio Ranzato, Sumit Chopra, Michael Auli, and Wojciech Zaremba. 2015. Sequence level training with recurrent neural networks. *arXiv preprint arXiv:1511.06732.*

Lifeng Shang, Zhengdong Lu, and Hang Li. 2015. Neural responding machine for short-text conversation. *arXiv preprint arXiv:1503.02364.*

Shiqi Shen, Yong Cheng, Zhongjun He, Wei He, Hua Wu, Maosong Sun, and Yang Liu. 2015. Minimum risk training for neural machine translation. *arXiv preprint arXiv:1512.02433.*

Yixuan Su, Lei Shu, Elman Mansimov, Arshit Gupta, Deng Cai, Yi-An Lai, and Yi Zhang. 2021. Multi-task pre-training for plug-and-play task-oriented dialogue system. *arXiv preprint arXiv:2109.14739.*

Richard S Sutton and Andrew G Barto. 2018. *Reinforcement learning: An introduction.* MIT press.

Laurens Van der Maaten and Geoffrey Hinton. 2008. Visualizing data using t-sne. *Journal of machine learning research*, 9(11).

Oriol Vinyals and Quoc Le. 2015. A neural conversational model. *arXiv preprint arXiv:1506.05869.*

Tsung-Hsien Wen, Milica Gasic, Nikola Mrksic, Pei-Hao Su, David Vandyke, and Steve Young. 2015. Semantically conditioned lstm-based natural language generation for spoken dialogue systems. *arXiv preprint arXiv:1508.01745.*

Jason D Williams, Antoine Raux, and Matthew Henderson. 2016. The dialog state tracking challenge series: A review. *Dialogue & Discourse*, 7(3):4–33.

Ronald J Williams. 1992. Simple statistical gradient-following algorithms for connectionist reinforcement learning. *Machine learning*, 8(3):229–256.

Sam Wiseman and Alexander M Rush. 2016. Sequence-to-sequence learning as beam-search optimization. *arXiv preprint arXiv:1606.02960.*

Chien-Sheng Wu, Steven Hoi, Richard Socher, and Caiming Xiong. 2020. Tod-bert: Pre-trained natural language understanding for task-oriented dialogue. *arXiv preprint arXiv:2004.06871.*

Chien-Sheng Wu, Andrea Madotto, Ehsan Hosseini-Asl, Caiming Xiong, Richard Socher, and Pascale Fung. 2019. Transferable multi-domain state generator for task-oriented dialogue systems. *arXiv preprint arXiv:1905.08743.*

Jingjing Xu, Xuancheng Ren, Junyang Lin, and Xu Sun. 2018. Diversity-promoting gan: A cross-entropy based generative adversarial network for diversified text generation. In *Proceedings of the 2018 conference on empirical methods in natural language processing*, pages 3940–3949.

Yao Yao. 2015. A review of corpus-based statistical models of language variation. In *Proceedings of the 29th Pacific Asia Conference on Language, Information and Computation*, pages 11–15.

Steve Young, Milica Gašić, Blaise Thomson, and Jason D Williams. 2013. Pomdp-based statistical spoken dialog systems: A review. *Proceedings of the IEEE*, 101(5):1160–1179.

Lantao Yu, Weinan Zhang, Jun Wang, and Yong Yu. 2017. Seqgan: Sequence generative adversarial nets with policy gradient. In *Proceedings of the AAAI conference on artificial intelligence*, volume 31.

Tianyi Zhang, Varsha Kishore, Felix Wu, Kilian Q Weinberger, and Yoav Artzi. 2019a. Bertscore: Evaluating text generation with bert. *arXiv preprint arXiv:1904.09675.*

Yizhe Zhang, Siqi Sun, Michel Galley, Yen-Chun Chen, Chris Brockett, Xiang Gao, Jianfeng Gao, Jingjing Liu, and Bill Dolan. 2019b. Dialogpt: Large-scale generative pre-training for conversational response generation. *arXiv preprint arXiv:1911.00536.*

Yuan Zhang, Regina Barzilay, and Tommi Jaakkola. 2017. Aspect-augmented adversarial networks for domain adaptation. *Transactions of the Association for Computational Linguistics*, 5:515–528.

Tiancheng Zhao, Ran Zhao, and Maxine Eskenazi. 2017. Learning discourse-level diversity for neural dialog models using conditional variational autoencoders. *arXiv preprint arXiv:1703.10960.*

Hao Zhou, Minlie Huang, Tianyang Zhang, Xiaoyan Zhu, and Bing Liu. 2018. Emotional chatting machine: Emotional conversation generation with internal and external memory. In *Proceedings of the AAAI Conference on Artificial Intelligence*, volume 32.

A BERT-Scroe

Experimental Setup : We randomly selected 100 samples from the data set to obtain the results of MLE and ADV. Furthermore, respectively calculate samples with USER's text the similarity degree. After 100 Bert-Scores were calculated, the average was calculated.The result are reported below:

Method	BERT-score
MLE	89.18%
ADV	**89.67%**

Table 8: Random sampling of 100 samples of BERT-score results

In order to prevent uneven distribution, the test data were divided into 10 groups and the BERT-score of the mean MLE model and ADV model are calculated respectively. The main results are shown below:

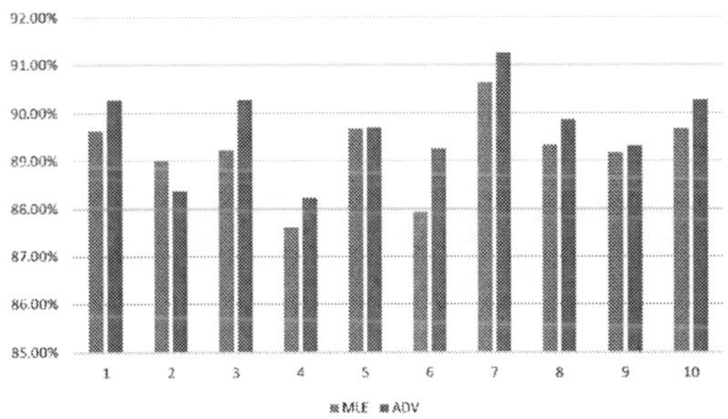

Figure 5: An overview of bert-score.

According to the Figure 5, the average Bert-score of group 2 is higher than that of ADV, and the similarity of the texts generated by ADV model is higher than that generated by MLE model in the other 9 groups, which proves the effectiveness of the algorithm.

B Human evaluation

Table 9 and Table 10 represent the experimental details statement fluency, and the conditions of slot value, contained for the human evaluation of the GRU-based model, respectively. Table 11 and Table 12 represent the same experimental details for the T5-based model, respectively.

Statement Fluency						
	USER		MLE		ADV	
	average value	≥3(%)	average value	≥3(%)	average value	≥3(%)
expert1	4.81	96%	4.12	81%	4.49	87%
expert2	4.38	97%	3.79	86%	3.92	94%
expert3	4.57	96%	4.09	96%	4.06	95%
average	4.59	96.30%	4	87.70%	**4.16**	**92%**

Table 9: Statement fluency experiment with GRU model.A total of 3 experts participated in the evaluation. Sentences are scored on a scale of 1 to 5. The average value represents the average score, and ≥3(%) represents the proportion of the sentence evaluation score greater than or equal to three points in all sentences

The conditions of slot value contained						
	USER		MLE		ADV	
	Contain /Part /No	Acc	Contain /Part /No	Acc	Contain /Part /No	Acc
expert1	79/12/9	79%	53/28/19	53%	64/19/17	64%
expert2	82/11/7	82%	53/26/21	53%	66/20/14	66%
expert3	81/13/6	81%	54/31/15	54%	62/23/15	62%
average	-	80.70%	-	53.30%	-	**64%**

Table 10: The conditions of slot value contained with GRU-based model.Contain, Part, and No respectively represent whether the answer of the dialogue is fully contained, partially contained, or not containing the dialogue state. Accuracy is only calculated for cases where the dialogue state is completely contained.

Statement Fluency						
	USER		MLE		ADV	
	average value	≥3(%)	average value	≥3(%)	average value	≥3(%)
expert1	4.84	100%	4.49	98%	4.71	98%
expert2	4.8	100%	4.71	98%	4.75	98%
expert3	4.71	100%	4.9	100%	4.98	100%
average	4.78	100.00%	4.70	98.67%	**4.81**	**98.67%**

Table 11: Statement fluency experiment with T5-based model. A total of 3 experts participated in the evaluation. Sentences are scored on a scale of 1 to 5. The average value represents the average score, and ≥3(%) represents the proportion of the sentence evaluation score greater than or equal to three points in all sentences.

The conditions of slot value contained						
	USER		MLE		ADV	
	Contain /Part /No	Acc	Contain /Part /No	Acc	Contain /Part /No	Acc
expert1	36/12/3	70.6%	39/8/4	76.5%	40/7/4	78.4%
expert2	37/10/4	72.5%	39/8/4	76.5%	41/6/4	80.4%
expert3	36/12/3	70.6%	39/9/3	76.5%	41/6/4	80.4%
average	–	71.23%	–	76.5%	–	**79.73%**

Table 12: The conditions of slot value contained with T5-based model.Contain, Part, and No respectively represent whether the answer of the dialogue is fully contained, partially contained, or not containing the dialogue state. Accuracy is only calculated for cases where the dialogue state is completely contained.

Information Extraction and Human-Robot Dialogue towards Real-life Tasks: A Baseline Study with the MobileCS Dataset

Hong Liu[1,3,†], **Hao Peng**[1,3,†], **Zhijian Ou**[1,3,*], **Juanzi Li**[1,3], **Yi Huang**[2,3], **Junlan Feng**[2,3]
[1]Tsinghua University, Beijing, China
[2]China Mobile Research Institute, Beijing, China
[3]Tsinghua University-China Mobile Communications Group Co., Ltd. Joint Institute, Beijing, China
{liuhong21,peng-h21}@mails.tsinghua.edu.cn,
{ozj,lijuanzi}@tsinghua.edu.cn,
{huangyi,fengjunlan}@chinamobile.com

Abstract

Recently, there have merged a class of task-oriented dialogue (TOD) datasets collected through Wizard-of-Oz simulated games. However, the Wizard-of-Oz data are in fact simulated data and thus are fundamentally different from real-life conversations, which are more noisy and casual. Recently, the SereTOD challenge is organized and releases the MobileCS dataset, which consists of real-world dialog transcripts between real users and customer-service staffs from China Mobile. Based on the MobileCS dataset, the SereTOD challenge has two tasks, not only evaluating the construction of the dialogue system itself, but also examining information extraction from dialog transcripts, which is crucial for building the knowledge base for TOD. This paper mainly presents a baseline study of the two tasks with the MobileCS dataset. We introduce how the two baselines are constructed, the problems encountered, and the results. We anticipate that the baselines can facilitate exciting future research to build human-robot dialogue systems for real-life tasks.

1 Introduction

Building human-robot dialogue systems is an important research question not only for artificial intelligence applications but also for artificial intelligence itself. In the Turing test, if the human evaluator finds that human-robot dialogue and human-human dialogue are indistinguishable, the robot would be said to exhibit intelligent behaviour and pass the test (Turing, 1950). So presumably, the best strategy to build an intelligent dialogue system may be to train the system over a large amount of real human-to-human conversations to mimic human behaviors. This approach was once pursued and several human-human dialogue datasets have been released, such as the Twitter dataset (Ritter et al., 2010), the Reddit conversations (Schrading et al., 2015), and the Ubuntu technical support corpus (Lowe et al., 2015). It is argued in (Budzianowski et al., 2018) that the lack of grounding conversations onto an existing knowledge base (KB) limits the usability of the systems developed over these human-human dialogue datasets.

So a class of Wizard-of-Oz simulated games have emerged to collect human-human conversations (Wen et al., 2017b; El Asri et al., 2017; Budzianowski et al., 2018; Zhu et al., 2020; Quan et al., 2020), particularly for task-oriented dialogue (TOD) systems which help users accomplish specific goals such as finding restaurants or booking flights and usually require a task-related KB. In the Wizard-of-Oz set-up, through random sampling based on an ontology and a KB (both are pre-defined), a task template is created for each dialogue session between two crowd workers. One worker acts as the role of a user and the other performs the role of a clerk (i.e. the system side). In practice, multiple workers may contribute to one dialogue session. In this way, annotations of belief states and systems acts become easy, and grounding conversations onto the KB is realized.

However, dialogue data collected in the Wizard-of-Oz set-up are in fact simulated data and thus are fundamentally different from real-life conversations. During the Wizard-of-Oz collection, specific instructions (e.g., goal descriptions for the user side and task descriptions for the system side) are provided for crowd workers to follow. In contrast, real-life dialogues are more casual and free-style, without instructions. Even with some goals in mind, chit-chat or redundant turns are often exist in real-life conversations, e.g., asking for repeating or confirming key information. In some sense, we could say that real-life dialogues are more *noisy*. Moreover, spoken conversations in real-world have a distinct style with those well-written conversations and are full of extra noise from grammatical errors, influences or barge-ins (Kim et al., 2021).

*Corresponding author, †Equal contribution

Proceedings of the Towards Semi-Supervised and Reinforced Task-Oriented Dialog Systems (SereTOD), pages 75 - 84
December 7, 2022 ©2022 Association for Computational Linguistics

For building dialogue systems that are more applicable to real-life tasks, real human-human dialogue datasets with grounding annotations to KBs are highly desirable.

Recently, the SereTOD challenge is organized (Ou et al., 2022) and releases a new human-human dialogue dataset, called the MobileCS (Mobile Customer Service) dataset. It consists of real-world dialog transcripts between real users and customer-service staffs from China Mobile. Based on the observation and analysis of those dialogue transcripts, a schema is summarized to our best[1], according to which about 10,000 dialogues are annotated with entities, attribute triples and speaker's intents for every turn. The annotated part of the MobileCS dataset is randomly split into a train, development and test set, which consists of 8975, 1025 and 962 dialogues, respectively.

Based on the MobileCS dataset, the SereTOD challenge not only evaluates the construction of the dialogue system itself (Task 2), but also examines information extraction from dialog transcripts (Task 1), which is crucial for building the KB. The MobileCS data are more noisy and challenging, as compared to previous Wizard-of-Oz data. It is non-trivial to establish baseline systems on such dataset. This paper mainly presents a baseline study of the two tasks with the MobileCS dataset. Two baseline systems are constructed for the two tasks respectively, which both are released as open source[2] and provided to the participating teams in the SereTOD challenge. We introduce how the two baselines are constructed, the problems encountered, and the results. The results clearly show the challenge for information extraction and human-robot dialogue, when trained and tested on real human-human data. We anticipate that the baselines can facilitate exciting future research to build human-robot dialogue systems for real-life tasks.

2 Related Work

2.1 Dialogue Datasets

According to Budzianowski et al. (2018), existing dialog datasets (whether task-oriented or not) can be grouped into three categories: machine-to-machine, human-to-machine, and human-to-human. The machine-to-machine datasets may ensure full coverage of all possible dialogue outcomes within a certain domain, but they do not consider noisy conditions in real life, which poses a risk of a mismatch between training data and real interactions. The human-to-machine datasets, however, depend on the provision of an existing working dialogue system, which limits the practicality of the datasets. The human-to-human datasets address the problems in the above two classes of datasets. However, previous human-to-human datasets lack knowledge base and explicit goal in the conversation, making that systems trained with these corpus struggle in generating consistent and diverse responses (Li et al., 2016).

It is non-trivial to collect a TOD dataset with knowledge base and user goals. Previous TOD datasets are either collected through Wizard-of-Oz simulated games (Wen et al., 2017b; El Asri et al., 2017; Budzianowski et al., 2018; Zhu et al., 2020; Quan et al., 2020), or collected by converting machine-generated outlines to natural languages using crowd workers (Shah et al., 2018; Rastogi et al., 2020; Lee et al., 2022). However, during the collection of these previous datasets, specific instructions are provided for crowd workers, which is different from real-life conversation scenarios and leads to a gap between collected data and dialogues in real-life. The MobileCS dataset, introduced in SereTOD Challenge, comes from real-world dialogue transcripts and represents a step advancing to remedy the above deficiencies.

2.2 Dialogue Information Extraction

Dialogue information extraction is the task of extracting structured information, e.g., entities and attributes, from dialogue transcripts. Different from the traditional information extraction in general domain text (Sarawagi et al., 2008; Li et al., 2020b; Han et al., 2020), dialogue transcirpts are more verbalized and loose with more irregular expressions and grammar errors. Previous works have explored how to extract user information (Catizone et al., 2010; Hirano et al., 2015; Wu et al., 2019), clinical information (Kannan et al., 2018; Peng et al., 2021), and relations between speakers and mentioned entities in dialogues (Yu et al., 2020; Jia et al., 2021). However, there is no previous work focusing on extracting information on real-world dialogue transcripts between real users and customer-service staffs. In the paper, we develop a modern dialogue information extraction baseline, based on the Mo-

[1] How to build an "optimal" schema for a real-life task is still an open research problem. Further investigation of the schema for the MobileCS dataset is an interesting future work.

[2] https://github.com/SereTOD/SereTOD2022

bileCS dataset, which contains dialogue transcripts from China Mobile.

2.3 Task-oriented Dialogue System

The methodology for building TOD systems is gradually advancing from separate training of individual modules (Williams et al., 2016; Mrkšić et al., 2017; Dai et al., 2018) to the end-to-end (E2E) trainable approach (Wen et al., 2017a; Liu and Lane, 2017; Lei et al., 2018; Shu et al., 2019; Zhang et al., 2020; Gao et al., 2020; Zhang et al., 2020). In early E2E methods, the sequential turns of a dialog are modeled with LSTM-based backbones. Recently, self-attention based Transformer neural networks (Vaswani et al., 2017) have shown their superiority in capturing long-term dependencies over LSTM based networks. Transformer based pretrained language models (PLM), such as GPT2 (Radford et al., 2019) and T5 (Raffel et al., 2020), have been leveraged to build generative E2E TOD systems in the pretraining-and-finetuning paradigm, which have shown improved performance over LSTM-based ones. Examples include GPT2-based SimpleTOD (Hosseini-Asl et al., 2020), SOLOIST (Li et al., 2020a), AuGPT (Kulhánek et al., 2021) and UBAR (Yang et al., 2021), and T5-based PPTOD (Su et al., 2021) and MT-TOD (Lee, 2021), among others. However, these previous TOD systems are mainly examined on simulated data collected by crowd workers. It is not clear what the potential performance of the current methodology of building TOD systems is in real-life tasks. In this paper, we present our effort to answer this question, by developing a TOD system on the MobileCS data, which are from real-life customer-service.

3 MobileCS Dialogue Dataset

The MobileCS dialogue dataset contains 10,000 dialogue labeled by crowd-sourcing and around 90,000 unlabeled dialogues. For each dialogue turn, the annotations consist of entities, attribute triples, and speaker's intents within the scope of the schema. Another around 1000 dialogs are put aside as the test data. More detailed information about the MobileCS dataset can be found in the challenge description paper for the SereTOD challenge (Ou et al., 2022).

The two tasks defined over the MobileCS dataset for the SereTOD challenge require different annotations. For information extraction (Task 1), the annotations of entities and attribute triples are needed for training and evaluating the system. For TOD system construction (Task 2), user intents, system intents and a local knowledge base (*local KB*, which covers personal information and relevant public knowledge in a dialogue) are required. A *global KB*, which covers and fuses all public knowledge and all personal information in the MobileCS domain, is difficult to obtain during the research phase. Thus, the SereTOD challenge introduces the concept of a local KB, which could be viewed as being composed of the relevant local snapshots from the global KB for each dialog. The local KB is obtained automatically by integrating all the annotations of entities and attributes into a sequence of entities[3]. Besides, user goals are needed for evaluating the performance of TOD systems in Task 2. Similarly, user goals are obtained automatically by integrating user intents and all the entities and attributes mentioned by the user. The examples of local KB and user goal can be found in Listing 1 in the challenge description paper (Ou et al., 2022).

Data Quality The MobileCS data were annotated by two professional data labeling teams according to well documented guidelines as described in (Ou et al., 2022). Quality control was enforced by sampling the annotated data and performing crossing check of the annotations by the two teams. Nevertheless, there still exist annotation errors in such a large dataset. Some annotation errors can be corrected by rules. A typical example of errors is the granularity error of entity types. In the schema, entity types have inheritance relationships, for example, "main package" inherits from "package" and contains all its properties. Therefore, there are quite a few annotation confusions between parent types and child types in the data. To correct those type errors, the most fine-grained type for each entity was selected according to the attributes held by the entity. By combining the schema with manual rules, more annotation errors can be corrected. The updated MobileCS dataset is called v1.1, which is released in the SereTOD challenge and used in the experiments in this paper.

[3] An interesting future problem is to study the quality of the local KBs constructed in such a way and their influence on the performance of the dialogue system.

4 Tasks

4.1 Task 1: Information Extraction from Dialog Transcripts

Task 1 aims to extract structured information from real-world dialogue transcripts for constructing KB for the TOD system. This task consists of two subtasks: entity extraction and slot filling. The entity extraction task aims to extract entities, involving named entity recognition and entity coreference resolution. And the slot filling task aims to extract the attributes and values of entities, and the status of user accounts. Compared to the information extraction tasks on general domain texts, this task poses more challenges. First, dialogue transcripts are more verbalized, loose and noisy, which requires more robust models. Second, dialogue transcripts contain more pronouns and referents, some of which even span several rounds. This requires coreference resolution and long context modeling.

4.2 Task 2: Task-Oriented Dialog Systems

The basic task for the TOD system is, for each dialog turn, given the dialog history, the user utterance and the local KB, to predict the user intent, query the local KB and generate appropriate system intent and response according to the queried information. Compared with previous work, this task has the following characteristics. First, there is no global KB but only a local KB for each dialog, containing all the information in entity and attribute annotations and representing the unique information for each user, e.g., the user's package plan and remaining phone charges. Second, the user's constraints on entities are relatively simple, e.g., 38M data package, so the customer service system usually can confirm the entities that the user refers to in one dialogue turn, without the need of dialogue state accumulation.

5 Baseline Models

5.1 Task 1 Baseline

Task 1 involves two challenging sub-tasks: entity extraction and slot filling. Therefore, we design a pipeline method to extract information from dialogue transcripts. For entity extraction, the pipeline is two-step: named entity recognition and entity coreference resolution. For slot filling, the pipeline is also two-step: slot recognition and entity slot alignment. For each step, we first utilize a text encoder backbone to encode utterances and then a task-specific module to extract specific information based on the encoded representations of the utterances. In our experiments, we adopt three text encoders: LSTM (Lai et al., 2015), BERT (Kenton and Toutanova, 2019), and RoBERTa (Liu et al., 2019). The overall model architecture is illustrated in Figure 1. The hyper-parameters are shown in Table 1. The details of each step are as follows.

Named Entity Recognition First, we utilize a sequence labeling method to extract entity mentions in dialogue transcripts as in Yamada et al. (2020a). Specifically, after encoding utterances, we adopt conditional random field (Lafferty et al., 2001) on the top of hidden representations to label entity mentions from each utterance of the dialogue transcripts.

Entity Coreference Resolution After extracting entity mentions from dialogue transcripts, we utilize an entity coreference resolution method to group the mentions that refer to the same entity, as the local KB organizes knowledge in entity level instead of mention level. Specifically, after encoding dialogues, we adopt the dot product between the representation vectors of the two entity mentions as the metric to assess whether two mentions refer to the same entity. The representation vector of an entity mention is defined by the mean pooling of the representations of the tokens of the entity mention, as did in Yao et al. (2019). We then utilize the binary cross entropy loss as the objective to fine-tune the backbone encoders.

Slot Recognition Slot recognition aims to recognize slots from plain texts, regardless of which entity the slot belongs to. We utilize a sequence labeling method to recognize the slots, i.e., to label certain spans in the utterance as slots, which are the attributes of entities and the status of users. Specifically, we utilize the same model architecture as in Named Entity Recognition to label slots from each utterance of the dialogue transcripts.

Entity Slot Alignment To construct a local KB, the final procedure is to link slots to the corresponding entities. We formulate the task as a sequence classification task. Specifically, we highlight an entity and a slot using special markers and then encode the text to the contextual representation, which is inspired by Soares et al. (2019). We adopt a linear classification head to classify whether the

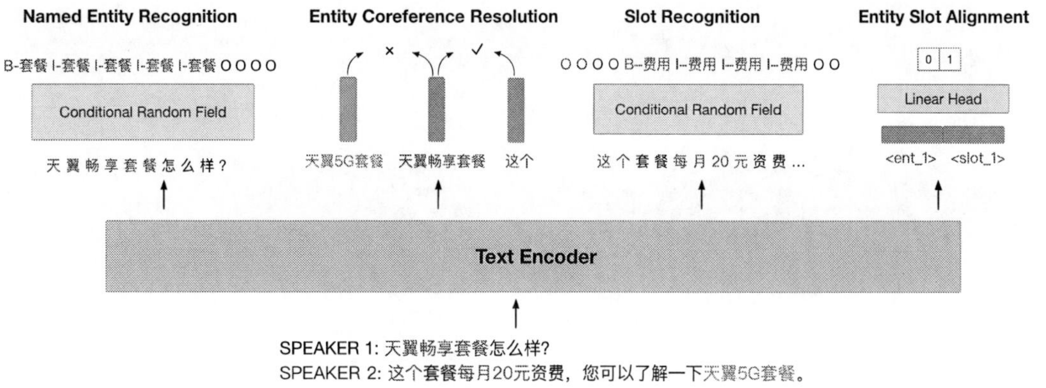

Figure 1: The overall model architecture of the pipeline model for Task 1. For the sub-task entity slot alignment, we utilize marker (e.g., <ent_1>*entity mention*<\ent_1>) to highlight entities and slots in the original text input.

Hyper-parameter	LSTM	PLMs
Learning Rate	1×10^{-3}	3×10^{-5}
Batch Size	64	64
Epoch	20	5

Table 1: Hyper-parameters of fine-tuning LSTM and PLMs (BERT, RoBERTa) on Track1 task.

slot corresponds to the entity.

5.2 Task 2 Baseline

KB Query We need to design a KB query function to help the TOD system access information from the local KB. After observing the dataset, we find that user queries can be divided into three different types. We encapsulate all query scenarios into one function and list their inputs (i.e. the arguments of the query function) and outputs as follows.

- Query the attribute of a specified entity. The input is the entity name and the attribute to be queried, the output is the attribute value in the local KB.
- Query entities of specified types. The input is entity type, the output is the entity names of this type.
- Query the attribute for users. The input is the attribute to be queried, the output is the queried attribute value in the local user profile (part of the local KB).

With the above query function, the TOD system can use the predicted user intent to access information from the local KB.

Baseline Architecture We divide the TOD system into several sub-tasks. For every dialog turn, the system needs to perform the following steps in order: 1) predict the entity name mentioned or referred to by the user; 2) predict the user intent (including the arguments of the query function); 3) query the local KB using the predicted user intent and obtain the KB result; 4) predict the system intent; 5) predict the system response. Note that there are many pronouns and co-references of entity names, so that the system may not be able to predict correct entity name with only the user utterance in current turn. To solve this problem, dialogue history information is needed. However, in real-life dialogues, the dialogue history is particularly long and contains plenty of characters, which will seriously hurt the training efficiency of the model (Liu et al., 2022). Therefore, we maintain a list of entity names mentioned by the user in all previous turns (entity name history) to replace the dialogue history. The entity name history and user utterance are fed into the model as the conditioning input to complete the above sub-tasks. Similar to Hosseini-Asl et al. (2020); Li et al. (2020a); Kulhánek et al. (2021); Yang et al. (2021); Liu et al. (2022), we employ a sequence generation architecture based on Chinese GPT-2 (Du, 2019) to implement the dialog system, which is depicted in Figure 2.

Data Analysis As described in Section 1, there are chit-chat or redundant turns in real-life dialogues. As observed from MobileCS, we find that these redundant turns can be divided into three cases: 1) one speaker asks for repetition and the other repeats what he/she said before; 2) one speaker confirms information and the other re-

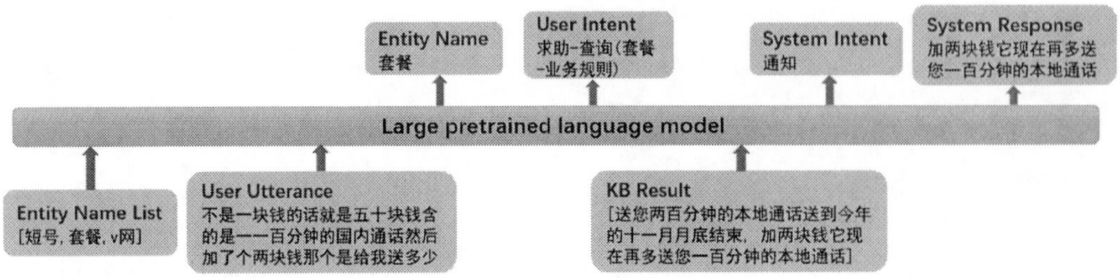

Figure 2: The baseline model architecture for Task 2. Examples are provided under the title of each box.

sponds to it passively; 3) the user interrupts the agent with some simple interjections, and then the agent continues to speak. Three examples corresponding to the three cases are shown in Table 2.

These redundant turns are interesting new phenomena revealed from the MobileCS data, which are transcribed from spoken conversations. Remarkably, the repetition and confirmation may be caused by that the staff did not hear clearly due to the accent or low quality of the user speech. The interjection is a special feature for spoken dialogues. However, after transcription of speech, the speech modality is missing, since only text is remained. Thus, the system in textual dialogues receives no relevant input from the user and is thus unable to respond properly. We leave further study of this problem for future work. In this work, we perform some pre-processing on the data to reduce the noise brought by the three cases. Specifically, for the first two cases, we simply delete the whole redundant turn (including utterances on both user and system sides) in the dialogue. For the third case, we merge the redundant turn with its previous turn by deleting the user utterance and merge the agent response with the previous one. Finally, we obtain a cleaned dataset with 15% fewer turns than the original one.

user	成那改成那最便宜那是打打那个长途是多少钱呢
system	呃呃您再说一下
user	我说改成那种你说那个便宜的是打打那个长途是多少钱一分钟呢
user	沈那中学里面
system	沈那中学是吗
user	对
system	三十八我看这边是流量送您六百兆通话送您两百分钟
user	嗯
system	前三个月每个月还送您二十块钱话费和一g的流量

Table 2: Examples of three types of redundant turns in MobileCS. The redundant utterances are marked in blue.

6 Evaluation

6.1 Task 1 Results

Metrics The evaluation metrics are two-fold. The metric for entity extraction is the span-level F1, following previous named entity recognition work (Yamada et al., 2020b). The metric for slot filling is the triple-level F1: a predicted *entity-slot-value* triple is correct if and only if the entity, slot and value are all correct. The evaluation for slot filling is a combinatorial optimization problem, as the entity is also predicted. We hence utilize the Hungarian algorithm (Kuhn, 1955) to find a best entity matching between predictions and golden labels before calculating the metric for slot filling.

Results The models are trained on the training set for a certain number of epochs (as shown in Table 1), selected according to performance over the dev set, and evaluated on the official test set[4]. The results are shown in Table 3. It can be seen that even with powerful pre-trained language models as text encoders, the performance of the baseline model is poorer on the MobileCS dataset, especially for the named entity recognition and slot recognition sub-tasks, as compared to results on other datasets reported in the literature (Yamada et al., 2020a). These results demonstrate how demanding the MobileCS dataset is, and indicate that extracting structured information from long and loose texts, e.g. dialogue transcripts, remains challenging for existing models, which urges more powerful and robust models.

6.2 Task 2 Results

Metrics In order to measure the performance of TOD systems, both automatic evaluation and human evaluation are conducted. For automatic evaluation, metrics include **Precision/Recall/F1 score, Success rate and BLEU score**. P/R/F1 are calculated for both predicted user intents and system

[4]Notably, the challenge leaderboad for Track 1 are ranked by the results tested over 500 dialogues, which is only a subset of the official test set and were held out by the Challenge Organizers and not sent to the teams.

Backbone	F1 (NER)	Golden Labels			Pipeline
		B^3 (ECR)	F1 (SR)	Acc. (ESA)	F1 (SF)
LSTM (Lai et al., 2015)	35.02	85.84	43.89	76.84	31.37
BERT$_{BASE}$ (Kenton and Toutanova, 2019)	34.21	88.09	46.46	76.50	33.24
RoBERTa$_{BASE}$ (Liu et al., 2019)	33.74	88.02	45.59	77.32	33.28
RoBERTa$_{LARGE}$ (Liu et al., 2019)	**35.06**	**89.42**	**46.89**	**78.07**	**34.95**

Table 3: Experimental results of Task 1 on the official test set, with different text encoder backbones. "Golden Labels" means using golden prerequisite labels (e.g. golden entities for entity coreference resolution) for each pipeline step. "Pipeline" represents using previous predictions for each pipeline step. The evaluation metric is micro F1 for named entity recognition and entity slot alignment, B-cubed metric (Bagga and Baldwin, 1998) for entity coreference resolution, and accuracy for entity slot alignment. NER: Named Entity Recognition. ECR: Entity Coreference Resolution. SR: Slot Recognition. ESA: Entity Slot Alignment. SF: Slot Filling.

Dataset	U-P/R/F1	S-P/R/F1	BLEU	Success
Original	0.681/0.569/0.620	0.635/0.501/0.502	3.79	0.268
Cleaned	0.686/0.595/0.637	0.656/0.547/0.596	4.13	0.279

Table 4: The results of Task 2 baseline on the official dev set. U-P/R/F1 and S-P/R/F1 denote P/R/F1 for the user side and the system side, respectively.

Fluency	Coherency	Success
2.76	2.18	2.24

Table 5: Human evaluation of the Task 2 baseline system (trained on the cleaned dataset).

intents. Success rate is the percentage of generated dialogs that achieve user goals. Specifically, for each dialogue, we extract the information requested in the user goal from the local KB, then we regard this dialogue as a success if the generated responses contain all the requested information. BLEU score evaluates the fluency of generated responses by comparing them with oracle responses. For human evaluation, 5 testers (staffs from China Mobile) interacted with the system, and each tester should interact for at least 10 dialogues with the system. The tester would score the system on a 5-point scale (1 to 5) by the following 3 metrics. Success measures if the system successfully completes the user goal by interacting with the user. Coherency measures whether the system's response is logically coherent with the dialogue context. Fluency measures the fluency of the system's response.

Results Based on the analysis in Section 5.2, we conduct experiments on the original dataset and the cleaned dataset, respectively. The models are trained on the official training set for 40 epochs, and tested on the official dev set. The results are shown in Table 4. It can be seen that the model trained on the cleaned dataset outperforms the model trained on the original dataset in all metrics, which demonstrates the benefit of cleaning up redundant conversations. Nevertheless, the results on the cleaned MobileCS still fall behind by a large margin in comparison to the results on other Wizard-of-Oz datasets. For example, the Success rate of state-of-the-art models on MultiWOZ2.1 is around 75%, while it is lower than 30% on MobileCS. The BLEU score on MobileCS is much lower than that on CrossWOZ (Liu et al., 2021). Note that both TOD systems on MobileCS and CrossWOZ are based on Chinese GPT-2, though not strictly comparable. These results demonstrate how challenging of building TOD systems for real-life tasks is. The agent responses from real-life are much more difficult to be modeled, as compared those in the Wizard-of-Oz scenarios.

We further perform human evaluation for the best baseline model (i.e. the model trained on the cleaned dataset) and the average scores of all tested dialogues are shown in Table 5. The scores of the three metrics are relatively low (lower than 3), which shows that in most cases, responses generated by the baseline system are neither fluent nor coherent enough, and can not provide requested information satisfactorily. In a word, building a TOD system that can perform well on real-life dialogues is very challenging, and there is much room for the baseline TOD system to be improved. The MobileCS dataset offers a valuable and challenging testbed for future research of building human-robot dialogue systems for real-life tasks.

7 Discussion and Conclusion

The performance of task-oriented dialogue systems on Wizard-of-Oz datasets have been improved continuously to a high level, for example, as shown in MultiWOZ[5]. However, Wizard-of-Oz dialogue data are in fact simulated data and thus are fundamentally different from real-life conversations, which are more noisy and casual. For further advancement of human-robot dialogue technology, real human-human dialogue data with grounding annotations to KBs are highly desirable. Further, noting that the KB is an indispensable part for TOD systems and usually is not readily available for real-life tasks, it is very important to investigate not only the dialogue system itself but also information extraction to construct the KB.

With the MobileCS dataset released by the SereTOD challenge, this paper presents a baseline study of both information extraction (Task 1) and human-robot dialogue (Task 2) over real human-human dialogue data. We introduce how the baselines for the two tasks are constructed, the problems encountered, and the results. It is found that the MobileCS dataset offers a challenging testbed for both tasks, with interesting open problems. Our baselines provide an easy entry to investigate the new dataset, and we anticipate that the baselines can facilitate exciting future research to build human-robot dialogue systems for real-life tasks.

References

Amit Bagga and Breck Baldwin. 1998. Entity-based cross-document coreferencing using the vector space model. In *COLING 1998 Volume 1: The 17th International Conference on Computational Linguistics*.

Paweł Budzianowski, Tsung-Hsien Wen, Bo-Hsiang Tseng, Iñigo Casanueva, Stefan Ultes, Osman Ramadan, and Milica Gašić. 2018. MultiWOZ - a large-scale multi-domain Wizard-of-Oz dataset for task-oriented dialogue modelling. In *Proceedings of the 2018 Conference on Empirical Methods in Natural Language Processing*, pages 5016–5026, Brussels, Belgium. Association for Computational Linguistics.

Roberta Catizone, Alexiei Dingli, and Robert J. Gaizauskas. 2010. Using dialogue corpora to extend information extraction patterns for natural language understanding of dialogue. In *Proceedings of the International Conference on Language Resources and Evaluation, LREC 2010, 17-23 May 2010, Valletta, Malta*. European Language Resources Association.

Yinpei Dai, Zhijian Ou, Dawei Ren, and Pengfei Yu. 2018. Tracking of enriched dialog states for flexible conversational information access. In *2018 IEEE International Conference on Acoustics, Speech and Signal Processing (ICASSP)*, pages 6139–6143. IEEE.

[5]https://github.com/budzianowski/multiwoz

Zeyao Du. 2019. GPT2-chinese: Tools for training GPT2 model in chinese language. `https://github.com/Morizeyao/GPT2-Chinese`.

Layla El Asri, Hannes Schulz, Shikhar Kr Sarma, Jeremie Zumer, Justin Harris, Emery Fine, Rahul Mehrotra, and Kaheer Suleman. 2017. Frames: a corpus for adding memory to goal-oriented dialogue systems. In *Proceedings of the 18th Annual SIGdial Meeting on Discourse and Dialogue*, pages 207–219.

S. Gao, Y. Zhang, Z. Ou, and Z. Yu. 2020. Paraphrase augmented task-oriented dialog generation. In *Proceedings of the 58th Annual Meeting of the Association for Computational Linguistics*.

Xu Han, Tianyu Gao, Yankai Lin, Hao Peng, Yaoliang Yang, Chaojun Xiao, Zhiyuan Liu, Peng Li, Maosong Sun, and Jie Zhou. 2020. More data, more relations, more context and more openness: A review and outlook for relation extraction. *arXiv preprint arXiv:2004.03186*.

Toru Hirano, Nozomi Kobayashi, Ryuichiro Higashinaka, Toshiro Makino, and Yoshihiro Matsuo. 2015. User information extraction for personalized dialogue systems. *SEMDIAL 2015 goDIAL*, page 67.

Ehsan Hosseini-Asl, Bryan McCann, Chien-Sheng Wu, Semih Yavuz, and Richard Socher. 2020. A simple language model for task-oriented dialogue. *arXiv preprint arXiv:2005.00796*.

Qi Jia, Hongru Huang, and Kenny Q Zhu. 2021. Ddrel: A new dataset for interpersonal relation classification in dyadic dialogues. In *Proceedings of the AAAI Conference on Artificial Intelligence*, volume 35, pages 13125–13133.

Anjuli Kannan, Kai Chen, Diana Jaunzeikare, and Alvin Rajkomar. 2018. Semi-supervised learning for information extraction from dialogue. In *Interspeech*, pages 2077–2081.

Jacob Devlin Ming-Wei Chang Kenton and Lee Kristina Toutanova. 2019. Bert: Pre-training of deep bidirectional transformers for language understanding. In *Proceedings of NAACL-HLT*, pages 4171–4186.

Seokhwan Kim, Yang Liu, Di Jin, Alexandros Papangelis, Karthik Gopalakrishnan, Behnam Hedayatnia, and Dilek Hakkani-Tür. 2021. "how robust r u?": Evaluating task-oriented dialogue systems on spoken conversations. In *2021 IEEE Automatic Speech Recognition and Understanding Workshop (ASRU)*, pages 1147–1154.

Harold W Kuhn. 1955. The hungarian method for the assignment problem. *Naval research logistics quarterly*, 2(1-2):83–97.

Jonáš Kulhánek, Vojtěch Hudeček, Tomáš Nekvinda, and Ondřej Dušek. 2021. AuGPT: Dialogue with pre-trained language models and data augmentation. *arXiv preprint arXiv:2102.05126*.

John D. Lafferty, Andrew McCallum, and Fernando C. N. Pereira. 2001. Conditional random fields: Probabilistic models for segmenting and labeling sequence data. In *Proceedings of the Eighteenth International Conference on Machine Learning (ICML 2001), Williams College, Williamstown, MA, USA, June 28 - July 1, 2001*, pages 282–289. Morgan Kaufmann.

Siwei Lai, Liheng Xu, Kang Liu, and Jun Zhao. 2015. Recurrent convolutional neural networks for text classification. In *Twenty-ninth AAAI conference on artificial intelligence*.

Harrison Lee, Raghav Gupta, Abhinav Rastogi, Yuan Cao, Bin Zhang, and Yonghui Wu. 2022. Sgd-x: A benchmark for robust generalization in schema-guided dialogue systems. In *Proceedings of the AAAI Conference on Artificial Intelligence*, volume 36, pages 10938–10946.

Yohan Lee. 2021. Improving end-to-end task-oriented dialog system with a simple auxiliary task. In *Findings of the Association for Computational Linguistics: EMNLP 2021*.

Wenqiang Lei, Xisen Jin, Min-Yen Kan, Zhaochun Ren, Xiangnan He, and Dawei Yin. 2018. Sequicity: Simplifying task-oriented dialogue systems with single sequence-to-sequence architectures. In *56th Annual Meeting of the Association for Computational Linguistics (ACL)*.

Baolin Peng Chunyuan Li, Jinchao Li, Shahin Shayandeh, Lars Liden, and Jianfeng Gao. 2020a. SOLOIST: Building task bots at scale with transfer learning and machine teaching. *Transactions of the Association for Computational Linguistics (TACL), 2021*.

Jing Li, Aixin Sun, Jianglei Han, and Chenliang Li. 2020b. A survey on deep learning for named entity recognition. *IEEE Transactions on Knowledge and Data Engineering*, 34(1):50–70.

Jiwei Li, Michel Galley, Chris Brockett, Jianfeng Gao, and William B Dolan. 2016. A diversity-promoting objective function for neural conversation models. In *Proceedings of the 2016 Conference of the North American Chapter of the Association for Computational Linguistics: Human Language Technologies*, pages 110–119.

Bing Liu and Ian Lane. 2017. An end-to-end trainable neural network model with belief tracking for task-oriented dialog. *Proc. Interspeech 2017*, pages 2506–2510.

Hong Liu, Yucheng Cai, Zhenru Lin, Zhijian Ou, Yi Huang, and Junlan Feng. 2021. Variational latent-state GPT for semi-supervised task-oriented dialog systems. *arXiv preprint arXiv:2109.04314*.

Hong Liu, Yucheng Cai, Zhijian Ou, Yi Huang, and Junlan Feng. 2022. Revisiting markovian generative architectures for efficient task-oriented dialog systems. *ArXiv preprint arXiv:2204.06452*.

Yinhan Liu, Myle Ott, Naman Goyal, Jingfei Du, Mandar Joshi, Danqi Chen, Omer Levy, Mike Lewis, Luke Zettlemoyer, and Veselin Stoyanov. 2019. Roberta: A robustly optimized bert pretraining approach. *arXiv preprint arXiv:1907.11692*.

Ryan Lowe, Nissan Pow, Iulian Serban, and Joelle Pineau. 2015. The ubuntu dialogue corpus: A large dataset for research in unstructured multi-turn dialogue systems. In *SIGDIAL Conference*.

Nikola Mrkšić, Diarmuid Ó Séaghdha, Tsung-Hsien Wen, Blaise Thomson, and Steve Young. 2017. Neural belief tracker: Data-driven dialogue state tracking. In *Proceedings of the 55th Annual Meeting of the Association for Computational Linguistics (ACL)*.

Zhijian Ou, Junlan Feng, Juanzi Li, Yakun Li, Hong Liu, Hao Peng, Yi Huang, and Jiangjiang Zhao. 2022. A challenge on semi-supervised and reinforced task-oriented dialog systems. *arXiv preprint arXiv:2207.02657*.

Shuang Peng, Mengdi Zhou, Minghui Yang, Haitao Mi, Shaosheng Cao, Zujie Wen, Teng Xu, Hongbin Wang, and Lei Liu. 2021. A dialogue-based information extraction system for medical insurance assessment. *arXiv preprint arXiv:2107.05866*.

Jun Quan, Shian Zhang, Qian Cao, Zizhong Li, and Deyi Xiong. 2020. RiSAWOZ: A large-scale multi-domain Wizard-of-Oz dataset with rich semantic annotations for task-oriented dialogue modeling. In *Proceedings of the 2020 Conference on Empirical Methods in Natural Language Processing (EMNLP)*, pages 930–940, Online. Association for Computational Linguistics.

Alec Radford, Jeffrey Wu, Rewon Child, David Luan, Dario Amodei, and Ilya Sutskever. 2019. Language models are unsupervised multitask learners. *OpenAI Blog*, 1(8):9.

Colin Raffel, Noam Shazeer, Adam Roberts, Katherine Lee, Sharan Narang, Michael Matena, Yanqi Zhou, Wei Li, and Peter J. Liu. 2020. Exploring the limits of transfer learning with a unified text-to-text transformer. *Journal of Machine Learning Research*, 21(140):1–67.

Abhinav Rastogi, Xiaoxue Zang, Srinivas Sunkara, Raghav Gupta, and Pranav Khaitan. 2020. Towards scalable multi-domain conversational agents: The schema-guided dialogue dataset. In *Proceedings of the AAAI Conference on Artificial Intelligence*, volume 34, pages 8689–8696.

Alan Ritter, Colin Cherry, and William B. Dolan. 2010. Unsupervised modeling of twitter conversations. In *NAACL*.

Sunita Sarawagi et al. 2008. Information extraction. *Foundations and Trends® in Databases*, 1(3):261–377.

Nicolas Schrading, Cecilia Ovesdotter Alm, Raymond W. Ptucha, and Christopher Homan. 2015. An analysis of domestic abuse discourse on reddit. In *EMNLP*.

Pararth Shah, Dilek Hakkani-Tür, Gokhan Tür, Abhinav Rastogi, Ankur Bapna, Neha Nayak, and Larry Heck. 2018. Building a conversational agent overnight with dialogue self-play. *arXiv preprint arXiv:1801.04871*.

Lei Shu, Piero Molino, Mahdi Namazifar, Hu Xu, Bing Liu, Huaixiu Zheng, and Gökhan Tür. 2019. Flexibly-structured model for task-oriented dialogues. In *Proceedings of the 20th Annual SIGdial Meeting on Discourse and Dialogue*.

Livio Baldini Soares, Nicholas FitzGerald, Jeffrey Ling, and Tom Kwiatkowski. 2019. Matching the blanks: Distributional similarity for relation learning. *arXiv preprint arXiv:1906.03158*.

Yixuan Su, Lei Shu, Elman Mansimov, Arshit Gupta, Deng Cai, Yi-An Lai, and Yi Zhang. 2021. Multi-task pre-training for plug-and-play task-oriented dialogue system. *CoRR*, abs/2109.14739.

A. M. Turing. 1950. Computing machinery and intelligence. *Mind*, 49:433–460.

Ashish Vaswani, Noam Shazeer, Niki Parmar, Jakob Uszkoreit, Llion Jones, Aidan N Gomez, Łukasz Kaiser, and Illia Polosukhin. 2017. Attention is all you need. In *Advances in neural information processing systems*, pages 5998–6008.

Tsung-Hsien Wen, David Vandyke, Nikola Mrkšić, Milica Gasic, Lina M Rojas Barahona, Pei-Hao Su, Stefan Ultes, and Steve Young. 2017a. A network-based end-to-end trainable task-oriented dialogue system. In *Proceedings of the 15th Conference of the European Chapter of the Association for Computational Linguistics*.

Tsung-Hsien Wen, David Vandyke, Nikola Mrkšić, Milica Gašić, Lina M. Rojas-Barahona, Pei-Hao Su, Stefan Ultes, and Steve Young. 2017b. A network-based end-to-end trainable task-oriented dialogue system. In *Proceedings of the 15th Conference of the European Chapter of the Association for Computational Linguistics: Volume 1, Long Papers*, pages 438–449, Valencia, Spain. Association for Computational Linguistics.

Jason D Williams, Antoine Raux, and Matthew Henderson. 2016. The dialog state tracking challenge series: A review. *Dialogue & Discourse*, 7(3):4–33.

Chien-Sheng Wu, Andrea Madotto, Zhaojiang Lin, Peng Xu, and Pascale Fung. 2019. Getting to know you: User attribute extraction from dialogues. *arXiv preprint arXiv:1908.04621*.

Ikuya Yamada, Akari Asai, Hiroyuki Shindo, Hideaki Takeda, and Yuji Matsumoto. 2020a. Luke: deep contextualized entity representations with entity-aware self-attention. *arXiv preprint arXiv:2010.01057*.

Ikuya Yamada, Akari Asai, Hiroyuki Shindo, Hideaki Takeda, and Yuji Matsumoto. 2020b. LUKE: deep contextualized entity representations with entity-aware self-attention. In *Proceedings of the 2020 Conference on Empirical Methods in Natural Language Processing, EMNLP 2020, Online, November 16-20, 2020*, pages 6442–6454. Association for Computational Linguistics.

Yunyi Yang, Yunhao Li, and Xiaojun Quan. 2021. UBAR: Towards fully end-to-end task-oriented dialog system with GPT-2. In *Proceedings of the AAAI Conference on Artificial Intelligence (AAAI)*.

Yuan Yao, Deming Ye, Peng Li, Xu Han, Yankai Lin, Zhenghao Liu, Zhiyuan Liu, Lixin Huang, Jie Zhou, and Maosong Sun. 2019. Docred: A large-scale document-level relation extraction dataset. *arXiv preprint arXiv:1906.06127*.

Dian Yu, Kai Sun, Claire Cardie, and Dong Yu. 2020. Dialogue-based relation extraction. *arXiv preprint arXiv:2004.08056*.

Yichi Zhang, Zhijian Ou, Min Hu, and Junlan Feng. 2020. A probabilistic end-to-end task-oriented dialog model with latent belief states towards semi-supervised learning. In *Proc. of the Conference on Empirical Methods in Natural Language Processing (EMNLP)*.

Yichi Zhang, Zhijian Ou, and Zhou Yu. 2020. Task-oriented dialog systems that consider multiple appropriate responses under the same context. In *The Thirty-Fourth AAAI Conference on Artificial Intelligence (AAAI)*.

Qi Zhu, Kaili Huang, Zheng Zhang, Xiaoyan Zhu, and Minlie Huang. 2020. CrossWOZ: A large-scale chinese cross-domain task-oriented dialogue dataset. *Transactions of the Association for Computational Linguistics*.

A Generative User Simulator with GPT-based Architecture and Goal State Tracking for Reinforced Multi-Domain Dialog Systems

Hong Liu[1,3], Yucheng Cai[1,3], Zhijian Ou[1,3]*, Yi Huang[2,3], Junlan Feng[2,3]

[1]Speech Processing and Machine Intelligence (SPMI) Lab, Tsinghua University, Beijing, China

[2]China Mobile Research Institute, Beijing, China

[3]Tsinghua University-China Mobile Communications Group Co., Ltd. Joint Institute, Beijing, China

{liuhong21,cyc22}@mails.tsinghua.edu.cn,
ozj@tsinghua.edu.cn,
{huangyi,fengjunlan}@chinamobile.com

Abstract

Building user simulators (USs) for reinforcement learning (RL) of task-oriented dialog systems (DSs) has gained more and more attention, which, however, still faces several fundamental challenges. First, it is unclear whether we can leverage pretrained language models to design, for example, GPT-2 based USs, to catch up and interact with the recently advanced GPT-2 based DSs. Second, an important ingredient in a US is that the user goal can be effectively incorporated and tracked; but how to flexibly integrate goal state tracking and develop an end-to-end trainable US for multi-domains has remained to be a challenge. In this work, we propose a generative user simulator (GUS) with GPT-2 based architecture and goal state tracking towards addressing the above two challenges. Extensive experiments are conducted on MultiWOZ2.1. Different DSs are trained via RL with GUS, the classic agenda-based user simulator (ABUS) and other ablation simulators respectively, and are compared for cross-model evaluation, corpus-based evaluation and human evaluation. The GUS achieves superior results in all three evaluation tasks.

1 Introduction

Task-oriented dialog (TOD) systems are mainly designed to help users accomplish specific goals, such as finding restaurants or booking flights. The dialog system (DS) usually consists of several modules - dialog state tracking (DST), database querying (DB), dialog policy (DP) and natural language generation (NLG). Recent studies recast these modules all as conditional generation of tokens and build on some pretrained language model (PLM) such as GPT-2 (Radford et al., 2019) as the backbone. Fine-tuning PLM over annotated dialog datasets via supervised learning (SL) has shown state-of-the-art results (Hosseini-Asl et al., 2020; Li et al., 2020; Kulhánek et al., 2021; Yang et al., 2021; Lee, 2021), thanks to the powerful generation ability of PLMs.

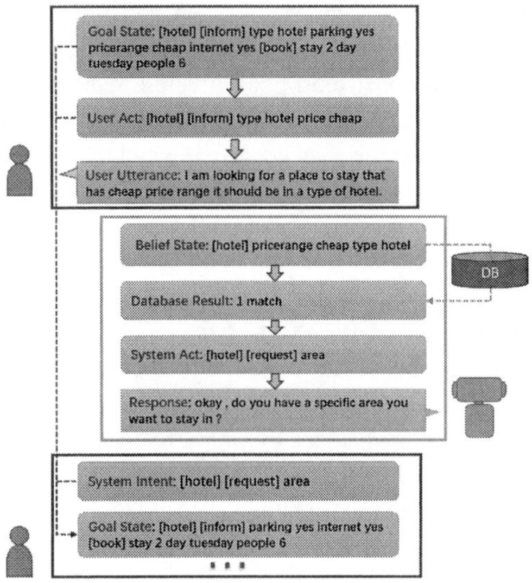

Figure 1: The information flow in a task-oriented dialog. Domains and intents are enclosed by square brackets.

However, supervised trained agents could become biased by the annotations, and it has long been recognized that reinforcement learning (RL) could be applied to policy learning for the agent (Young et al., 2013), which aims at goal-directed learning from interaction between the dialog agent and the user. Interaction with human users is expensive and time-consuming in practice. Therefore, an alternative approach, building user simulators (USs), has gained more and more attention, which, however, still faces several fundamental challenges.

First, note that the recent research on building dialog agents has been significantly advanced with the end-to-end trainable generative approach based on PLMs such as GPT-2. However, prior work on user simulators are mostly LSTM-based, not utilizing any PLMs, as reviewed in Table 1. It is unclear whether we can leverage PLMs to design, for ex-

*Corresponding author. The code is released at https://github.com/thu-spmi/GUS

Proceedings of the Towards Semi-Supervised and Reinforced Task-Oriented Dialog Systems (SereTOD), pages 85 - 97
December 7, 2022 ©2022 Association for Computational Linguistics

ample, GPT-2 based[1] user simulators, to catch up and interact with the GPT-2 based dialog agents. This has not ever been systematically examined, to the best of our knowledge. We leave detailed discussion to Related Work section, where we review prior work on USs from a number of important features in building USs.

Second, an important ingredient in a US is that the user goal can be incorporated and tracked. Task-oriented dialog systems are characterized by a user goal, which is composed of user constraints and requests. The user goal ensures that the user behaves in a consistent, goal-directed manner, and the system agent is considered successful if it is able to fulfill the user goal by the end of a dialog session. Thus, it is desirable for the US to track the completion process of the goal explicitly (which we call goal state tracking in this paper), as did in the classic agenda-based user simulator (ABUS) (Schatzmann et al., 2007). However, the goal state tracking process is overlooked in later data-driven USs (Asri et al., 2016; Gür et al., 2018; Papangelis et al., 2019), or realized by binary vectors (Kreyssig et al., 2018; Lin et al., 2021; Tseng et al., 2021), or only works at the semantic level (Takanobu et al., 2020). How to flexibly integrate goal state tracking and develop an end-to-end trainable US for multi-domains has remained to be a challenge.

In this work, we propose a generative user simulator (GUS) with GPT-2 based architecture and goal state tracking towards addressing the above two challenges in building end-to-end trainable USs for reinforced multi-domain dialog systems. Basically, a US, interacting with a DS in natural languages, needs several modules - natural language understanding (NLU) of system responses, goal state tracking (GST) to refresh the remained constrains and requests that need to send subsequently, user policy (UP), and natural language generation (NLG). The information flow in a task-oriented dialog between a US and a DS is illustrated in Figure 1. In generative user simulator (GUS), we recast these modules in US all as conditional generation of tokens, similar to the recent approach of fine-tuning PLMs such as GPT-2 to build end-to-end trainable generative DSs.

To be specific in this paper, we use the GPT-2 based architecture for GUS to generate user acts and user utterances, and constantly track the goal

[1]It can be seen that the discussion and the proposed method in the remainder of this paper can also be applied to other PLMs such as T5 (Raffel et al., 2020), not limited to GPT-2.

US	PLM	Goal State Tracking	Cross-model Evaluation	Compared with DS-SL	Natural Lang. Interaction	Multi-Domain
Schatzmann et al. (2007)	N	Y	N	N	N	N
Asri et al. (2016)	N	N	N	N	N	N
Liu and Lane (2017)	N	N	N	Y	Y	N
Gür et al. (2018)	N	N	N	N	N	N
Kreyssig et al. (2018)	N	Y	Y	N	Y	N
Papangelis et al. (2019)	N	N	N	Y	Y	N
Shi et al. (2019)	N	N	Y	N	Y	N
Takanobu et al. (2020)	N	Y	N	Y	N	Y
Lin et al. (2021)	N	Y	Y	N	N	Y
Tseng et al. (2021)	N	Y	N	Y	Y	Y
GUS	Y	Y	Y	Y	Y	Y

Table 1: Comparison of prior different user simulators from a number of important features in building USs. DS-SL denotes dialog system (DS) trained by supervised learning (SL). See Section 2 for detailed meaning of each feature by column.

state according to the user acts and system acts of the previous turn, which is shown in Figure 2. In this work, the definition of goal state is similar to the agenda in ABUS (Schatzmann et al., 2007), which represents a collection of pending user acts that are needed to elicit the information specified in the goal. The maintenance of goal state includes not only removing the completed user acts, but also changing the user goal when the system cannot find a requested entity.

Extensive experiments are conducted on MultiWOZ2.1 (Eric et al., 2020). Different DSs are trained via RL with GUS, ABUS and other ablation simulators respectively, and are compared for cross-model evaluation, corpus-based evaluation and human evaluation. The GUS achieves superior results in all three evaluation tasks.

2 Related Work

Novelty In Table 1, we review prior work on USs from a number of important features in building USs, including whether or not the US is based on any PLMs, the US conducts goal state tracking, the cross-model evaluation (Schatztnann et al., 2005) is conducted to assess the performance of the US, the DS trained via RL with the US is compared to the DS trained via supervised learning, the US and the DS interact in natural languages [2], the US is designed to work for multi-domain dialogs. It is clear from Table 1 that our proposed GUS is distinctive, which represents the first US that possesses all these desirable features, to the best of our knowledge. More discussions are provided in the

[2]This means that during reinforcement training of the DS with the US, the US accepts the system response in natural language. In contrast, for those USs with 'N' marked in the 'Natural Lang. Interaction' column, the system acts are directly fed to the US so that the US does not need a natural language understanding module. For such as case, the US is also said to work at the semantic level.

following.

US Architecture A variety of user simulators have been studied, either rule-based or data-driven. A classic rule-based US is the agenda-based user simulator (ABUS) (Schatzmann et al., 2007). Different data-driven US models are proposed with different architectures and characteristics. Asri et al. (2016) develops a LSTM-based seq2seq US on the single-domain DSTC2 dataset and generates semantic-level user acts. Gür et al. (2018) proposes a GRU-based hierarchical seq2seq framework for US (HUS) and further introduces a latent variable to control the diversity of dialogue (VHUS). NUS (Kreyssig et al., 2018) extracts feature vectors related to current goal states and feeds to a LSTM seq2seq model to output natural languages. Shi et al. (2019) make extensive comparisons for six user simulators, based on two user policy modules (seq2seq or agenda based) and three NLG modules (template, retrieval or seq2seq). TUS in (Lin et al., 2021) designs domain-independent features and implements the user policy as multi-class classification so that TUS could be easily adapted to new domains. Some studies aim to jointly optimize DS and US. The USs used in these studies are mostly based on LSTM seq2seq architectures (Liu and Lane, 2017; Papangelis et al., 2019; Tseng et al., 2021), or simply as multi-class classification for action selection with feed-forward networks (Takanobu et al., 2020).

Goal State Tracking in US ABUS is classic in goal state tracking, where the pending user acts are tracked in a stack-like structure, called agenda. ABUS is rule-based, generating user acts by pushing and popping hand-crafted rules from agenda. The goal state tracking process is overlooked in some later studies of data-driven USs (Asri et al., 2016; Gür et al., 2018; Papangelis et al., 2019), where the US is always conditioned on the whole initial user goal at each turn. Some data-driven USs explicitly track goal states but employ binary vectors (Kreyssig et al., 2018; Lin et al., 2021; Tseng et al., 2021). The US in (Takanobu et al., 2020) represents goal states by tokens, which is flexible, but the US only interacts with the DS at the semantic level (not end-to-end trainable).

3 Preliminaries

Notations According to the information flow in a task-oriented dialog between a US and a DS as

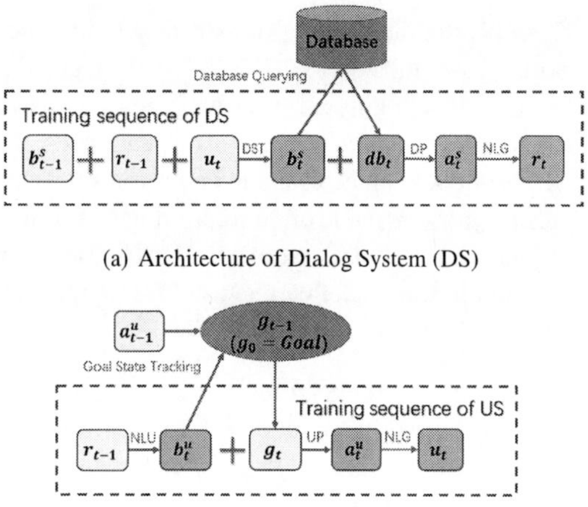

(a) Architecture of Dialog System (DS)

(b) Architecture of User Simulator (US)

Figure 2: The generative architecture of dialog system and user simulator in our experiments.Yellow boxes represent the conditioning input of the model during generation, and green boxes the targeting output.

illustrated in Figure 1, we let g_t denote the user goal state, a_t^u the user act, u_t the user utterance, b_t^s the system belief state, db_t the database result, a_t^s the system act, and r_t the system response, respectively, at turn $t = 1, \cdots, T$, for a dialog of T turns. Moreover, in this paper we are interested in building end-to-end trainable US that can interact with the DS in natural languages. Thus, we introduce a NLU module in the US, which takes the system response r_t as input and infer system intent. The NLU result is denoted by b_t^u, or loosely speaking, referred to as the user belief state. Notably, the US belief state b_t^u denotes the US's understanding only about the previous system response, and accordingly is labeled as a_{t-1}^s in training. b_t^u is not of accumulated nature, since the US uses the goal state g_t to summarize the dialog history encountered by the US[3].

GPT-2-based Generative Architecture In this work, all variables defined in the last paragraph for the US and DS are converted to token sequences, like in DAMD (Zhang et al., 2020). So pretrained language models (LMs) such as GPT-2 can be finetuned to build end-to-end trainable DS and US, as will be introduced later. To be clear, GPT-2 (Radford et al., 2019) in this paper refers to the particular class of causal LMs, which computes conditional probabilities for next-token generation

[3]In contrast, the system belief state b_t^s summarizes the dialog history encountered by the DS. This subtle difference makes sense, since the roles of the DS and US are different.

via self-attention based Transformer neural network (Vaswani et al., 2017). Given a particular form of conditional model, $p(output|input)$, where $input$ and $output$ are token sequences, the GPT-2 model can be finetuned over training samples $(input, output)$ (often referred to as training sequences (Hosseini-Asl et al., 2020)), and after finetuning, the model can be used for generation, i.e., generating $output$ after receiving $input$.

Generative Dialog System The main task for a dialog system (DS) is, for each dialog turn t, to generate (or say, predict)[4] b_t^s, a_t^s and r_t, given u_t and dialog history $u_1, r_1, \cdots, u_{t-1}, r_{t-1}$. A recent progress in building DS is that all variables are represented by token sequences, and the workflow of a dialog system (DST, DP and NLG) is unified into a single sequence generation problem, which can be accomplished by a causal LM such as GPT-2 (Hosseini-Asl et al., 2020; Liu et al., 2022). In this paper, we employ the Markov generative architecture (MGA) for DS, which is introduced in Liu et al. (2022) and shows efficiency advantages in memory, computation and learning over non-Markov DS models like SimpleTOD (Hosseini-Asl et al., 2020). Specifically, for DS to predict b_t^s, a_t^s and r_t at each turn t, we use only the belief state b_{t-1} and response r_{t-1} from previous turn along with current user utterance u_t, as shown in Figure 2(a). The DS can thus be trained via finetuning GPT-2 by maximizing the following conditional likelihood over labeled training sequences for supervised learning (SL):

$$\begin{aligned}\mathcal{J}_{\text{DS-SL}} &= \log p_\theta(b_t^s, a_t^s, r_t | b_{t-1}^s, r_{t-1}, u_t) \\ &= \sum_{i=1}^{|b_t^s \oplus a_t^s \oplus r_t|} \log p_\theta(c_i | b_{t-1}^s, r_{t-1}, u_t, c_{<i})\end{aligned} \quad (1)$$

where $\oplus$ denotes the concatenation of sequences, $|b_t^s \oplus a_t^s \oplus r_t|$ denotes the length in tokens, and c_i denotes the i-th token. The DS parameters are actually a set of GPT-2 parameters, collectively denoted by θ.

4 Method: Generative User Simulator

An end-to-end trainable US needs several modules - natural language understanding (NLU) of system responses, goal state tracking (GST), user policy (UP), and natural language generation (NLG). Inspired by the recent approach of finetuning PLMs such as GPT-2 to build end-to-end trainable generative DSs, we propose an end-to-end trainable generative user simulator (GUS), which generally refer to the approach of recasting all the modules in the US (NLU, UP, and NLG) as conditional generation of tokens based on finetuning PLMs such as GPT-2. In the following, we first introduce the GUS model including goal state tracking and GPT-2 based architecture. Then, we describe how GUS is trained and used for reinforcement training of the DS.

4.1 GUS Model

Goal State Definition Crucially, the interaction between the user and the system is motivated by the user goal, which is composed of user constraints and requests such as booking a cheap hotel. The goal state, in this paper, is defined as the uncompleted part of the user goal at each turn. Similar to Kreyssig et al. (2018), we accumulate the annotated user acts backwards turn by turn to obtain the goal state annotation at each turn. The accumulation process is illustrated in Appendix A.1.The goal state obtained at the first turn corresponds to the initial user goal for the whole dialog session.

Goal State Tracking Given the goal state annotations at each turn, the US can be trained via teacher-forcing to mimic the user behaviors. When the US is applied to interact with the DS for evaluation or for reinforcement training of the DS, the US needs to track the completion process of the goal to update the goal state turn by turn, which we call goal state tracking. There are three types of user intents in the goal state g_t - *inform, book and request*. The slots and values for the first two types of intents in g_t are denoted by $g_t^{constraint}$ and those of the *request* intent as $g_t^{request}$. The update rule of g_t at turn t is designed to be as follows:

$$\begin{aligned}g_t^{constraint} &= g_{t-1}^{constraint} \ominus a_{t-1}^{u,inform} \\ g_t^{request} &= g_{t-1}^{request} \ominus b_t^{u,inform}\end{aligned} \quad (2)$$

where $a_{t-1}^{u,inform}$, $b_t^{u,inform}$ are the informable slots and values in user act a_{t-1}^u and user belief state b_t^u respectively and $\ominus$ denotes removing the corresponding slots and values. Moreover, the slot values in the initial user goal may be changed during the interaction (i.e., goal change). When the DS expresses *no-offer* intent, which means no entities in the database satisfy the constraints of the

[4] Note that database result db_t is deterministically obtained by querying database using the predicted b_t^s. We omit db_t in the discussion for simplicity.

goal, we randomly select one slot in the *no-offer* intent and replace its value with another value in the ontology.

GPT-2-based Architecture The main task for a US is, conditional on the user goal, to iteratively understand the system response, track goal state, decide user act, and generate user utterance. In this work, we find that the recent approach of finetuning GPT-2 for conditional generation can be similarly applied to build US. Specifically, we employ Markov generative architecture (Liu et al., 2022). The US is designed to firstly infer the system intent, i.e., user belief state b_t^u of turn t from the previous system response r_{t-1}, which could be modeled as $p_\phi(b_t^u|r_{t-1})$. After obtaining b_t^u, the goal state will be updated according to the rule in Eq. (2). Then, the US will generate user act and user utterance sequentially conditioned on the previous system response, user belief state, and the updated goal state. The resulting US is called GUS and could be modeled as $p_\phi(a_t^u, u_t|r_{t-1}, b_t^u, g_t)$. The GUS parameters are actually another set of GPT-2 parameters, collectively denoted by ϕ.

4.2 GUS Training

The GUS model can thus be trained via finetuning GPT-2 by maximizing the following conditional likelihood over labeled training sequences for supervised learning (SL):

$$\begin{aligned}\mathcal{J}_{\text{US-SL}} &= \log p_\phi(b_t^u|r_{t-1}) \\ &+ \log p_\phi(a_t^u, u_t|r_{t-1}, b_t^u, g_t)\end{aligned} \tag{3}$$

Note that during supervised learning, the user belief state b_t^u is labeled by directly copying the system act a_{t-1}^s from the previous turn.

4.3 Reinforcement Optimization of DS through Interaction with US

RL Setup The DS and US described above will first be trained using supervised learning with the objectives in Eq. (1) and Eq. (3) respectively. After supervised learning, we can perform RL optimization on the DS through interactions with the US. The DS agent view the US as the environment and use its conditional model $p_\theta(b_t^s, a_t^s, r_t|b_{t-1}^s, r_{t-1}, u_t)$ as its policy. Here the policy of the DS involves generating not only system act a_t^s, but also belief state b_t^s and system response r_t. This is different from some previous studies of learning reinforced DS, e.g., (Liu and Lane, 2017; Papangelis et al., 2019; Tseng et al., 2021), which only use RL to optimize the selection of system acts (but all use traditional LSTM seq2seq architectures). However, thanks to the representation power of GPT-2, recursively predict (or say, decide about) b_t^s, a_t^s and r_t in one policy yields the best performance in our experiment. In Section 7.3, we compare different schemes for policy definition for the DS agent with more discussions.

RL Optimization We apply the policy gradient method (Sutton et al., 2000) to optimize the DS for RL. We first let the two agents interact with each other based on the user goals from the goal generator provided by ConvLab-2 (Zhu et al., 2020). Then we calculate the reward R_t for each turn, as detailed below. The return $U_{i,t}$ for the action of turn t at the i-th step is $\gamma^{|A_t|-i}R_t$, where γ is the discounting factor and $|A_t|$ is the policy sequence length of turn t. We update the DS with the following policy gradients:

$$\nabla_\theta \mathcal{J}_{\text{DS-RL}} = \sum_{i=1}^{|b_t^s \oplus a_t^s \oplus r_t|} U_{i,t} \nabla_\theta \log p_\theta(c_i) \tag{4}$$

where $p_\theta(c_i)$ denotes $p_\theta(c_i|b_{t-1}^s, r_{t-1}, u_t, c_{<i})$.

Reward Settings A number of different settings for reward have been studied, as described in the following. The three settings are separately tested, and the experimental results are given in Section 7.2.

1) Success. If a dialog is successful, we set the reward of each turn to 1, otherwise it is set to be 0;
2) A turn-level synthetic reward similar to Tseng et al. (2021); Takanobu et al. (2020), which consists of requesting reward (+0.1 for each), repeating punishment (-0.5 for each) and task completion reward (the proportion of tasks completed) of the DS;
3) A Sigmoid synthetic reward obtained by mapping the synthetic reward to [0,1] interval using the Sigmoid function. This setting is designed to exclude the influence of the value range of reward because the value range is different between the Success reward and the synthetic reward.

5 Experiments

5.1 Dataset

Experiments are conducted on MultiWOZ2.1 (Eric et al., 2020), which is an English multi-domain task-oriented dialog dataset of human-human conversations. It contains 10.4k dialogs, collected in a Wizard-of-Oz setup over seven domains. The dataset contains the annotations of system belief state, system act, and user act for every turn.

5.2 Evaluation Metrics

Evaluating the quality of a US is not trivial. The performance of the reinforced DS trained with a specific US gives an *indirect* assessment of the quality of the US. Considering that a main purpose of developing USs is to help train RL based DSs, this indirect assessment makes sense and is widely employed (Kreyssig et al., 2018; Shi et al., 2019; Lin et al., 2021). We conduct both automatic evaluation and human evaluation of the DSs trained with different USs. Additionally, we also ask human graders to *directly* assess the performance of different USs, by reading and scoring the generated utterances from the USs.

Automatic Evaluation It could be interaction-based or corpus-based. For both manners, we can calculate *Inform* and *Success* for measuring the performance of the DSs. *Inform Rate* measures how often the entities provided by the system are correct. *Success Rate* refers to how often the system is able to answer all the requested attributes by user. *BLEU Score* is used to measure the fluency of the generated system responses when conducting corpus-based evaluation.

Human Evaluation We conduct human evaluation, where human graders are recruited to assess the quality of dialogs generated by the US and the DS trained with it. Similar to Su et al. (2021), for each dialog, the grader will score the conversation on a 3-point scale (0, 1, or 2)[5] by the following 3 metrics for the DS and 2 metrics for the US:

- Success. This metric measures if the DS successfully completes the user goal by interacting with the US;
- DS Coherency (DS-coh). This metric measures whether the system's response is logically coherent with the dialogue context;
- DS Fluency (DS-Flu). This metric measures the fluency of the system's response.
- US Coherency (US-Coh). This metric measures whether the simulator's utterance is logically coherent with the dialogue context;
- US Fluency (US-Flu). This metric measures the fluency of the simulator's utterance.

[5]Three scales (0, 1 and 2) denote three degrees - not at all, partially and completely, respectively.

5.3 Baseline

The DS model is as described in Section 3. We compare GUS with the classic rule-based simulator ABUS (Schatzmann et al., 2007). We use the simulator in the ConvLab-2 (Zhu et al., 2020) toolkit, which provides an instantiation of ABUS on MultiWOZ (Budzianowski et al., 2018), including BERT-based NLU and template-based NLG. The ABUS in ConvLab-2 has a goal generator module, which we use for driving the interaction between the DSs and the proposed GUS. Remarkably, the TUS paper (Lin et al., 2021) has revealed the shortcoming of VHUS (Gür et al., 2018), which performs much worse than ABUS. Also, it is concluded that TUS has a comparable performance to the rule-based ABUS in cross-model evaluation. Thus, in this paper, we mainly compare GUS with ABUS, which is a very strong baseline.

6 Main Results

6.1 Cross-Model Evaluation

Cross-model evaluation is a type of automatic evaluation (Schatztnann et al., 2005) to compare different USs. The main idea is that if the DS trained with a specific US performs well on all USs (not just on the one that the DS was trained with), it indicates the specific US with which the DS was trained is of good quality (realistic), and thus the DS is likely to perform better on real users.

Specifically, we first train a DS and a US separately on training data based on the supervised learning objectives described in Eq. (1) and Eq. (3). The resulting models are referred to as DS-SL and GUS respectively. Then we further optimize DS-SL by policy gradient in Eq. (4) on interaction with either ABUS or GUS, and obtain DS-ABUS and DS-GUS respectively. For either of ABUS and GUS, RL trainings (all starting from DS-SL) are independently taken for three times with different random seeds. Each specific DS model is then tested on both ABUS and GUS. We use the same 1000 randomly generated goals for each test. Further implementation details can be found in Appendix A.2. Table 2 shows the cross-model evaluation results[6].

It can be seen from Table 2 that the DS trained with GUS (DS-GUS) performs well on both ABUS

[6]Similar tables to Table 2 have been used in previous work such as NUS (Kreyssig et al., 2018) and TUS (Lin et al., 2021). A common practice of reading such tables is row-by-row comparison. This is exactly what the cross-model evaluation means.

DS \ US	ABUS		GUS	
	Inform	Success	Inform	Success
DS-SL	0.864	0.791	0.781	0.736
DS-ABUS$_{best}$	0.885	0.816	0.783	0.741
DS-GUS$_{best}$	0.881	0.810	0.864	0.808
DS-ABUS$_{avg}$	0.889	0.793	0.793	0.735
DS-GUS$_{avg}$	0.872	0.801	0.859	0.802

Table 2: Cross-model evaluation results. The subscripts $best$ and avg denote the best and the average from 3 independent RL experiments with different random seeds.

DS	Inform	Success	BLEU	Combined
AuGPT (Kulhánek et al., 2021)	76.6	60.5	16.8	85.4
SOLOIST (Li et al., 2020)	82.3	72.4	13.6	90.9
UBAR (Yang et al., 2021)	83.4	70.3	17.6	94.4
DS-SL	84.10	72.10	19.24	97.34
DS-ABUS$_{best}$	84.20	71.00	19.44	97.04
DS-ABUS$_{avg}$	85.37	69.70	19.10	96.64
DS-GUS$_{best}$	85.70	74.60	19.80	99.95
DS-GUS$_{avg}$	85.17	73.33	19.83	99.01

Table 3: Corpus-based evaluation. Above the dashed line are GPT-2-based results from the official website of MultiWOZ. Below are the results from DS-SL and the DSs trained with ABUS and GUS respectively.

and GUS, while the DS trained with ABUS (DS-ABUS) only performs well on ABUS and achieves much lower Inform and Success when tested with GUS. This indicates the superiority of GUS over ABUS, being more helpful in training reinforced DSs that perform well on both USs. Moreover, DS-GUS also outperforms the supervised baseline (DS-SL) on both USs. This shows the practical benefit brought by training DSs via RL on interaction with the proposed GUS. Such comparison of RL and SL is overlooked in some prior work, as reviewed in Table 1.

6.2 Corpus-based Evaluation

Corpus-based evaluation has become a widely-used type of automatic evaluation to compare different end-to-end DSs. In the context of studying USs, it is relevant to conduct corpus-based evaluation for the following two aspects. First, running testing of the DS trained with a specific US over a fixed testing set of dialogs could be an indirect assessment of the quality of the US. Second, it is possible for the trained DS via RL to achieve high task success and yet not generate human language (Zhao et al., 2019), particularly when the reward is mainly defined to encourage task success. With the fixed testing set, we could calculate BLEU which measures the NLG performance of the trained DS.

We use the standard evaluation scripts from Nekvinda and Dušek (2021) for corpus-based evaluation. The results are shown in Table 3 with some interesting findings. First, the DS trained with GUS (DS-GUS) achieves higher combined score than the DS trained with ABUS (DS-ABUS). This is consistent with the results in Table 2 and again demonstrate the advantage of GUS over ABUS. Second, note that DS-GUS is initialized from DS-SL and further trained via RL on interaction with GUS, and Table 2 shows that DS-GUS improves over DS-SL not only in Inform and Success but also in BLEU. This result indicates that RL training of the DS with GUS does not suffer from the tradeoff problem between policy learning and NLG in offline RL (Zhao et al., 2019)[7], achieving higher success and being faithful to human language. See more discussions in Section 7.3.

6.3 Human Evaluation

We further perform human evaluation of the performances of USs and DSs. For each pair of US and DS, 100 dialogs were gathered, which were scored by 5 human graders. The details of evaluation metrics have been described in Sec. 5.2 and the results are shown in Table 4. For convenience, we refer to the results of each row by the name of the DS in the table. It can seen that the overall performance of DS-GUS is superior over both DS-ABUS and DS-SL. Further, we conduct significance tests by comparing either DS-ABUS or DS-SL with DS-GUS respectively, using the matched-pairs method (Gillick and Cox, 1989) and add a superscript * to the score in the first two rows in Table 4 if the p-value is less than 0.05. All the specific p-values can be seen in Appendix A.4. The results show that DS-GUS significantly improves over DS-SL for Success and US-Coh, while the differences in terms of DS-Coh, DS-Flu and US-Flu are not significant. Moreover, all the human evaluation metrics by DS-GUS are stronger than or equal to those by DS-ABUS. Particularly, DS-GUS significantly outperforms DS-ABUS for DS-Flu, US-Coh and US-Flu. This indicates that GUS is able to generate more coherent and fluent utterances than ABUS. To illustrate this point, we provide some generated dialogues in Appendix A.3.

[7]This problem for offline RL is further studied and alleviated in Lubis et al. (2020).

DS	US	Success	DS-Coh	DS-Flu	US-Coh	US-Flu
DS-ABUS	ABUS	1.71	1.51	1.65*	1.27*	1.30*
DS-SL	GUS	1.73*	1.60	1.85	1.61*	1.88
DS-GUS	GUS	1.84	1.52	1.79	1.75	1.90

Table 4: Human evaluation of the dialogs generated by different DSs and USs. The score with * in the first two rows denotes the difference between this score and the score in the last row (DS-GUS with GUS) is significant (p-value<0.05); otherwise, the difference is not significant (p-value>=0.05).

US	Inform	Success
ABUS	0.863	0.790
GUS	0.825	0.777
GUS w/o GST	0.743	0.502

Table 5: The ablation results about goal state tracking (GST). The DS trained with GUS w/o GST is tested on ABUS, GUS and GUS w/o GST respectively.

Reward	Inform	Success
None	0.781	0.736
Success	0.842	0.787
Synthetic	0.864	0.808
Sigmoid synthetic	0.850	0.780

Table 6: Interaction-based results of testing DS-GUS on GUS under different reward settings, as introduced in Section 7.2. "None" denotes the testing results of DS-SL with GUS, as also reported in the first row in Table 2.

Policy	Inform	Success
$b_t^s \oplus a_t^s \oplus r_t$	0.864	0.808
$a_t^s \oplus r_t$	0.845	0.770
a_t^s	0.848	0.796

Table 7: The ablation experiments of using different policy schemes.

7 Ablation Study

7.1 The Importance of Goal State Tracking

In our GUS model, we use Eq. (2) to update the goal state at every turn. In the section, we consider a variant of GUS, which sets the goal state at all turns to be the initial goal, that is, $g_t = g_0, t = 1, ..., T$, like in Asri et al. (2016); Gür et al. (2018); Papangelis et al. (2019). Such model is referred to as GUS w/o GST, and could be similarly trained according to Eq. (3). Then we train a DS with this US (called "DS-GUS w/o GST") and test it with ABUS, GUS and GUS w/o GST respectively. The results are shown in Table 5. We can see that the Inform and Success rates obtained by "DS-GUS w/o GST" are lower than those by DS-GUS as shown in Table 2, when testing on ABUS and GUS. This indicates the importance of using GST in GUS. Besides, we can see that the results are pretty low when testing on GUS w/o GST. Presumably, this is because GUS w/o GST cannot accurately distinguish the uncompleted part in the complex goal, which will easily cause omission and repetition when generating user acts.

7.2 Different Reward Settings

The results of optimizing DS on GUS using different reward settings are reported in Table 6. It is found that all reward settings achieve better results than supervised baseline (Reward=None) and the synthetic reward setting achieves the best result, which is reasonable since the fine-grained rewards reflect more than simple success rate in terms of the nature of the tasks (Tseng et al., 2021). All RL results in this paper are based on this setting of reward, unless here for ablation study.

7.3 Different Policy Schemes for DS

The policy in RL refers to the probabilistic mapping from states to actions. Previous studies of learning reinforced DS, e.g., (Liu and Lane, 2017; Papangelis et al., 2019; Tseng et al., 2021), mainly employ RL to optimize the policy module, i.e., use system acts for actions. In contrast, the policy of DS-GUS and DS-ABUS involves generating not only system act a_t^s, but also belief state b_t^s and system response r_t, which can be represented as $b_t^s \oplus a_t^s \oplus r_t$, as illustrated in Eq. (4). To compare policy schemes for reinforced DS, we try two other policy schemes when optimizing DS-GUS. The first policy scheme only involves the generation of system act a_t^s and the second one involves the generation of both system act a_t^s and system response r_t. We denote the two policy schemes as a_t^s and $a_t^s \oplus r_t$ respectively. Table 7 shows the interaction results when the DS-GUS trained under different policy schemes is tested with GUS.

It can be seen from Table 7 that using $b_t^s \oplus a_t^s \oplus r_t$ for policy achieves the highest Inform and Success rate. We provide two points, which may explain the advantage of our model in using $b_t^s \oplus a_t^s \oplus r_t$ for RL. First, since the DST, DP and NLG modules in GPT-2 based DS share the model parameters, parameter adjust in one module will affect other modules. Only optimizing DP during RL without considering other modules may mislead other modules. Using

$b_t^s \oplus a_t^s \oplus r_t$ leads to better overall optimization and decision-making. Second, the balance between policy learning and NLG, which was a concern in previous studies when using modular or small-capacity architectures (Zhao et al., 2019), could be relieved, thanks to the high-capacity of GPT-2.

8 Conclusion

In this paper, towards developing an end-to-end trainable US for multi-domains, a generative user simulator (GUS) with GPT-2 based architecture and goal state tracking is proposed and systematically evaluated. We train GPT-2 based DSs and USs and conduct cross-model evaluation, corpus-based evaluation and human evaluation. The results show that the DS trained with GUS outperforms both the supervised trained DS and the DS trained with ABUS. The human evaluation further confirms the superiority of GUS and shows that GUS can generate much more coherent and fluent utterances than ABUS. Moreover, GUS is simple and easy to use, in addition to its strong performance. Hope this work will stimulate further work on developing and using user simulators in the study of building dialog systems.

9 Limitations

There are some limitations of this work. First, due to computational constraints, both the DSs and the USs are experimented based on a distilled version of GPT-2. Studies using larger GPT-2 and other classes of larger PLMs such as T5 (Raffel et al., 2020) would enhance our results in this paper. Second, we only utilize the policy gradient method for RL in this paper. Other advanced RL methods such as proximal policy optimization (PPO) and actor-critic are also worth trying in future work. Those being said, while we agree that experimenting with larger PLMs and more complex RL methods are meaningful, we believe the extensive experiments presented in this paper (cross-model evaluation, corpus-based evaluation, human evaluation, and ablation studies) can well support the evaluations of GUS and should not affect the main finding and contribution of this paper.

References

Layla El Asri, Jing He, and Kaheer Suleman. 2016. A sequence-to-sequence model for user simulation in spoken dialogue systems. In *INTERSPEECH*.

Paweł Budzianowski, Tsung-Hsien Wen, Bo-Hsiang Tseng, Iñigo Casanueva, Ultes Stefan, Ramadan Osman, and Milica Gašić. 2018. Multiwoz - a large-scale multi-domain wizard-of-oz dataset for task-oriented dialogue modelling. In *Proceedings of the 2018 Conference on Empirical Methods in Natural Language Processing (EMNLP)*.

Mihail Eric, Rahul Goel, Shachi Paul, Abhishek Sethi, Sanchit Agarwal, Shuyang Gao, Adarsh Kumar, Anuj Kumar Goyal, Peter Ku, and Dilek Hakkani-Tür. 2020. Multiwoz 2.1: A consolidated multi-domain dialogue dataset with state corrections and state tracking baselines. In *LREC*.

Laurence Gillick and Stephen J Cox. 1989. Some statistical issues in the comparison of speech recognition algorithms. In *International Conference on Acoustics, Speech, and Signal Processing*, pages 532–535. IEEE.

Izzeddin Gür, Dilek Hakkani-Tür, Gokhan Tür, and Pararth Shah. 2018. User modeling for task oriented dialogues. In *2018 IEEE Spoken Language Technology Workshop (SLT)*, pages 900–906.

Ehsan Hosseini-Asl, Bryan McCann, Chien-Sheng Wu, Semih Yavuz, and Richard Socher. 2020. A simple language model for task-oriented dialogue. *arXiv preprint arXiv:2005.00796*.

Florian Kreyssig, Iñigo Casanueva, Paweł Budzianowski, and Milica Gašić. 2018. Neural user simulation for corpus-based policy optimisation of spoken dialogue systems. In *Proceedings of the 19th Annual SIGdial Meeting on Discourse and Dialogue*, pages 60–69, Melbourne, Australia. Association for Computational Linguistics.

Jonáš Kulhánek, Vojtěch Hudeček, Tomáš Nekvinda, and Ondřej Dušek. 2021. Augpt: Dialogue with pre-trained language models and data augmentation. *arXiv preprint arXiv:2102.05126*.

Yohan Lee. 2021. Improving end-to-end task-oriented dialog system with a simple auxiliary task. In *Findings of the Association for Computational Linguistics: EMNLP 2021*, pages 1296–1303, Punta Cana, Dominican Republic. Association for Computational Linguistics.

Baolin Peng Chunyuan Li, Jinchao Li, Shahin Shayandeh, Lars Liden, and Jianfeng Gao. 2020. Soloist: Building task bots at scale with transfer learning and machine teaching. *Transactions of the Association for Computational Linguistics (TACL), 2021*.

Hsien-chin Lin, Nurul Lubis, Songbo Hu, Carel van Niekerk, Christian Geishauser, Michael Heck, Shutong Feng, and Milica Gasic. 2021. Domain-independent user simulation with transformers for task-oriented dialogue systems. In *Proceedings of the 22nd Annual Meeting of the Special Interest Group on Discourse and Dialogue*, pages 445–456, Singapore and Online. Association for Computational Linguistics.

Bing Liu and Ian R. Lane. 2017. Iterative policy learning in end-to-end trainable task-oriented neural dialog models. In *2017 IEEE Automatic Speech Recognition and Understanding Workshop, ASRU 2017, Okinawa, Japan, December 16-20, 2017*, pages 482–489. IEEE.

Hong Liu, Yucheng Cai, Zhijian Ou, Yi Huang, and Junlan Feng. 2022. Building Markovian generative architectures over pretrained LM backbones for efficient task-oriented dialog systems. *ArXiv preprint arXiv:2204.06452*.

Nurul Lubis, Christian Geishauser, Michael Heck, Hsien-Chin Lin, Marco Moresi, Carel van Niekerk, and Milica Gasic. 2020. LAVA: Latent action spaces via variational auto-encoding for dialogue policy optimization. In *Proceedings of the 28th International Conference on Computational Linguistics*, pages 465–479.

Tomáš Nekvinda and Ondřej Dušek. 2021. Shades of BLEU, flavours of success: The case of MultiWOZ. In *Proceedings of the 1st Workshop on Natural Language Generation, Evaluation, and Metrics (GEM 2021)*, pages 34–46, Online. Association for Computational Linguistics.

Alexandros Papangelis, Yi-Chia Wang, Piero Molino, and Gokhan Tur. 2019. Collaborative multi-agent dialogue model training via reinforcement learning. In *Proceedings of the 20th Annual SIGdial Meeting on Discourse and Dialogue*, pages 92–102, Stockholm, Sweden. Association for Computational Linguistics.

Alec Radford, Jeffrey Wu, Rewon Child, David Luan, Dario Amodei, and Ilya Sutskever. 2019. Language models are unsupervised multitask learners. *OpenAI Blog*, 1(8):9.

Colin Raffel, Noam Shazeer, Adam Roberts, Katherine Lee, Sharan Narang, Michael Matena, Yanqi Zhou, Wei Li, and Peter J. Liu. 2020. Exploring the limits of transfer learning with a unified text-to-text transformer. *Journal of Machine Learning Research*, 21(140):1–67.

Victor Sanh, Lysandre Debut, Julien Chaumond, and Thomas Wolf. 2019. Distilbert, a distilled version of bert: smaller, faster, cheaper and lighter. *arXiv preprint arXiv:1910.01108*.

Jost Schatzmann, Blaise Thomson, Karl Weilhammer, Hui Ye, and Steve Young. 2007. Agenda-based user simulation for bootstrapping a POMDP dialogue system. In *Human Language Technologies 2007: The Conference of the North American Chapter of the Association for Computational Linguistics; Companion Volume, Short Papers*, pages 149–152, Rochester, New York. Association for Computational Linguistics.

Jost Schatztnann, Matthew N Stuttle, Karl Weilhammer, and Steve Young. 2005. Effects of the user model on simulation-based learning of dialogue strategies. In *IEEE Workshop on Automatic Speech Recognition and Understanding, 2005.*, pages 220–225. IEEE.

Weiyan Shi, Kun Qian, Xuewei Wang, and Zhou Yu. 2019. How to build user simulators to train RL-based dialog systems. In *Proceedings of the 2019 Conference on Empirical Methods in Natural Language Processing and the 9th International Joint Conference on Natural Language Processing (EMNLP-IJCNLP)*, pages 1990–2000, Hong Kong, China. Association for Computational Linguistics.

Yixuan Su, Lei Shu, Elman Mansimov, Arshit Gupta, Deng Cai, Yi-An Lai, and Yi Zhang. 2021. Multi-task pre-training for plug-and-play task-oriented dialogue system. *CoRR*, abs/2109.14739.

Richard S Sutton, David A McAllester, Satinder P Singh, and Yishay Mansour. 2000. Policy gradient methods for reinforcement learning with function approximation. In *Advances in neural information processing systems*, pages 1057–1063.

Ryuichi Takanobu, Runze Liang, and Minlie Huang. 2020. Multi-agent task-oriented dialog policy learning with role-aware reward decomposition. In *Proceedings of the 58th Annual Meeting of the Association for Computational Linguistics*, pages 625–638, Online. Association for Computational Linguistics.

Bo-Hsiang Tseng, Yinpei Dai, Florian Kreyssig, and Bill Byrne. 2021. Transferable dialogue systems and user simulators. In *Proceedings of the 59th Annual Meeting of the Association for Computational Linguistics and the 11th International Joint Conference on Natural Language Processing (Volume 1: Long Papers)*, pages 152–166, Online. Association for Computational Linguistics.

Ashish Vaswani, Noam Shazeer, Niki Parmar, Jakob Uszkoreit, Llion Jones, Aidan N Gomez, Łukasz Kaiser, and Illia Polosukhin. 2017. Attention is all you need. In *Advances in neural information processing systems*, pages 5998–6008.

Yunyi Yang, Yunhao Li, and Xiaojun Quan. 2021. Ubar: Towards fully end-to-end task-oriented dialog system with gpt-2. In *Proceedings of the AAAI Conference on Artificial Intelligence (AAAI)*.

Steve Young, Milica Gašić, Blaise Thomson, and Jason D. Williams. 2013. Pomdp-based statistical spoken dialog systems: A review. *Proceedings of the IEEE*, 101(5):1160–1179.

Yichi Zhang, Zhijian Ou, Min Hu, and Junlan Feng. 2020. A probabilistic end-to-end task-oriented dialog model with latent belief states towards semi-supervised learning. In *Proc. of the Conference on Empirical Methods in Natural Language Processing (EMNLP)*.

Yichi Zhang, Zhijian Ou, and Zhou Yu. 2020. Task-oriented dialog systems that consider multiple appropriate responses under the same context. In *The Thirty-Fourth AAAI Conference on Artificial Intelligence (AAAI)*.

Tiancheng Zhao, Kaige Xie, and Maxine Eskenazi. 2019. Rethinking action spaces for reinforcement learning in end-to-end dialog agents with latent variable models. In *Proceedings of the 2019 Conference of the North American Chapter of the Association for Computational Linguistics: Human Language Technologies, Volume 1 (Long and Short Papers)*, pages 1208–1218, Minneapolis, Minnesota. Association for Computational Linguistics.

Qi Zhu, Zheng Zhang, Yan Fang, Xiang Li, Ryuichi Takanobu, Jinchao Li, Baolin Peng, Jianfeng Gao, Xiaoyan Zhu, and Minlie Huang. 2020. Convlab-2: An open-source toolkit for building, evaluating, and diagnosing dialogue systems. In *Proceedings of the 58th Annual Meeting of the Association for Computational Linguistics*.

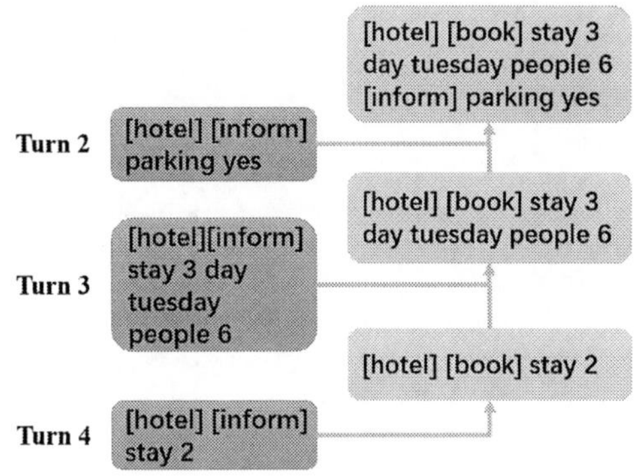

Figure 3: An example of how turn-level goal state annotations are obtained. The blue boxes are user acts and the yellow ones are goal states.

SNG0616	
User	Sorry, actually I need an expensive restaurant in the north. The first on your list would be great.
Bspan	[restaurant] pricerange expensive area north
Act	[restaurant] [inform] name
Resp	Sure how about [value_name]?
Bspan$_{SL}$	[restaurant] pricerange expensive area north food north
Act$_{SL}$	[restaurant] [nooffer] food area [request] food
Resp$_{SL}$	I am sorry, there are no [value_food] restaurants in the [value_area] . Would you like to try a different type of cuisine?
Bspan$_{RL}$	[restaurant] pricerange expensive area north
Act$_{RL}$	[restaurant] [inform] choice price area [request] food
Resp$_{RL}$	There are [value_choice] [value_price] restaurants in the [value_area] . What type of food would you like?

Table 8: One dialog turn in the test set. Bspan and Act denote the sequence forms of belief state and system act. The subscript SL and RL represent the supervised trained model DS-SL and the RL model DS-GUS respectively.

A Appendices

A.1 Data Processing

We delexicalize system responses following Zhang et al. (2020) to reduce surface language variability. Specifically, we replace values in the ontology with specific placeholders such as $[value\_name]$ and $[value\_price]$. The proposed DS and US are both trained on the delexicalized dataset. During human evaluation or interaction with ABUS, the system responses need to be lexicalized. We then replace those placeholders with corresponding values in the predicted entities by querying the given database with the predicted belief states.

For building US, we need to accumulate the annotated user acts backwards turn by turn to obtain the goal state annotation at each turn as we described in Sec 4. The accumulation process is depicted in Figure 3.

A.2 Implementation Details

We use Huggingface Transformers repository. GPT-2 based DSs and USs are initialized with DistilGPT-2 (Sanh et al., 2019), a distilled version of GPT-2, with 6 transformer decoder layer. During supervised learning, we use the AdamW optimizer and a linear scheduler with 20% warm up steps and maximum learning rate 10^{-4}. The minibatch base size is set to be 8 with gradient accumulation steps of 4. During RL, we no longer use scheduler and fix the learning rate to 2×10^{-5}. The minibatch base size is set to be 16 with gradient accumulation steps of 12. For each interaction, the dialog will end in the following three cases: 1) both the DS and US generate `bye` intent; 2) the goal state of the US is empty; 3) the content of the current turn is exactly the same as that of the previous turn. Besides, to increase the diversity of dialogues, beam search decoding is applied during generating user acts and system acts. The beam size is set to be 10 and the final act will be sampled by probability from the 10 candidates. All the SL and RL experiments are conducted on a single 16GB Tesla-P100 GPU.

A.3 Case Study

Interaction Case To illustrate the advantage of GUS over ABUS, we let DS-ABUS and DS-GUS interact with their corresponding USs under the same user goal. The generated dialogs are shown in Table 9. It can be seen that the user utterances generated by ABUS are unlike natural languages and sometimes logically coherent. For instance, ABUS says "I want a train" when it has said "please book the train for me" before in the first turn. On the contrary, GUS can generates very fluent and logically coherent utterances, and is able to understand the system response and provide necessary information to complete the dialogue.

Corpus-based Evaluation Case We can see from Table 3 that DS-GUS improves the Success rate over DS-SL on test set. We show an dialog example in Table 8 to explain how the RL improves the DS performance. In this turn, DS-SL predicts a wrong Bspan with a redundant slot "food" and incorrect value "north". As a result, no entity can be found when querying database and DS-SL generates "nooffer" intent, which finally leads to an unsuccess dialog. However, DS-GUS can predict a correct Bspan and generate an appropriate system act in this turn. This indicates that RL can improve the ability of dialog state tracking of DS, thus improving the success rate. In fact, this advantage

User Goal
Train: Inform (arrive=12:45; day=Thursday; departure=Birmingham new street; destination: Cambridge), Book (people=8)
Attraction: Inform (area=centre), Request (postcode, phone)
Dialogue generated through the interaction between DS-ABUS and ABUS
$user_1$: Please book the train for me. I am departing from Birmingham new street. I want a train leaving on Thursday. I would like to go to Cambridge please.
$resp_1$: There are 19 trains that meet your criteria. What time would you like to leave?
$user_2$: Please pick one for me. I don't care about the leave of the train.
$resp_2$: Tr4235 leaves at 05:40. Would you like me to book it for you?
$user_3$: I want to get there by 12:45.
$resp_3$: Tr4235 arrives at 08:23. Would you like me to book it for you?
$user_4$: I would like 8 tickets please.
$resp_4$: Booking was successful, the total fee is 600.8 pounds payable at the station. Reference number is: 0000002206. Is there anything else I can help you with?
$user_5$: Can you help me plan a trip to see a particular attraction? I'd like something in the centre.
$resp_5$: There are 44 theatre and architecture in the centre of town. What type of attraction are you interested in?
$user_6$: Just select one for me. I don't care about the type of the attraction.
$resp_6$: There are 44 museums in the centre of town. May I suggest Adc theatre ?
$user_7$: Sounds good. Could I get the phone number of the attraction? Can you give me the postcode of the attraction?
$resp_7$: The phone number is 01223300085 and the postcode is CB58AS. Is there anything else I can help you with?
$user_7$: That's all the help I need. Take care. Bye.
$resp_7$: Thank you for contacting us and have a nice day.
Dialogue generated through the interaction between DS-GUS and GUS
$user_1$: I am looking for places to go in the centre of town.
$resp_1$: There are 44 attractions in the centre. Do you have a specific type in mind?
$user_2$: No, I don't have a preference.
$resp_2$: I would recommend Adc Theatre on Park Street. It is free to get in.
$user_3$: That sounds great. Can I get the phone number and postcode?
$resp_3$: The phone number is 01223300085 and the postcode is CB58AS. Is there anything else i can help you with?
$user_4$: I am also looking for a train going to Cambridge.
$resp_4$: Where will you be departing from and what day would you like to travel?
$user_5$: I will be departing from Birmingham new street on Thursday.
$resp_5$: There are 19 trains that meet your criteria. Do you have a preferred departure or arrival time?
$user_6$: I would like to arrive by 12:45. I would like to book for 8 people.
$resp_6$: Booking was successful, the total fee is 600.8 pounds payable at the station. Reference number is: 0000002206.
$user_7$: Thank you so much! that is all I need.
$resp_7$: Thank you for contacting us and have a nice day.

Table 9: Dialogs generated through the interaction between DSs and USs.

comes from the special policy scheme employed in this paper, as discussed in Sec 7.3.

A.4 Significance Test

In Sec. 6.3, we conduct significance tests to show whether the differences between the first two groups and the last group in Table 4 are significant. The p-values are listed in Table 10.

DS	Success	DS-Coh	DS-Flu	US-Coh	US-Flu
DS-ABUS vs DS-GUS	0.065	0.535	0.036	0.000	0.000
DS-SL vs DS-GUS	0.045	0.220	0.273	0.020	0.639

Table 10: Significance tests for human evaluation. We refer to the results of each row in Table 4 by the name of the DS.

Offline-to-Online Co-Evolutional User Simulator and Dialogue System

Dafeng Chi[1,4], Yuzheng Zhuang[4,*], Yao Mu[2,4], Bin Wang[4], Jianzhu Bao[3,4], Yasheng Wang[4],Yuhan Dong[1,*], Xin Jiang[4], Qun Liu[4], Jianye Hao[4]
[1]Tsinghua University, [2]The University of Hong Kong,
[3]Harbin Institute of Technology(Shenzhen) [4]Huawei Noah's Ark Lab
{cdf20@mails,dongyuhan@sz}.tsinghua.edu.cn,
muyao@connect.hku.hk, jianzhubao@gmail.com
{zhuangyuzheng,wangbin158,wangyasheng,Jiang.Xin,qun.liu,haojianye}@huawei.com

Abstract

Reinforcement learning (RL) has emerged as a promising approach to fine-tune offline pretrained GPT-2 model in task-oriented dialogue (TOD) systems. In order to obtain human-like online interactions while extending the usage of RL, building pretrained user simulators (US) along with dialogue systems (DS) and facilitating jointly fine-tuning via RL becomes prevalent. However, joint training brings distributional shift problem caused by compounding exposure bias. Existing methods usually iterative update US and DS to ameliorate the ensued non-stationarity problem, which could lead to sub-optimal policy and less sample efficiency. To take a step further for tackling the problem, we introduce an **O**ffline-to-o**N**line **C**o-**E**volutional (**ONCE**) framework, which enables bias-aware concurrent joint update for RL-based fine-tuning whilst takes advantages from GPT-2 based end-to-end modeling on US and DS. Extensive experiments demonstrate that ONCE builds high-quality loops of policy learning and dialogues data collection, and achieves state-of-the-art online and offline evaluation results on MultiWOZ2.1 dataset. Open-sourced code will be implemented with Mindspore (MS, 2022) and released on our homepage [1].

1 Introduction

Traditionally, task-oriented dialogue (TOD) systems are trained via pipeline approaches by decomposing the task into multiple independent modules (Wen et al., 2017; Chen et al., 2020). Recently, recasting the TOD as a unified language modeling task with leveraging pretrained language model like GPT-2 (Radford et al., 2019) becomes prevailing, which thoroughly avoids the cross-module error accumulation problem in the pipeline approach. However, GPT-2 suffers from exposure bias (He et al., 2019; Zhang et al., 2020a; Arora et al., 2022) problem that the model has never been exclusively exposed to its own predictions during training thus leads to accumulated errors in the output generation process during test. To avoid such problem, leveraging reinforcement learning (RL) could be one of the antidotes (Keneshloo et al., 2020) because the optimization direct relies on its own outputs with rewards (e.g., success rate) as update guidance rather than the ground-truths.

RL requires large amounts of online interactions for training. However, interacting with human users is time-consuming and costly. An intuitive way for establishing communications with an RL-based dialogue system (DS) is training a GPT-2 based user simulator (US) which learns from real data to mimic human behavior (Shi et al., 2019). Such interaction paradigm brings additional exposure bias problem that DS exposed to both unseen input and output distributions. To resolve such problem, prior works extended the usage of RL for online joint fine-tuning (Tseng et al., 2021). However, serving as each other's environment to interact with, joint update makes both US and DS learning under non-stationarity conditions (Liu and Lane, 2017), which is challenging since the need of continuous adaptation of distribution shift (Al-Shedivat et al., 2018) caused by the introduced compounding exposure bias. To be specific, the compounding exposure bias is the deviation due to self-carrying bias and unseen input distribution from the environment in the process of online interactions.

Existing methods usually employ iterative joint update (Fig. 1(a)) to implicitly address the problem of distribution shift along the fine-tuning process. Unfortunately, such paradigm ameliorates the problem by sacrificing sample efficiency and might lead to sub-optimal policy. In order to take a step further for tackling the distributional shift problem, we propose an **O**ffline-to-o**N**line **C**o-**E**volutional (**ONCE**)

[1] https://gitee.com/mindspore/models/tree/master/research/rl/CETOD.

Proceedings of the Towards Semi-Supervised and Reinforced Task-Oriented Dialog Systems (SereTOD), pages 98 - 113
December 7, 2022 ©2022 Association for Computational Linguistics

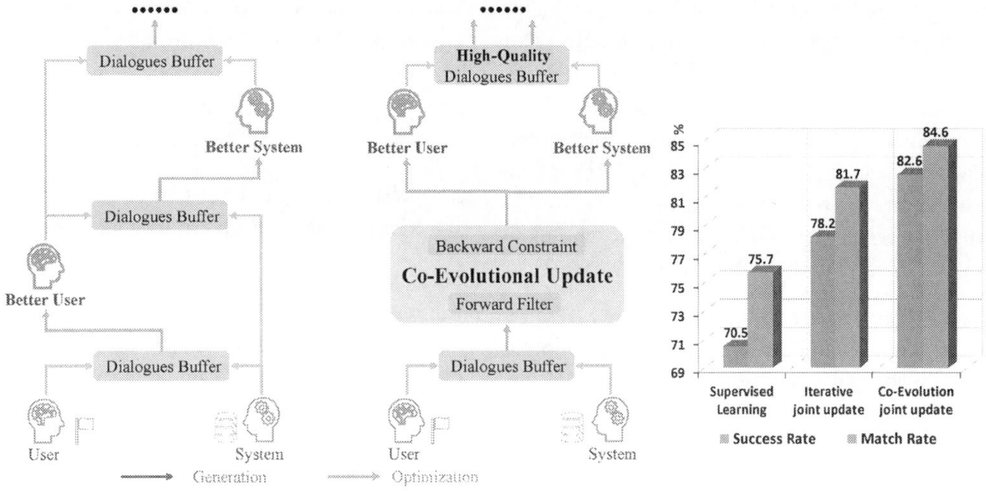

(a) Iterative joint update (b) Co-Evolutional joint update (c) Online evaluation

Figure 1: (a) Iterative joint update usually serial update US first and then update DS, while (b) co-evolutional joint update use the same batch of data to update US and DS simultaneously. The online evaluation results (c) show that our update method is superior to iterative update regarding dialogue success rate and inform rate. The co-evolutional joint update aims to build high-quality loops for policy learning and data collection.

framework, which enables bias-aware concurrent joint update for RL-based fine-tuning with forward filter and backward constraint through the same batch of online data (Fig. 1(b)) whilst takes advantages from GPT-2 based end-to-end modeling on US and DS. The forward filter enables continued training from pretrained models by picking out fatal biased samples via human priors. The backward constraint performs on both US and DS by taking uncertainty of transitions (Yu et al., 2020) into consideration to address the problem of distribution shift by trading off the risk of making mistakes and the benefit of diverse exploration. With such a dual mechanism, we build high-quality loops for policy learning and online data collection as shown in Fig. 1(b). Our contributions can be summarized as follows:

- We propose a novel bias-aware concurrent joint update framework for US and DS policy fine-tuning while ameliorating the distributional shift problem with engaging the components of forward filter and backward constraint.
- ONCE provides end-to-end modeling on US and DS based on GPT-2 with the full ability to understand, make decisions, generate language, and enable naturally joint fine-tuning with the rewards that been explored from both different hierarchical granularity and dialogue sub-task optimization combinations.
- Extensive experiments demonstrate that ONCE outperforms state-of-the-art methods on MultiWOZ2.1 and has achieved 79.0 success rate, 87.5 inform rate and the 101.5 combined score.

2 Related Work

Pretrained language model for US and DS. The approaches of solving TOD have been transformed from traditional pipeline methods (Zhong et al., 2018; Zhang et al., 2019a; Chen et al., 2019) to end-to-end manner (Madotto et al., 2018; Lei et al., 2018; Zhang et al., 2020b; Zhao et al., 2022). With the development of pretrained language models such as GPT-2, GPT-based methods become dominant in TOD, e.g., SimpleTOD (Hosseini-Asl et al., 2020), SOLOIST (Peng et al., 2020), AuGPT (Kulhánek et al., 2021), UBAR (Yang et al., 2021). The literature of US modeling can be roughly summarized into two types: one is rule-based simulation such as the agenda-based user simulator (Li et al., 2016; Shah et al., 2018a), easy to apply but very limited under complex scenarios; the other is data-driven US modeling, (Eshky et al., 2012; Asri et al., 2016; Kreyssig et al., 2018; Shi et al., 2019; Shah et al., 2018a; Zhang et al., 2019b), which is more robust but requires large amounts of manual annotations and system-corresponding data. The most widely used benchmark dataset MultiWOZ (Budzianowski et al., 2018b) have about 8000 dialogues. Smaller datasets such as DSTC2 (Henderson et al., 2014) and M2M (Shah et al., 2018b) contain 1600 and 1500 dialogues respectively. In this work, ONCE leverages GPT-2 for end-to-end modeling of US and DS with MultiWOZ2.1 dataset.

Reinforcement Learning methods in TOD. Reinforcement learning aims to learn optimal policy to maximize long-term cumulative rewards. With different data collecting paradigm for policy update, (Sutton and Barto, 1998) divides RL into online RL and offline RL. Apply offline RL in TOD can avoid explicit construction of US and directly learn from offline dataset (Zhou et al., 2017; Lin et al., 2021; Jeon and Lee, 2022). However, offline RL struggles with a major challenge (Kumar et al., 2020) that it may fail due to overestimation of values caused by distribution shift between dataset and learning policies. Online RL (Gur et al., 2018; Tseng et al., 2021) needs to design a US to interact with DS (acting as their opponent's environment) and generate dialogues data which can be further used for policy optimization. To improve the sample efficiency of deep RL, (Wu et al., 2020) apply model-based RL which incorporates a model-based critic for the TOD system. ONCE builds the framework of US and DS through offline supervised learning (SL) to online RL. The offline stage focuses on building US and DS that communicate using natural language, whereas the online stage optimizes dialogue policy using high-quality generated data.

Joint update of US and DS. The joint optimization scheme for end-to-end US and DS is the most relevant research direction of our work. (Takanobu et al., 2020) follows the idea of multi-agent reinforcement learning, which treats DS and US as two dialogue agents and utilizes role-aware reward decomposition in joint optimization. (Papangelis et al., 2019) learn both US and DS, but only applied in the single-domain dataset (DSTC2). In addition, most of them are based on traditional network architectures LSTM (Liu and Lane, 2017; Tseng et al., 2021), (Liu et al., 2022) firstly build a GPT-2 based trainable US. And in the way of joint update implementation, they (Liu and Lane, 2017; Liu et al., 2022) usually employ iterative joint update to weaken non-stationarity problem, which chooses to fix the system and update user first, and update system after obtaining a better user (Fig. 1(a)). ONCE is a co-evolutional joint fine-tuning framework (Fig. 1(b)) to tackle the distribution shift problem, which ameliorates the compounding exposure bias while ensuring stationarity.

3 Offline Supervised Learning for User Simulator and Dialogue System

To enable our online co-evolutional joint update framework, we first build DS and US via SL on the MultiWOZ2.1 dataset to establish communications via natural language between them. Offline-to-online is a paradigm that leverages online RL to fine-tune offline pretrained models and co-evolutional update was only conducted in the online RL.

3.1 Architecture Design

To simulate the entire dialogue process and information flow in real world, the end-to-end architecture of US and DS is designed as shown in Fig. 2(b). During the training phase, a pretrained language model such as GPT-2 is tuned to produce a conditional generative model. The whole input sequence c_t as described below: for US, the natural language sequential pairs $\{sr, uu\}_{1:t-1}$ of system response sr_t and user utterance uu_t is concatenated with the user's understanding un_t of dialogue history, dynamic goal state g_t, user act ua_t, and current user utterance uu_t, i.e.,

$$c_t^{\text{US}} = \{sr, uu\}_{1:t-1} \oplus un_t \oplus g_t \oplus ua_t \oplus uu_t \quad (1)$$

where $\oplus$ serves as the operation of concatenation, specific details are shown in Fig. 2(b). The natural language sequential pairs $\{uu, sr\}_{1:t-1}$ is highly symmetric for DS and is concatenated with the belief state bs_t, database query result db_t, system act sa_t and current system response sr_t, i.e.,

$$c_t^{\text{DS}} = \{uu, sr\}_{1:t-1} \oplus bs_t \oplus db_t \oplus sa_t \oplus sr_t \quad (2)$$

3.2 Offline Supervised Learning

The training objective of offline supervised learning is the language modeling conditional likelihood objective (Bengio et al., 2000) as shown in Eq. 3:

$$L_{\text{SL}}^{\#} = \sum_{i}^{|C|} \log P(c_i^{\#} | c_{<i}^{\#}) \quad (3)$$

where # denote US or DS, and $|\cdot|$ is the length of sequence, which maximizes the probability of

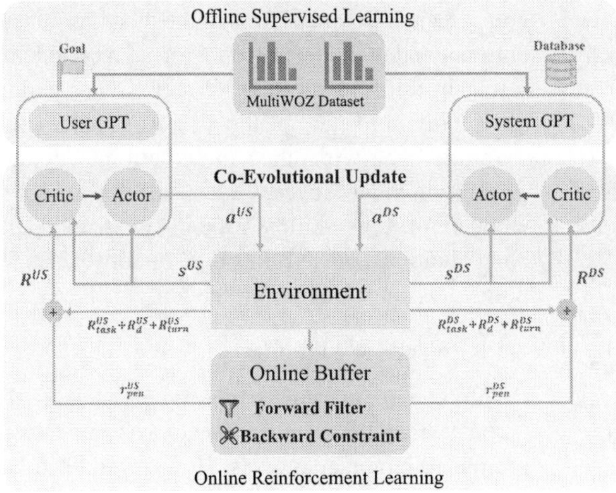

(a) Overall view of framework: ONCE.

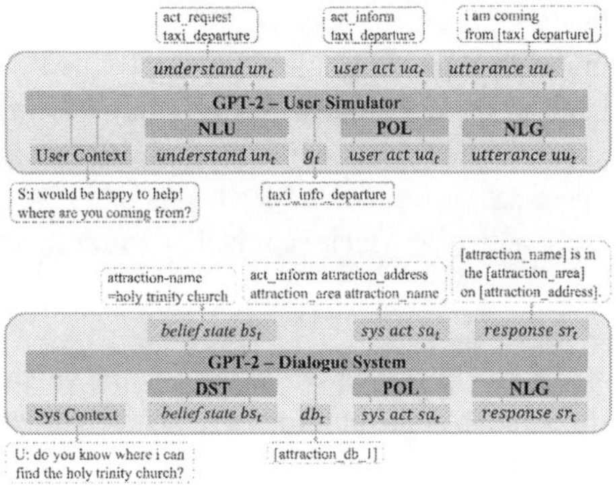

(b) Architecture of US and DS.

Figure 2: (a) The overall view of our framework ONCE. We first obtain US and DS through offline SL and then use online RL and co-evolutional update with forward filter and backward constraint to further optimize dialogue policies. (b) The architecture of our end-to-end (NLU or DST, POL, and NLG) US and DS.

the next word prediction, and it is the same for US and DS. In the online interactive phase, the US generates under the condition of a completed goal and history, while the DS is conditioned on the external database and history. First, they generate an understanding un_t or bs_t of the content based on previous context history. Then the goal state g_t and db_t are added to form a new sequence, lastly producing their corresponding actions ua_t or sa_t and delexicalized responses sr_t or uu_t.

4 Online Reinforcement Learning for User Simulator and Dialogue System

With US and DS obtained from offline learning as policy initialization, co-evolutional updates are performed with forward filter and backward constraint. We present how online RL works and the corresponding hierarchical dense reward settings in the following section.

4.1 Co-Evolutional Joint Update

In TOD tasks, US tries to fully express the entire goal and responds to DS, while DS searches for entities that meet the requirements and replies in accordance with the request of US, finally they complete the dialogue goal successfully; it is essential to joint update which improves coordination and synchronization between US and DS.

In our framework ONCE shown in Fig. 2(a), it is crucial to accelerate online RL using offline learned policies of US π_θ^{US} and DS π_θ^{DS}. However, DS and US tend to express their own perspectives and generate poor quality dialogue data under the existing iterative update paradigm due to distribution shift; detailed examples are illustrated in Appendix B. ONCE improves their dialogue policies by concurrent joint update, which uses the same batch of data generated by the interaction between US and DS every epoch to concurrently optimize dialogue policy.

We apply PPO2 (Schulman et al., 2017) in our online RL framework, which has the advantage of trust region policy optimization (TRPO (Schulman et al., 2015)), and it is easier to implement, more generic, and empirically has better sample complexity. The objective proposed is the following:

$$
\begin{aligned}
L_\pi(\theta^\#) = &\hat{\mathbb{E}}_t[\frac{\pi_{\theta^\#}(a_t|s_t)}{\pi_{\theta^\#_{old}}(a_t|s_t)}\hat{A}_t, \\
&\text{clip}(\frac{\pi_{\theta^\#}(a_t|s_t)}{\pi_{\theta^\#_{old}}(a_t|s_t)}, 1-\epsilon, 1-\epsilon)\hat{A}_t)]
\end{aligned}
\tag{4}
$$

where # denote US or DS, θ is the parameter of the policy network, s_t, a_t is the state and action in the markov decision process (MDP), which are token by token for GPT's input and output of our ONCE, the state is represented by the context of previous dialogue turns, the action is the response generated by the model each turn, and their space is composed of the generated tokens in an orderly manner, ϵ is a hyper-parameter, $\hat{A}_t$ is advantage function, the specific calculation formula can refer to PPO2 (Schulman et al., 2017). In order to fully exploit the performance of GPT-2 without generating redundant parameter models, we treat GPT-2 itself as the actor network for policy learning. To approximate the value function, we connect a small linear network to the hidden layers of GPT-2 as the critic network, which is aimed at minimizing:

$$L_V(\phi^{\#}) = (V_{\phi^{\#}}(s_t) - V_{\#}^{\text{target}})^2 \tag{5}$$

denote US or DS, where $V_{\phi^{\#}}$ is the value function, and ϕ is the parameter of the value network. According to the visualization of data distribution results in Sec. 6, co-evolutional joint update can effectively ameliorate the compounding exposure bias between US and DS, thus preventing policy from falling into the sub-optimal range. Online interaction evaluation in Sec. 5 also demonstrates that it improves the sample efficiency compared to iterative update.

4.2 Forward Filter

During the start stage of online fine-tuning, distribution shift may result in severe bootstrap errors. Updates in an unseen regime can lead to erroneous policy evaluations and arbitrary policy updates may ruin the initial learned policy. To ensure the purity of our dialogue date in online buffer and continued training during the RL phase, a handcrafted rule-based forward filter is applied to pick out fatal dialogues that impact the optimization process: 1) A large number of repetitions of meaningless words appear in the sentence; 2) The key special token representing the start or end of the sequence does not appear; etc. Forward filter plays an important component in our high-quality loop.

4.3 Backward Constraint

We also propose a penalty reward based on the uncertainty of our learned transitions. Referring to the penalty reward of uncertainty in MOPO (Yu et al., 2020), $r_{\text{pen}}^{\#}$ is related to the probability of the generated output token in GPT-2:

$$r_{\text{pen}}^{\#} = \lambda\left(1 - \frac{\sum \mathit{Num}(\mathit{prob} > \mathit{prob}^{\star})}{\sum \mathit{Num}}\right) \tag{6}$$

λ and $prob^{\star}$ are two hyperparameters, $prob^{\star}$ is the artificially set threshold, *Num* represents the number of eligible tokens. In general, the backward constraint is used for dealing with untrusted data. We use the penalty reward mechanisms to guide policy learning and ensure that the data it produces does not end up in untrusted regions. Experimental results in Table 4 indicate that backward constraints are important to state-of-the-art performance.

Intuitively, with the co-evolutional update, greater dialogue success rates can be achieved while improving sample efficiency. As a result, co-evolutional update forms high-quality cycles for policy learning and data collection.

4.4 Reward Assignment

Reinforcement learning methods help to solve the inconsistency between train/test measurements in pretrained language models. However, it becomes difficult for policy learning when RL algorithms take place in an environment where rewards are sparse, so we explore the hierarchical dense reward with different levels of granularity and divide the reward into different levels:

Task Reward R_{task}: the success of the online dialogue is used as the Task Reward R_{task}, which can only be observed at the end of the conversation, and are shared for US and DS. R_{task} serves as the most important motivational signal to facilitate policy learning and performance improvement.

Domain Reward R_d: the success for a domain is defined as Domain Reward R_d, which is also shared for US and DS. In the dialogue of multiple domains, R_d assists in smoothing the process of policy learning at the node of domain conversion.

Turn Reward $R_{\text{turn}}^{\#}$: is designed separately for US and DS, and it can be observed at every turn.

1) US Turn Reward $R_{\text{turn}}^{\text{US}}$ concludes: it provides a new inform about the slot; it asks about a new attribute about an entity; and it correctly replies to the request from the DS side.

2) DS Turn Reward $R_{\text{turn}}^{\text{DS}}$ involves: it requests a new slot; it successfully provides the entity; and it correctly answers all attributes from the US side.

The experimental results show that all the different types of rewards plays an essential role in performance improvement. In summary, the composition of our global reward $R^{\#}$ is as follows:

$$R^{\#} = R_{\text{task}} + R_d + R_{\text{turn}}^{\#} + r_{pen}^{\#} \tag{7}$$

5 Experiments

Dataset. We perform all experiments using MultiWOZ2.1 (Eric et al., 2020), which is currently still widely being used in TOD, and the results published on the official leaderboard are all using Mul-

Model	Pretrained Model	RL-based	Inform Rate	Success Rate	BLEU	Combined Score
SimpleTOD (Hosseini-Asl et al., 2020)	DistilGPT2	w/o	84.4	70.1	15.0	92.3
AuGPT (Kulhánek et al., 2021)	variantGPT-2	w/o	76.6	60.5	16.8	85.4
SOLOIST (Peng et al., 2020)	GPT-2	w/o	82.3	72.4	13.6	90.9
UBAR (Yang et al., 2021)	DistilGPT2	w/o	83.4	70.3	17.6	94.4
PPTOD (Su et al., 2022)	T5models	w/o	83.1	72.7	18.2	96.1
BORT (Sun et al., 2022)	T5-small	w/o	85.5	77.4	17.9	99.4
MTTOD (Lee, 2021)	T5-base	w/o	85.9	76.5	19.0	100.2
GALAXY (He et al., 2021)	UniLM	w/o	85.4	75.7	**19.64**	100.2
MTTOD (Lee, 2021)	T5-base	w/o	85.9	76.5	19.0	100.2
JOUST (Tseng et al., 2021)	LSTM	w	83.2	73.5	17.6	96.0
SGA-JRUD (Liu et al., 2022)	DistilGPT-2	w	85.0	74.0	19.11	98.61
ONCE-DS(Ours)	DistilGPT2	w	**87.5**	**79.0**	18.25	**101.5**

Table 1: Empirical comparison of End-to-End TOD systems models in the official leaderboard. ONCE achieve the state-of-the-art results of Success, Inform and the Combined Score.

tiWOZ2.0/2.1. It is a large-scale multi-domain Wizard of Oz dataset for TOD. There are 3406 single-domain conversations that include booking if the domain allows for that and 7032 multi-domain conversations consisting of at least 2 to 5 domains. Each dialogue consists of a goal, multiple user utterances, and system responses. Also, each turn contains a belief state and a set of dialogue actions with slots for each turn. TOD system is usually defined by an ontology, which defines all entity properties called slots and all possible slot values. Details can be found in the appendix E. The user's understanding works as a reception of DS's output messages, and it's not available in MultiWOZ, we use dst.tar.gz according to JOUST, which is open sourced.

Evaluation Metrics. Three automatic metrics are included to ensure better interpretation of the results. Among them, the first two metrics evaluate the completion of dialogue tasks: whether the system has provided an appropriate entity (*Inform rate*) and then answered all the requested attributes (*Success rate*); while fluency is measured via *BLEU* score (Papineni et al., 2002). Following (Mehri et al., 2019) ,the *Combined Score* performance (Combined) is also reported, calculated as (0.5*(Inform + Success) + BLEU). The overall goal in TOD domain is getting a strong DS, which is achieved by fair Offline evaluation compared to other methods(such as JOUST, SGA-JRUD etc. on the leaderboard). Online evaluation is used to measure the respective method's performance in the joint update process.

Training Procedure. First, we train US and DS with offline supervision on the MultiWOZ2.1 (Eric et al., 2020) dataset, defined as SL-US and SL-DS. We implement our framework with HuggingFace's Transformers (Wolf et al., 2019) of DistilGPT2 (Sanh et al., 2019), a distilled version of GPT-2. Then we collect online interactive data through the communication between SL-US and SL-DS for later RL experiments with the objective Eq. 4 and Eq. 5, and the constructed goal is sampled from the train or dev dataset. Thus we get two co-evolutional update models defined as ONCE-US and ONCE-DS. More details about the experiments and hyper-parameters can be found in Appendix A.

Offline Benchmark Evaluation. We first show the offline benchmark results of different supervised-trained DS in an end-to-end manner in Table 1. All the contents we use are ground truth from the US side; it mainly evaluates the ability of DS. The scripts [2] we strictly followed are released by Paweł Budzianowski from Cambridge Dialogue Systems Group (Budzianowski et al., 2018a; Ramadan et al., 2018; Eric et al., 2020; Zang et al., 2020). Those end-to-end pretrained model-based methods use the dialogue history as input to generate the belief states, actions, and responses simultaneously. Regardless of the type of pretrained model and whether the RL methods are used, ONCE achieves state-of-the-art results: success rate of 79.0, inform rate of 87.5, and combined score of 101.5 points.

Online Interactive Evaluation. In order to verify the effectiveness of our online RL optimization, we let US and DS interact with each other. In this process, the US can only receive the information from the goal and system response, and DS feeds back the entities through the database according to user utterance; there is no ground truth in the

[2]The evaluation code is released at `https://github.com/budzianowski/multiwoz`.

Diversity	SL-US	ONCE-US	SL-DS	ONCE-DS
distinct-1(‰)↑	5.961	**6.249**	4.872	**5.125**
distinct-2(‰)↑	31.848	**32.098**	26.549	**27.617**
Self-BLEU(%)↓	24.722	**21.025**	27.008	**22.161**

Table 2: Results of diversity matrix distinct.

Percentage(%)	SL-US + SL-DS	ONCE-US + ONCE-DS
Success	36.0	**64.0**
US Humanoid	40.0	**60.0**
DS Quality	43.0	**57.0**
Fluency	38.0	**62.0**

Table 3: Results of human evaluation.

process of online interactive dialogues. In addition to DS, this evaluation also indicates the capabilities of the US. Note that we do not show the BLEU score since there is no reference available in online interactions. Some existing methods are not compared here because of the inconsistent evaluation methods (the reason why SGA-JRUD has better performance under online evaluation is that they used different and uncommonly used evaluation scripts (Shi et al., 2019)). The experimental results are shown in Table 4 and Fig. 3.

Under the same test method, the success rate of ONCE is significantly better than JOUST (Tseng et al., 2021), which verifies that our ONCE achieves the purpose of an efficient loop of data collection and policy learning. During the stage of co-evolutional joint update, the bias of US is passed to the DST of DS, resulting in a decrease of inform rate, while JOUST adopts an iterative update method, MADPL is not an end-to-end approach, SGA-JRUD uses different scripts between online and offline evaluation. Table 2 shows the results of distinct-k, which measures the degree of diversity by calculating the number of distinct uni-grams and bi-grams in generated responses. It can be seen that the text generated with our RL optimization is of higher diversity, and A lower Self-BLEU (Zhu et al., 2018) score also implies more diversity of the document.

Human Evaluation. Human evaluation of dialogue quality is performed on the Amazon Mechanical Turk platform to confirm the improvement of our proposed method ONCE. It is to verify that method has improved from SL to RL. We randomly sample 100 dialogues by US and DS, and each dialogue is evaluated by five turkers. Four evaluation indicators involve: **1) Success**: Which interactive dialogue completes the goal of the task more successfully? **2) US Humanoid**: Which US behaves more like a real human user and whether the US expresses the constraints completely in an organized way? **3) DS Quality**: Which DS behaves more intelligently and provides US with the required information? **4) Fluency**: Which dialogue is more natural, fluent, and efficient?

The results of the human evaluation shown in Table 3 are consistent with the results of the online evaluation. DS is more efficient at completing dialogues with our proposed online RL optimization. Furthermore, joint optimization of US can produce behavior more closely resembling that of a human. Improvements under two agents produce a more natural and efficient dialogue flow.

6 Ablation Study

Hierarchical Dense Rewards. A major challenge of putting RL into practice is the sparsity of reward feedback (Rengarajan et al., 2022). As described in Sec. 4.1, we specially design fine-grained dialogue turn reward $R^{\#}_{\text{turn}}$, domain reward R_d and overall task reward R_{task} according to the characteristics of US and DS in TOD. The evaluation results are shown in the second row of Table 4. In Fig. 3(a), we plot the online interaction success rate curve, which is based on different reward settings during online RL optimization.

As we can see from the result, the three types of designed dense rewards all have final positive effects on the success of the task. It is worth noticing that R_{task} plays a major role. The success rate will dramatically drop if there is no R_{task}. R_d and $R^{\#}_{\text{turn}}$ both improve the performance of online and offline evaluation, which indicates the importance of our dense reward for realizing optimal performance.

Choice of RL Policy Scheme. In RL, the policy represents a probabilistic mapping from states to actions. ONCE's framework contains not only reinforced end-to-end DS, but also reinforced the end-to-end US, and their policies include executing action A_t, understanding context U_t, and generating natural language G_t.

We conduct three experiments and their RL policies are $U_t \oplus A_t \oplus G_t$, $U_t \oplus A_t$ and A_t respectively. Based on different policy schemes during online RL optimization, the success rate curves are shown in Fig. 3(b). The best performance results are obtained when only the dialogue policy is optimized, while adding the optimization of the component of understanding and generation does not enhance the success rate. It can be seen from Table 4 that using A_t for policy achieves the highest online evaluation

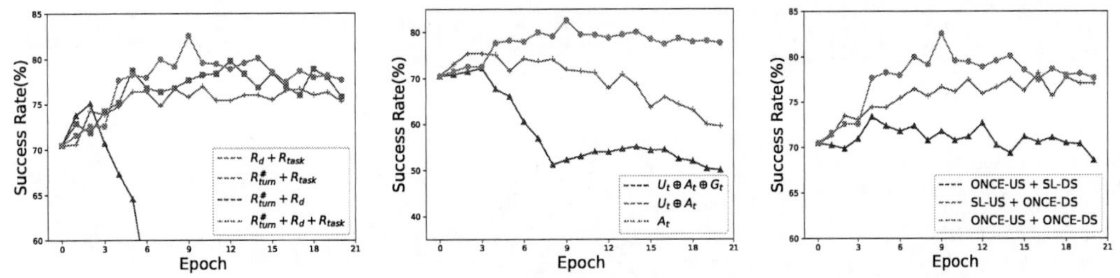

(a) Reward Settings (b) Policy Scheme (c) Update Pattern

Figure 3: Comparative analysis of different combinations of rewards settings, policy schemes and update patterns.

Model	Online Evaluation		Offline Evaluation			
	Inform	Success	Inform	Success	BLEU	Combined
JOUST (Tseng et al., 2021)	**84.6**	73.0	83.2	73.5	17.6	96.0
ONCE-w/o R_{task}	79.9	75.1	82	74.9	18.23	96.68
ONCE-w/o R_d	82.4	76.7	86.6	77.4	17.55	99.55
ONCE-w/o $R^{\#}_{\text{turn}}$	83.2	79.8	86.5	77.2	17.64	99.49
ONCE-[POL = $U_t \oplus A_t \oplus G_t$]	77.5	72.3	83.9	76.5	16.67	98.87
ONCE-[POL = $U_t \oplus A_t$]	80	75.4	84.6	76.5	**18.71**	99.26
ONCE-[SL-US + SL-DS]	75.7	70.5	70.5	69.8	18.1	91.95
ONCE-[ONCE-US + SL-DS]	78.8	73.4	70.5	69.8	18.1	91.95
ONCE-[SL-US + ONCE-DS]	81.7	78.2	85.2	77.4	17.98	99.28
ONCE-[Iterative Update]	82	78.6	85.9	77.2	17.51	99.06
ONCE-w/o R_{pen}	84	80.6	85.5	78	17.8	99.55
ONCE [ONCE-US + ONCE-DS] [POL = A_t], w R_{pen} w R_{task} R_d $R^{\#}_{\text{turn}}$ (Ours)	**84.6**	**82.6**	**87.5**	**79.0**	18.25	**101.5**

Table 4: Empirical comparison of interaction quality of generated dialogues using the 1k test corpus user goals.

results with large margins. In offline evaluation, using A_t also achieves the best results. The reason is that the quality of the policy directly influences the quality of the dialogue, and the generation module generally has an excellent performance in SL. In the case of three modules being optimized simultaneously, the training of the online RL process becomes more trembling and the guidance of reward becomes oblique and falls into sub-optimal.

Validity of Co-Evolutional joint update. The third row of Table 4 demonstrates the effectiveness of co-evolutional update. When we use RL to optimize only US or DS, the performance drops significantly compared with the co-evolutional update. In particular, when we only update the US, the performance improvement is even smaller. We also compare the performance between iterative update and co-evolutional joint update in our ONCE framework, iterative update is lower than ONCE but comparable to SGA-JRUD, especially the success rate and inform rate, which shows that co-evolutional update is efficient and better. The main reason is that the co-evolutional update helps US and DS coordinate with each other and effectively solve the problem of distribution shift. As shown in Fig. 3(c), the online interaction success rate curve based on different reinforced agents during online RL optimization also verifies the conclusion. The iterative update result of ONCE method is shown in Table 4, which is lower than ONCE but comparable to SGA-JRUD, especially the success rate and inform rate, which shows that co-evolutional update is better.

The forward filter helps continued training in the online process. The fourth row of Table 4 demonstrates the effectiveness of our backward constraint. Concretely, the penalty reward help ONCE maximizes a lower bound of the return in the true MDP, careful use of the model in regions outside of the data support, and find the optimal trade-off between the return and the risk (Yu et al., 2020). The forward filter is to filter out poor quality data and ensure the stability of the training in the initial stage. Removing the forward filter will cause severe policy deterioration leading to learning failure.

Visualization of Data Distribution. Following the work of Budzianowski et al. (2018b), as shown in Fig. 4, we calculate and plot the lengths of user act and system act, as well as the dialogue turn length. We compare the results of the original Dataset, supervised learning (SL-US + SL-DS), iterative update, and ONCE (final optimal ONCE-US + ONCE-DS). The visualization shown in Fig. 4 and KL divergence in Table 5 can help us clearly see the exposure bias problem from offline to online. Also, it can be seen that our method can make up for those invisible data parts in the pretrained model and help the learning of strategies.

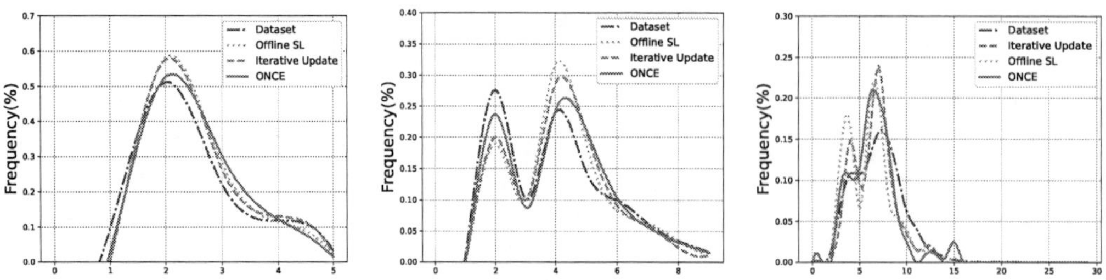

(a) User Act Length (b) System Act Length (c) Dialogue Length

Figure 4: The length of user act and system act, as well as the dialogue turn length.

KL divergence(%)	User Act	System Act	Dialogue
Offline SL	17.48	2.08	11.46
Iterative Update	17.0	2.23	8.76
ONCE	**4.27**	**0.58**	**1.95**

Table 5: Comparison of KL divergence results on user act, system act, and dialogue turn length between generation after different methods and MultiWOZ2.1 dataset.

7 Conclusion and Discussion

Our contribution is that we propose a bias-aware concurrent joint update framework compared to existing RL-based TOD systems, forward filter and backward constraint are modules that make the online RL process more stable and improve the final performance. Compared with the iterative update, concurrent joint update greatly reduces the proportion of manual operations, and optimizes it as an automated process, when terminating the optimization of US or DS is not easy and difficult to balance in iterative update. It performs offline SL on dataset to learn GPT-2-based end-to-end US and DS, both of which possess features of natural language understanding, dialogue policy management, and natural language generation. Then co-evolutional update of their dialogue policies through online RL with the help of forward filter and backward constraint, which takes a step further towards addressing the problem of non-stationarity and distribution shift caused by compounding exposure bias, and greatly improves the sampling efficiency. Finally, we achieved the current state-of-the-art results.

As for future work, ONCE will be applied to more complex dialogues tasks and other scenarios. Although ONCE currently achieves state-of-the-art results, its performance may still be limited by the pretrained language model and online reinforcement learning algorithms, so it will be interesting to explore stronger neural network models or robust RL algorithms. Last but not least, another research direction is to create the US with a variety of personalities to support DS policy learning.

Limitations

Throughout the perspective of distributional visualizations, the problem of distribution shift caused by compounding exposure bias and non-stationarity still persists. However, we have made claims about our desire to take a step further to address it, which can be proved from our experimental results and the gap of distribution between ours and the original dataset is shrunk. Thus we can focus on more effective methods in the future and provide a theoretical basis for solving this problem.

Meanwhile, due to a large amount of parameters of the GPT model, it is difficult and time-consuming to train the two GPT-based US and DS in the online RL process. At the same time, according to the conclusion of optimizing the GPT with different granularity of policy schemes. In future work, we can consider optimizing only parts of parameters of GPT itself to achieve better performance and improve the efficiency of RL algorithms and computing resources.

Ethics Statement

Our method and implementation are based on the existing public dataset MultiWOZ (Eric et al., 2020), without any personal identity and subjective feelings. While our approach has no negative effects on society, we also hope to contribute to the development of task-oriented dialogue. At the same time, we also pay attractive salaries to the turkers of Amazon Mechanical Turk; in addition to thanking them for their assistance in human evaluation, we also want to encourage more scholars to participate and offer part-time job opportunities.

References

2022. Mindspore. Software available from https://www.mindspore.cn/.

Maruan Al-Shedivat, Trapit Bansal, Yura Burda, Ilya Sutskever, Igor Mordatch, and Pieter Abbeel. 2018. Continuous adaptation via meta-learning in nonstationary and competitive environments. In *6th International Conference on Learning Representations, ICLR 2018, Vancouver, BC, Canada, April 30 - May 3, 2018, Conference Track Proceedings*. OpenReview.net.

Kushal Arora, Layla El Asri, Hareesh Bahuleyan, and Jackie Chi Kit Cheung. 2022. Why exposure bias matters: An imitation learning perspective of error accumulation in language generation. In *Findings of the Association for Computational Linguistics: ACL 2022, Dublin, Ireland, May 22-27, 2022*, pages 700–710. Association for Computational Linguistics.

Layla El Asri, Jing He, and Kaheer Suleman. 2016. A sequence-to-sequence model for user simulation in spoken dialogue systems. In *Interspeech 2016, 17th Annual Conference of the International Speech Communication Association, San Francisco, CA, USA, September 8-12, 2016*, pages 1151–1155. ISCA.

Yoshua Bengio, Réjean Ducharme, and Pascal Vincent. 2000. A neural probabilistic language model. In *Advances in Neural Information Processing Systems 13, Papers from Neural Information Processing Systems (NIPS) 2000, Denver, CO, USA*, pages 932–938. MIT Press.

Paweł Budzianowski, Tsung-Hsien Wen, Bo-Hsiang Tseng, Iñigo Casanueva, Ultes Stefan, Ramadan Osman, and Milica Gašić. 2018a. Multiwoz - a large-scale multi-domain wizard-of-oz dataset for task-oriented dialogue modelling. In *Proceedings of the 2018 Conference on Empirical Methods in Natural Language Processing (EMNLP)*.

Pawel Budzianowski, Tsung-Hsien Wen, Bo-Hsiang Tseng, Iñigo Casanueva, Stefan Ultes, Osman Ramadan, and Milica Gasic. 2018b. Multiwoz - A large-scale multi-domain wizard-of-oz dataset for task-oriented dialogue modelling. In *Proceedings of the 2018 Conference on Empirical Methods in Natural Language Processing, Brussels, Belgium, October 31 - November 4, 2018*, pages 5016–5026. Association for Computational Linguistics.

Lu Chen, Boer Lv, Chi Wang, Su Zhu, Bowen Tan, and Kai Yu. 2020. Schema-guided multi-domain dialogue state tracking with graph attention neural networks. In *The Thirty-Fourth AAAI Conference on Artificial Intelligence, AAAI 2020, The Thirty-Second Innovative Applications of Artificial Intelligence Conference, IAAI 2020, The Tenth AAAI Symposium on Educational Advances in Artificial Intelligence, EAAI 2020, New York, NY, USA, February 7-12, 2020*, pages 7521–7528. AAAI Press.

Wenhu Chen, Jianshu Chen, Pengda Qin, Xifeng Yan, and William Yang Wang. 2019. Semantically conditioned dialog response generation via hierarchical disentangled self-attention. In *Proceedings of the 57th Conference of the Association for Computational Linguistics, ACL 2019, Florence, Italy, July 28- August 2, 2019, Volume 1: Long Papers*, pages 3696–3709. Association for Computational Linguistics.

Mihail Eric, Rahul Goel, Shachi Paul, Abhishek Sethi, Sanchit Agarwal, Shuyang Gao, Adarsh Kumar, Anuj Kumar Goyal, Peter Ku, and Dilek Hakkani-Tür. 2020. Multiwoz 2.1: A consolidated multi-domain dialogue dataset with state corrections and state tracking baselines. In *Proceedings of The 12th Language Resources and Evaluation Conference, LREC 2020, Marseille, France, May 11-16, 2020*, pages 422–428. European Language Resources Association.

Aciel Eshky, Ben Allison, and Mark Steedman. 2012. Generative goal-driven user simulation for dialog management. In *Proceedings of the 2012 Joint Conference on Empirical Methods in Natural Language Processing and Computational Natural Language Learning, EMNLP-CoNLL 2012, July 12-14, 2012, Jeju Island, Korea*, pages 71–81. ACL.

Izzeddin Gur, Dilek Hakkani-Tür, Gökhan Tür, and Pararth Shah. 2018. User modeling for task oriented dialogues. In *2018 IEEE Spoken Language Technology Workshop, SLT 2018, Athens, Greece, December 18-21, 2018*, pages 900–906. IEEE.

Tianxing He, Jingzhao Zhang, Zhiming Zhou, and James R. Glass. 2019. Quantifying exposure bias for neural language generation. *CoRR*, abs/1905.10617.

Wanwei He, Yinpei Dai, Yinhe Zheng, Yuchuan Wu, Zheng Cao, Dermot Liu, Peng Jiang, Min Yang, Fei Huang, Luo Si, Jian Sun, and Yongbin Li. 2021. GALAXY: A generative pre-trained model for task-oriented dialog with semi-supervised learning and explicit policy injection. *CoRR*, abs/2111.14592.

Matthew Henderson, Blaise Thomson, and Jason D. Williams. 2014. The second dialog state tracking challenge. In *Proceedings of the SIGDIAL 2014 Conference, The 15th Annual Meeting of the Special Interest Group on Discourse and Dialogue, 18-20 June 2014, Philadelphia, PA, USA*, pages 263–272. The Association for Computer Linguistics.

Ehsan Hosseini-Asl, Bryan McCann, Chien-Sheng Wu, Semih Yavuz, and Richard Socher. 2020. A simple language model for task-oriented dialogue. In *Advances in Neural Information Processing Systems*, volume 33, pages 20179–20191. Curran Associates, Inc.

Hyunmin Jeon and Gary Geunbae Lee. 2022. DORA: towards policy optimization for task-oriented dialogue system with efficient context. *Comput. Speech Lang.*, 72:101310.

Yaser Keneshloo, Tian Shi, Naren Ramakrishnan, and Chandan K. Reddy. 2020. Deep reinforcement learning for sequence-to-sequence models. *IEEE Trans. Neural Networks Learn. Syst.*, 31(7):2469–2489.

Florian Kreyssig, Iñigo Casanueva, Pawel Budzianowski, and Milica Gasic. 2018. Neural user simulation for corpus-based policy optimisation of spoken dialogue systems. In *Proceedings of the 19th Annual SIGdial Meeting on Discourse and Dialogue, Melbourne, Australia, July 12-14, 2018*, pages 60–69. Association for Computational Linguistics.

Jonás Kulhánek, Vojtech Hudecek, Tomás Nekvinda, and Ondrej Dusek. 2021. Augpt: Dialogue with pre-trained language models and data augmentation. *CoRR*, abs/2102.05126.

Aviral Kumar, Aurick Zhou, George Tucker, and Sergey Levine. 2020. Conservative q-learning for offline reinforcement learning. In *Advances in Neural Information Processing Systems 33: Annual Conference on Neural Information Processing Systems 2020, NeurIPS 2020, December 6-12, 2020, virtual.*

Yohan Lee. 2021. Improving end-to-end task-oriented dialog system with A simple auxiliary task. In *Findings of the Association for Computational Linguistics: EMNLP 2021, Virtual Event / Punta Cana, Dominican Republic, 16-20 November, 2021*, pages 1296–1303. Association for Computational Linguistics.

Wenqiang Lei, Xisen Jin, Min-Yen Kan, Zhaochun Ren, Xiangnan He, and Dawei Yin. 2018. Sequicity: Simplifying task-oriented dialogue systems with single sequence-to-sequence architectures. In *Proceedings of the 56th Annual Meeting of the Association for Computational Linguistics, ACL 2018, Melbourne, Australia, July 15-20, 2018, Volume 1: Long Papers*, pages 1437–1447. Association for Computational Linguistics.

Xiujun Li, Zachary C. Lipton, Bhuwan Dhingra, Lihong Li, Jianfeng Gao, and Yun-Nung Chen. 2016. A user simulator for task-completion dialogues. *CoRR*, abs/1612.05688.

Zichuan Lin, Jing Huang, Bowen Zhou, Xiaodong He, and Tengyu Ma. 2021. Joint system-wise optimization for pipeline goal-oriented dialog system. *CoRR*, abs/2106.04835.

Bing Liu and Ian R. Lane. 2017. Iterative policy learning in end-to-end trainable task-oriented neural dialog models. In *2017 IEEE Automatic Speech Recognition and Understanding Workshop, ASRU 2017, Okinawa, Japan, December 16-20, 2017*, pages 482–489. IEEE.

Hong Liu, Zhijian Ou, Yi Huang, and Junlan Feng. 2022. Jointly Reinforced User Simulator and Task-oriented Dialog System with Simplified Generative Architecture. *arXiv e-prints*, page arXiv:2210.06706.

Andrea Madotto, Chien-Sheng Wu, and Pascale Fung. 2018. Mem2seq: Effectively incorporating knowledge bases into end-to-end task-oriented dialog systems. In *Proceedings of the 56th Annual Meeting of the Association for Computational Linguistics, ACL 2018, Melbourne, Australia, July 15-20, 2018, Volume 1: Long Papers*, pages 1468–1478. Association for Computational Linguistics.

Shikib Mehri, Tejas Srinivasan, and Maxine Eskénazi. 2019. Structured fusion networks for dialog. In *Proceedings of the 20th Annual SIGdial Meeting on Discourse and Dialogue, SIGdial 2019, Stockholm, Sweden, September 11-13, 2019*, pages 165–177. Association for Computational Linguistics.

Alexandros Papangelis, Yi-Chia Wang, Piero Molino, and Gökhan Tür. 2019. Collaborative multi-agent dialogue model training via reinforcement learning. In *Proceedings of the 20th Annual SIGdial Meeting on Discourse and Dialogue, SIGdial 2019, Stockholm, Sweden, September 11-13, 2019*, pages 92–102. Association for Computational Linguistics.

Kishore Papineni, Salim Roukos, Todd Ward, and Wei-Jing Zhu. 2002. Bleu: a method for automatic evaluation of machine translation. In *Proceedings of the 40th Annual Meeting of the Association for Computational Linguistics, July 6-12, 2002, Philadelphia, PA, USA*, pages 311–318. ACL.

Baolin Peng, Chunyuan Li, Jinchao Li, Shahin Shayandeh, Lars Liden, and Jianfeng Gao. 2020. SOLOIST: few-shot task-oriented dialog with A single pre-trained auto-regressive model. *CoRR*, abs/2005.05298.

Alec Radford, Jeff Wu, Rewon Child, David Luan, Dario Amodei, and Ilya Sutskever. 2019. Language models are unsupervised multitask learners.

Osman Ramadan, Paweł Budzianowski, and Milica Gasic. 2018. Large-scale multi-domain belief tracking with knowledge sharing. In *Proceedings of the 56th Annual Meeting of the Association for Computational Linguistics*, volume 2, pages 432–437.

Desik Rengarajan, Gargi Vaidya, Akshay Sarvesh, Dileep M. Kalathil, and Srinivas Shakkottai. 2022. Reinforcement learning with sparse rewards using guidance from offline demonstration. *CoRR*, abs/2202.04628.

Victor Sanh, Lysandre Debut, Julien Chaumond, and Thomas Wolf. 2019. Distilbert, a distilled version of BERT: smaller, faster, cheaper and lighter. *CoRR*, abs/1910.01108.

John Schulman, Sergey Levine, Pieter Abbeel, Michael I. Jordan, and Philipp Moritz. 2015. Trust region policy optimization. In *Proceedings of the 32nd International Conference on Machine Learning, ICML 2015, Lille, France, 6-11 July 2015*, volume 37 of *JMLR Workshop and Conference Proceedings*, pages 1889–1897. JMLR.org.

John Schulman, Filip Wolski, Prafulla Dhariwal, Alec Radford, and Oleg Klimov. 2017. Proximal policy optimization algorithms. *CoRR*, abs/1707.06347.

Pararth Shah, Dilek Hakkani-Tür, Bing Liu, and Gökhan Tür. 2018a. Bootstrapping a neural conversational agent with dialogue self-play, crowdsourcing and on-line reinforcement learning. In *Proceedings of the 2018 Conference of the North American Chapter of the Association for Computational Linguistics: Human Language Technologies, NAACL-HLT 2018, New Orleans, Louisiana, USA, June 1-6, 2018, Volume 3 (Industry Papers)*, pages 41–51. Association for Computational Linguistics.

Pararth Shah, Dilek Hakkani-Tür, Gökhan Tür, Abhinav Rastogi, Ankur Bapna, Neha Nayak, and Larry P. Heck. 2018b. Building a conversational agent overnight with dialogue self-play. *CoRR*, abs/1801.04871.

Weiyan Shi, Kun Qian, Xuewei Wang, and Zhou Yu. 2019. How to build user simulators to train rl-based dialog systems. In *Proceedings of the 2019 Conference on Empirical Methods in Natural Language Processing and the 9th International Joint Conference on Natural Language Processing, EMNLP-IJCNLP 2019, Hong Kong, China, November 3-7, 2019*, pages 1990–2000. Association for Computational Linguistics.

Yixuan Su, Lei Shu, Elman Mansimov, Arshit Gupta, Deng Cai, Yi-An Lai, and Yi Zhang. 2022. Multi-task pre-training for plug-and-play task-oriented dialogue system. In *Proceedings of the 60th Annual Meeting of the Association for Computational Linguistics (Volume 1: Long Papers), ACL 2022, Dublin, Ireland, May 22-27, 2022*, pages 4661–4676. Association for Computational Linguistics.

Haipeng Sun, Junwei Bao, Youzheng Wu, and Xiaodong He. 2022. BORT: back and denoising reconstruction for end-to-end task-oriented dialog. *CoRR*, abs/2205.02471.

Richard S. Sutton and Andrew G. Barto. 1998. *Reinforcement learning - an introduction*. Adaptive computation and machine learning. MIT Press.

Ryuichi Takanobu, Runze Liang, and Minlie Huang. 2020. Multi-agent task-oriented dialog policy learning with role-aware reward decomposition. In *Proceedings of the 58th Annual Meeting of the Association for Computational Linguistics, ACL 2020, Online, July 5-10, 2020*, pages 625–638. Association for Computational Linguistics.

Bo-Hsiang Tseng, Yinpei Dai, Florian Kreyssig, and Bill Byrne. 2021. Transferable dialogue systems and user simulators. In *Proceedings of the 59th Annual Meeting of the Association for Computational Linguistics and the 11th International Joint Conference on Natural Language Processing, ACL/IJCNLP 2021, (Volume 1: Long Papers), Virtual Event, August 1-6, 2021*, pages 152–166. Association for Computational Linguistics.

Tsung-Hsien Wen, Yishu Miao, Phil Blunsom, and Steve J. Young. 2017. Latent intention dialogue models. In *Proceedings of the 34th International Conference on Machine Learning, ICML 2017, Sydney, NSW, Australia, 6-11 August 2017*, volume 70 of *Proceedings of Machine Learning Research*, pages 3732–3741. PMLR.

Thomas Wolf, Lysandre Debut, Victor Sanh, Julien Chaumond, Clement Delangue, Anthony Moi, Pierric Cistac, Tim Rault, Rémi Louf, Morgan Funtowicz, and Jamie Brew. 2019. Huggingface's transformers: State-of-the-art natural language processing. *CoRR*, abs/1910.03771.

Yen-Chen Wu, Bo-Hsiang Tseng, and Milica Gasic. 2020. Actor-double-critic: Incorporating model-based critic for task-oriented dialogue systems. In *Findings of the Association for Computational Linguistics: EMNLP 2020, Online Event, 16-20 November 2020*, volume EMNLP 2020 of *Findings of ACL*, pages 854–863. Association for Computational Linguistics.

Yunyi Yang, Yunhao Li, and Xiaojun Quan. 2021. UBAR: towards fully end-to-end task-oriented dialog system with GPT-2. In *Thirty-Fifth AAAI Conference on Artificial Intelligence, AAAI 2021, Thirty-Third Conference on Innovative Applications of Artificial Intelligence, IAAI 2021, The Eleventh Symposium on Educational Advances in Artificial Intelligence, EAAI 2021, Virtual Event, February 2-9, 2021*, pages 14230–14238. AAAI Press.

Tianhe Yu, Garrett Thomas, Lantao Yu, Stefano Ermon, James Y. Zou, Sergey Levine, Chelsea Finn, and Tengyu Ma. 2020. MOPO: model-based offline policy optimization. In *Advances in Neural Information Processing Systems 33: Annual Conference on Neural Information Processing Systems 2020, NeurIPS 2020, December 6-12, 2020, virtual.*

Xiaoxue Zang, Abhinav Rastogi, Srinivas Sunkara, Raghav Gupta, Jianguo Zhang, and Jindong Chen. 2020. Multiwoz 2.2: A dialogue dataset with additional annotation corrections and state tracking baselines. In *Proceedings of the 2nd Workshop on Natural Language Processing for Conversational AI, ACL 2020*, pages 109–117.

Ranran Haoran Zhang, Qianying Liu, Aysa Xuemo Fan, Heng Ji, Daojian Zeng, Fei Cheng, Daisuke Kawahara, and Sadao Kurohashi. 2020a. Minimize exposure bias of seq2seq models in joint entity and relation extraction. In *Findings of the Association for Computational Linguistics: EMNLP 2020, Online Event, 16-20 November 2020*, volume EMNLP 2020 of *Findings of ACL*, pages 236–246. Association for Computational Linguistics.

Yichi Zhang, Zhijian Ou, and Zhou Yu. 2020b. Task-oriented dialog systems that consider multiple appropriate responses under the same context. In *The Thirty-Fourth AAAI Conference on Artificial Intelligence, AAAI 2020, The Thirty-Second Innovative Applications of Artificial Intelligence Conference, IAAI*

2020, The Tenth AAAI Symposium on Educational Advances in Artificial Intelligence, EAAI 2020, New York, NY, USA, February 7-12, 2020, pages 9604–9611. AAAI Press.

Zheng Zhang, Lizi Liao, Minlie Huang, Xiaoyan Zhu, and Tat-Seng Chua. 2019a. Neural multimodal belief tracker with adaptive attention for dialogue systems. In *The World Wide Web Conference, WWW 2019, San Francisco, CA, USA, May 13-17, 2019*, pages 2401–2412. ACM.

Zhirui Zhang, Xiujun Li, Jianfeng Gao, and Enhong Chen. 2019b. Budgeted policy learning for task-oriented dialogue systems. *CoRR*, abs/1906.00499.

Xinyan Zhao, Bin He, Yasheng Wang, Yitong Li, Fei Mi, Yajiao Liu, Xin Jiang, Qun Liu, and Huanhuan Chen. 2022. Unids: A unified dialogue system for chit-chat and task-oriented dialogues. In *Proceedings of the Second DialDoc Workshop on Document-grounded Dialogue and Conversational Question Answering, DialDoc@ACL 2022, Dublin, Ireland, May 26, 2022*, pages 13–22. Association for Computational Linguistics.

Victor Zhong, Caiming Xiong, and Richard Socher. 2018. Global-locally self-attentive encoder for dialogue state tracking. In *Proceedings of the 56th Annual Meeting of the Association for Computational Linguistics, ACL 2018, Melbourne, Australia, July 15-20, 2018, Volume 1: Long Papers*, pages 1458–1467. Association for Computational Linguistics.

Li Zhou, Kevin Small, Oleg Rokhlenko, and Charles Elkan. 2017. End-to-end offline goal-oriented dialog policy learning via policy gradient. *CoRR*, abs/1712.02838.

Yaoming Zhu, Sidi Lu, Lei Zheng, Jiaxian Guo, Weinan Zhang, Jun Wang, and Yong Yu. 2018. Texygen: A benchmarking platform for text generation models. In *The 41st International ACM SIGIR Conference on Research & Development in Information Retrieval, SIGIR 2018, Ann Arbor, MI, USA, July 08-12, 2018*, pages 1097–1100. ACM.

A Training Details

We implement US and DS models with Huggingface Transformers repository of version 4.2.2. We initialize it with DistilGPT-2, a distilled version of GPT-2. During offline supervised learning, the minibatch base size is set to be 2 with gradient accumulation steps of 16, we use AdamW optimizer and a linear scheduler with 20 warm up steps and maximum learning rate 1×10^{-4}, and the gradient clip is set to be 5. The total epochs are 30 (it takes about 20 hours on NVIDIA Tesla 2V100-SXM2-32GB) and we select the best model on the test set.

In the stage of online RL, we connect three linear layers (768*512 $\rightarrow$ ReLU $\rightarrow$ 512*512 $\rightarrow$ ReLU$\rightarrow$512*1) as our value network. The learning rate of policy and value are 1×10^{-6} and 5×10^{-6} respectively. The batch size for RL optimization is 4, and the hyper-parameters is PPO2: γ is 0.99, ϵ is 0.1 and τ is 0.95. Two important hyper-parameters in policy constraint λ we set to be 0.75 and the probability threshold is 0.9. The replay buffer size of our algorithm is 200. The whole RL optimized epoch is 20 (it takes about 4 hours on a single NVIDIA Tesla V100-SXM2-32GB), we will evaluate the online interaction quality after every epoch (about 1 hour) and choose the excellent model for offline evaluation (about 40 min).

The reward setting of our framework: Task Reward R_{task}, Domain Reward R_d and Turn Reward $R^{\#}_{\text{turn}}$ are listed in Table 6:

Reward Type	Success	Failure
R_{task}	20	-10
R_d	5	-5
User $R^{\#}_{\text{turn}}$	0 0 0	-1 -1 -1
System $R^{\#}_{\text{turn}}$	0 0 0	-2.5 -1 -2.5

Table 6: Reward setting of our online RL experiment.

B Examples of Bad Case

After offline supervised learning to obtain US and DS with dialogue ability, when we let them interact online, we will find that there are some problems in the dialogue, we regard it as low-quality data, of which the first type is to generate too much Tokens that are too long or redundantly repeated, and the second category is a token that does not generate the key to indicate the start or end of the sequence. These two types of data are shown in the Table 8:

C Examples of Improvement from RL

In order to demonstrate the effectiveness of the RL method, we show in Table 7 the DS obtained based on supervised learning and the DS after RL optimization with different feed backs for the input of the same goal and US. We enumerate the original failed dialogues and the successful dialogues after policy optimization.

	MUL0072.json
$Utter$	yes, i also need a hotel room with free wifi also in [$hotel\_area$], [$hotel\_stars$] star, and [$hotel\_pricerange$] please.
Act	act_inform hotel_name act_offerbook hotel_none
$Resp$	the [$hotel\_name$] meets your requirement -s. would you like me to book this for you?
Act_{SL}	act_inform hotel_choice act_request hotel_area
$Resp_{SL}$	there are [$value\_count$] hotel -s that meet your criteria. is there a certain area you would like to stay in?
Act_{RL}	act_inform hotel_choice hotel_internet hotel_name hotel_name hotel_name hotel_pricerange hotel_stars hotel_type act_offerbook hotel_none
$Resp_{RL}$	there are [$value\_count$] hotel -s that meet your criteria [$hotel\_name$], [$hotel\_name$], [$hotel\_name$], [$hotel\_name$], and [$hotel\_name$]. would you like to book [$value\_count$] of these?
	MUL0116.json
$Utter$	yes, i am looking for a [$restaurant\_pricerange$] -ly priced restaurant with [$restaurant\_food$] food.
Act	act_offerbook restaurant_none act_recommend restaurant_name
$Resp$	i can recommend [$restaurant\_name$]. would you like to book a table with them?
Act_{SL}	act_inform restaurant_area restaurant_choice restaurant_food restaurant_pricerange act_request restaurant_food
$Resp_{SL}$	i have [$value\_count$] [$restaurant\_pricerange$] [$restaurant\_food$] restaurant -s in the [$restaurant\_area$]. do you have a preferred area of town?
Act_{RL}	act_inform restaurant_name act_offerbook restaurant_none
$Resp_{RL}$	[$restaurant\_name$] fits your criteria. would you like me to book a table for you?

Table 7: Example of RL improvement.

D Examples of Diversity

Through the observation of online interactive dialogue, we can find that RL helps our model has the ability to generate richer dialog action. At the same time, our natural language generation is also richer and more diverse. We enumerate examples of which are shown in the Table 9, which also

Bad Type	Examples
Redundant sequence	• $< sos\_sa >$ [*act_inform*] [*attraction_type*] [*attraction_type*] [*attraction_type*] [*act_request*] [*attraction_type*] $< eos\_sa >$ $< sos\_sr >$ what type of attraction are you looking for? in the south, we have [*attraction_type*], [*attraction_type*], [*attraction_type*],[*attraction_type*],[*attraction_type*], ,[*attraction_type*] [*attraction_type*],[*attraction_type*],[*attraction_type*], [*attraction_type*], [*attraction_type*],[*attraction_type*],[*attraction_type*],and [*attraction_type*]. [*attraction_type*], if you tell me what you are looking for, we can narrow it • $<sos\_sa>$ [*act_inform*] [*hotel_area*] [*hotel_area*] [*hotel_area*] [*hotel_choice*] [*hotel_choice*] [*hotel_choice*] [*hotel_choice*] [*hotel_choice*] [*hotel_choice*] [*hotel_stars*] [*hotel_stars*] [*hotel_stars*] [*hotel_stars*] [*hotel_stars*] [*hotel_stars*] [*hotel_stars*] [*hotel_stars*] [*hotel_stars*] [*hotel_stars*] [*hotel_stars*][*hotel_stars*] [*hotel_stars*] [*hotel_stars*] [*hotel_stars*] [*hotel_stars*][*hotel_stars*] [*hotel_stars*] [*hotel_stars*]
No key special token	• $< sos\_ua >$ [*act_inform*] [*hotel_area*] [*hotel_stars*] star hotel -s in the [*hotel_area*]. $<eos\_uu>$ • $< sos\_ua >$ [*act_inform*] [*hotel_area*] [*hotel_stars*] star hotel -s in the [*hotel_area*]. $<eos\_uu>$ • $< sos\_ua >$ with free parking and wifi? $<eos\_uu>$ • $< sos\_ua >$ [*act_inform*] [*attraction_address*] [*attraction_area*] [*attraction_fee*] [*value_price*] pounds to enter. $<eos\_sr>$

Table 8: Low quality data in our online generation.

	SNG01290.json
$Utter_{GT}$	i am interesting in info about [hotel_stars] star hotel -s and such that offer free wifi.
$Resp_{GT}$	i have [value_count] hotel -s that match the description of [hotel_stars] star rating -s. are you looking for a hotel in the centre or south area?
$Utter1$	i am looking for a [hotel_pricerange] hotel with free wifi.
$Resp1$	i have [value_count] [hotel_pricerange] hotel -s with free wifi. is there a specific area you would like to stay in?
$Utter2$	i am looking for a [hotel_pricerange] place to stay with free wifi.
$Resp2$	i have [value_count] [hotel_pricerange] hotel -s with free wifi. is there a particular area you would like to stay in?
$Utter_{GT}$	the location does not matter so long as it has free wifi
$Resp_{GT}$	[hotel_name] is supposed to be great and it offers free wifi. would you like me to book you a room?
$Utter1$	i would like to stay in the centre of town, and i am open to place -s that have a [hotel_stars] star rating.
$Resp1$	[hotel_name] meets your criteria. would you like to book a room?
$Utter2$	i would like to stay in a hotel with a [hotel_stars] star rating please.
$Resp2$	i have [value_count] options for you to choose from. do you prefer a certain area of town?
$Utter_{GT}$	book it for [hotel_people] people and [hotel_stay] nights starting from [hotel_day].
$Resp_{GT}$	sorry, it looks like the hotel cannot accommodate you for that amount of time.
$Utter1$	yes, please. i need it for [hotel_stay] nights starting on [hotel_day]. there will be [hotel_people] people.
$Resp1$	booking was successful. reference number is [hotel_reference]. is there anything else i can help you with?
$Utter2$	no, i do not have a preference. i just need to book it for [value_count] people staying for [value_count] nights.
$Resp2$	i have booked you at the [hotel_name]. your reference number is [hotel_reference]. is there anything else i can help you with?
$Utter_{GT}$	perhaps starting [hotel_day] instead?
$Resp_{GT}$	great, your reference number is [hotel_reference]. is there anything else i can help with?
$Utter1$	no, that s all i need. thank you for your help.
$Resp1$	thank you for using our system!
$Utter2$	no, that s all i need. thank you!
$Resp2$	thank you for using our service. goodbye.!
$Utter_{GT}$	no that s it all. thanks for your help.
$Resp_{GT}$	wonderful. glad to help.
$Utter1$	
$Resp1$	
$Utter2$	
$Resp2$	

Table 9: Example of diversity.

explains why the BLEU value drops in our experiments.

E Ontology

The ontology defines all entity properties called slots and all possible values for each slot, which concludes goal slot, act slot and belief state slot, special token conclude the start and end token of sentences or actions, database query result and padding token. Special tokens and ontology are illustrated as shown in Table 10.

Type	Representations
Goal Slot Tokens	'restaurant_info_area', 'restaurant_info_food', 'restaurant_info_name', 'restaurant_info_pricerange','restaurant_book_day', 'restaurant_book_people', 'restaurant_book_time', 'restaurant_reqt_address', 'restaurant_reqt_area', 'restaurant_reqt_food', 'restaurant_reqt_phone', 'restaurant$_r$eqt$_p$ostcode', 'restaurant_reqt_pricerange', 'hotel_info_area', 'hotel_info_internet', 'hotel_info_name', 'hotel_info_parking', 'hotel_info_pricerange', 'hotel_info_stars', 'hotel_info_type', 'hotel_book_day', 'hotel_book_people', 'hotel_reqt_type', 'hotel_book_stay', 'hotel_reqt_address', 'hotel_reqt_area', 'hotel_reqt_internet', 'hotel_reqt_parking', 'hotel_reqt_phone', 'hotel_reqt_postcode', 'hotel_reqt_pricerange', 'hotel_reqt_stars', 'attraction_info_area', 'attraction_info_name', 'attraction_info_type', 'attraction_reqt_address', 'attraction_reqt_area', 'attraction_reqt_fee', 'attraction_reqt_phone', 'attraction_reqt_postcode′, 'attraction_reqt_type', 'train_info_arriveBy', 'train_info_day', 'train_info_departure', 'train_info_destination', 'train_info_leaveAt', 'train_book_people', 'train_reqt_arriveBy', 'train_reqt_duration', 'train_reqt_leaveAt', 'train_reqt_price', 'train_reqt_trainID', 'taxi_info_arriveBy', 'taxi_info_departure', 'taxi_info_destination', 'taxi_info_leaveAt', 'taxi_reqt_type', 'taxi_reqt_phone', 'police_reqt_address','police_reqt_phone', 'police_reqt_postcode', 'hospital_info_department', 'hospital_reqt_address', 'hospital_reqt_phone','hospital_reqt_postcode',
Special Tokens	'<pad>', '<unk>', '<eos_g>', '<eos_ua>', '<eos_uu>', '<eos_b>', '<eos_d>', '<eos_sa>', '<eos_sr>', '<sos_g>', '<sos_ua>','<sos_uu>', '<sos_b>', '<eos_d>', '<sos_sa>', '<sos_sr>', '<sos_db>', '<eos_db>', 'restaurant_db_0', 'restaurant_db_1','restaurant_db_2', 'hotel_db_0', 'hotel_db_1', 'hotel_db_2', 'attraction_db_0', 'attraction_db_1', 'attraction_db_2', 'train_db_0', 'train_db_1', 'train_db_2'
Action Slot Tokens	['act_inform', 'general_none', 'act_request', 'act_reqmore', 'restaurant_food', 'act_thank', 'act_offerbook', 'train_leaveAt', 'restaurant_name', 'restaurant_area', 'restaurant_pricerange', 'hotel_area', 'act_offerbooked', 'hotel_name', 'train_destination', 'hotel_type', 'train_departure', 'hotel_pricerange', 'attraction_type', 'train_arriveBy', 'train_day', 'attraction_area', 'act_bye', 'attraction_name', 'hotel_stars', 'act_welcome', 'hotel_stay','restaurant_none', 'act_recommend', 'attraction_address', 'hotel_none', 'train_trainID', 'restaurant_time', 'hotel_parking', 'hotel_internet', 'hotel_day', 'train_none', 'train_price', 'attraction_fee', 'restaurant_day', 'restaurant_address', 'restaurant_choice', 'attraction_phone','hotel_people', 'train_people', 'attraction_postcode', 'restaurant_people', 'restaurant_reference', 'act_nooffer', 'hotel_reference', 'train_reference', 'act_select', 'restaurant_phone', 'taxi_type', 'attraction_choice', 'act_greet', 'train_choice', 'restaurant_postcode', 'taxi_phone', 'taxi_departure', 'taxi_leaveAt', 'hotel_address', 'train_duration', 'taxi_destination', 'act_nobook', 'booking_none', 'hotel_phone', 'hotel_postcode', 'taxi_arriveBy', 'taxi_none', 'booking_day', 'attraction_none', 'booking_time', 'booking_people', 'hospital_postcode', 'hospital_phone','hospital_address', 'police_address', 'police_postcode', 'police_phone','hospital_department', 'hospital_none', 'police_name', 'attraction_pricerange', 'booking_stay', 'police_none', 'train_leaveat', 'booking_reference', 'train_arriveby', 'booking_name', 'taxi_leaveat','hotel_time', 'attraction_open', 'restaurant_stay', 'taxi_arriveby','hotel_choice']

Table 10: Speicial tokens and ontology defined in our experiment.

Author Index

Association for Computational Linguistics
209 N. Eighth Street
Stroudsburg, Pennsylvania 18360

ISBN 978-1-7138-9147-5

9 781713 891475

CURRAN ASSOCIATES INC.
proceedings.com